THE EVALUATION OF CULTURAL ACTION

D0913601

STUDIES IN INTERNATIONAL DEVELOPMENT
RESEARCH

Also published

Robert J. Moore: THIRD-WORLD DIPLOMATS IN
  DIALOGUE WITH THE FIRST WORLD

Further titles in preparation

THE EVALUATION OF CULTURAL ACTION

An Evaluative Study of the Parents and Children
Program (PPH)

HOWARD RICHARDS

*with the assistance of Horacio Walker and Luis Brahm and the advice of
Juan-Eduardo Garcia-Huidobro, Edmund V. Sullivan and Joel Weiss*

Foreword by Malcolm Parlett

in association with
INTERNATIONAL DEVELOPMENT
RESEARCH CENTRE

CENTRE DE RECHERCHES POUR LE
DÉVELOPPEMENT INTERNATIONAL
OTTAWA

First published 1985 by
THE MACMILLAN PRESS LTD
London and Basingstoke
Companies and representatives
throughout the world

Printed in Hong Kong

British Library Cataloguing in Publication Data
Richards, Howard
The evaluation of cultural action.
1.   Programa Padres e Hijos
2.   Community development – Chile
I.   Title
361.6'0983   HN298
ISBN 0–333–36338–8
ISBN 0–333–36339–6 Pbk

To Three Martyrs for Meaning
Gandhi, Martin Luther King Jr and Oscar Romero

... que la alegría del hombre
brote de muy dentro
darle fin a la hipocresía
que el amor sea su centro ...

(May the joy of man
bud out from deep inside
putting an end to hypocrisy.
May love be its centre.)

*(from a poem by a program
participant who prefers to be
identified not by name but as 'a
peasant woman from Cumilelfu')*

Contents

Acknowledgements

The study which led to this book was supported by the Ford Foundation and the International Development Research Centre. The program which is the subject and object of the study has been supported by CEBEMO of the Catholic Church of Holland, *Bröt für die Welt* of the Protestant Churches of West Germany, and the Capuchin Fathers.

Much of the inspiration for the program came from the earlier Maipu Project coordinated by Juan José Silva, and many of the methods used were developed by Carols Ortuzar.

Many of the people whose assistance has been indispensable are mentioned by name in the text. Others are Emily Vargas Adams, Regina de Assis, Carol Barton, Marilyn Campbell, Ramsay Derry, Raquel Fernandez, Guillermo Garcia, Denis Goulet, Bernardita Icaza, Ruth Jackson, Vera John, Robert Myers, Caroline Richards, Shelley Richards, Valery Rose, Rosa Saavedra, Jorge Martinez Sanchez, Sheldon Shaeffer, Alice Shaffer, Nelly Stromquist and José Martinez Terrero, S.J.

Acknowledgements

Foreword

Howard Richards has compiled a significant and satisfying book – or books, rather, for it is really two accounts in one. Here is a detailed evaluation report of a notable educational/community development project in Chile: the *Programa Padres e Hijos* (Parents and Children Program). It is designed for the very poor, it draws on the ideas of Paulo Freire, it is run by a Catholic organization, it is internationally financed, and it is having to survive and grow, as a project, in the harsh political climate of a repressive military dictatorship.

Simply as a documentation of this remarkable program the book deserves note. Yet there is another account too, running along beside it: a telling indictment of a research tradition that grips most of the evaluation activity in the world today, despite inadequacies of logic and methodology. The author carries out a painstaking dissection of this dominant tradition, testing it carefully himself, and finally abandoning it in favour of its alternative. The approach finally adopted has strategies, methods and assumptions of an altogether different kind from that of the dominant psychometrically and econometrically based traditions usually associated with evaluation.

The two parts of the account are therefore interdependent: the author's reporting of the study made and his reflective discussion of methodology proceed hand in hand, each effort strengthening the other.

Evaluation reports are not widely read. Even those who commission studies or who are the responsible decision-makers do not always scrutinize the body of the text: they may turn to 'executive summaries' and cast an eye briefly over the tables of results, but rarely do they actually *read* reports, think about them, enjoy them, and act upon them. Given that many reports are data-bound and jargon-ridden with no literary flair, wit, or analytic bite, such reluctance to read them is understandable.

The first commendation is that the present book is an

exception – here is an evaluation that can be read without experiencing tedium, that stimulates us to think hard about the very basis of what constitutes evaluation of a program, that is genuinely informative about what the program is like, and which at the same time is also entertaining. The unserious style of writing may offend those who like their prose plain and in the academic fashion. Equally, the embellishments and the tongue-in-cheekness will delight others who believe that it is possible to tackle issues of high seriousness without being pompous and writing leaden prose.

Not all problems of evaluation reports lie in their style of writing. They also suffer from their specificity – usually, the data relate to one program and examples are locally drawn. For those who have never met the people, or visited the site, or do not know the wider context of the country or the system, getting inside an evaluation report can be uphill work even if it is well written.

The problem of reader overload, of a surfeit of local detail, is largely avoided here. The case study of the program in Chile does not stand alone, as a mass of project specifics, with no generalizations or wider thought in sight. Instead, we find details of the program interweaving the accompanying theoretical discussion. We encounter the *centros* and Jorge Zuleta (the program's local director in Osorno) at one moment, and at the next moment are pitched into questioning the very nature of what evaluators can legitimately claim to do. What is this realm of human endeavour, Dr Richards asks us to consider, involving investigation of a series of organized events (called a 'project' or 'program') by someone from the outside (the 'evaluator')? And by what rules, prerogatives and working assumptions should an evaluation proceed?

Howard Richards' twin-purpose account makes a notable addition to the literature of evaluation. To combine empirical study – assiduously and intelligently pursued – with a blow-by-blow exploration of the philosophy and technical details of investigative practice is a rarer alliance than it should be, particularly in a field like evaluation. There are evaluation theorists – even well-known ones – who regularly put forward ideas with little experience of actually trying them out. And there are practitioners by the dozen who, in reporting their efforts, never seem to examine critically the fundamental nature of their craft. Both groups may feel chastened by the achievement represented here.

The report is designed for several different audiences: those in governments and international agencies concerned either with broadly similar programs to this one elsewhere in the world or, more generally, with how to evaluate *appropriately* educational and social action projects that are complex, varied, and that have multiple outcomes and purposes. Other audiences include the organizers of the Parents and Children Program themselves; evaluators and researchers who want to be stimulated to think hard about their own work; and members of the professional evaluation community who are interested in a well-developed exemplar of 'illuminative evaluation'.

Practised first at the Massachusetts Institute of Technology in 1967–9 and subsequently developed at Edinburgh University as an integrated methodological framework, illuminative evaluation has since been widely experimented with, mainly in the USA and Britain, and usually for sponsors or clients with an independent spirit or who have accumulated a sense of frustration with more conventional approaches. More generally, illuminative evaluators have become used to having to defend vigorously their choice of approach – with its custom-built research strategy, its relative lack of interest in formal statements of objectives, its scepticism concerning elaborate statistical procedures, its willingness to employ so-called 'subjective' methods (as used, inevitably, by historians and ethnographers as well), and its primary interest in the 'informing' function of evaluation, rather than the more usual 'inspectorial' or 'grading' functions. As an approach, it has more in common with producing serious, carefully researched documentaries and with policy analysis than it has with large-scale social science research of the type dominant in graduate schools.

Howard Richards' onslaught on the taken-for-granted ways of thinking and conducting traditional evaluations is provocative, and his defence of the illuminative alternative is one of the best yet put forward. He points out how most evaluators have allowed themselves to be trapped in a system of thought and practice that is, at best, exceedingly difficult to apply intelligently and, at worst, is humbug. Familiar claims are made for the usual stance: it is systematic, rigorous, quantitative, and the rest; but much of the conviction has long ago drained away. Routinely now, reservations and concerns are raised: is there not over-reliance on tests and surveys and similar techniques? Is the statistical virtuosity displayed in analysing data gathered by these means truly revealing, or has it become some kind of elaborate game? Is such research – dependent as it is on the literacy of informants, on technical mastery of the methods, and on accessible data-processing facilities – the most appropriate form of social science orthodoxy for graduate schools in the world's North to be exporting to graduate schools and practitioners in the South? Does the usual form of evaluation really help decision-makers to understand the nature of a program – its life, problems in practice, its implicit assumptions – or is it couched in a form that effectively removes the study from the hurly burly practicalities of real-world decision-making?

The questions are many. What Howard Richards concludes is what others have concluded too (though he puts it far more lucidly), and that is that no minor tinkering will suddenly bring the usually taught and practised methods of evaluation up to scratch; it is not a case of this powerful school of social science research having a few easily corrected flaws, some practical limitations requiring a little adjustment here and there to make it fit evaluation's demands. No, what is needed for a truly sensible evaluation methodology is an entire shift in perspective – in fundamental assumptions, working concepts, methodological tenets, research values. When this total re-think of evaluation occurs, the almost slavish-seeming adherence to dominating conventions of formal research design, elaborate statistical procedures, etc., is inevitably broken, as strategies, goals and outcomes become re-defined to accord more with the realities of everyday phenomena and less with methodological dictates.

Illuminative evaluation, and the similar approaches grown up beside it, is an attempt to articulate and practise a genuinely alternative approach. Thus, it is *holistic* – evaluators attending closely to the various contexts of a program being evaluated and seeking to portray the program as a working whole, as an individual organizational construction that needs to be examined simultaneously from many different perspectives. It is *responsive* – with researchers working closely to provide all concerned with a program with a genuinely helpful report, that might take many different forms and draw on many diverse sources and methods, but is designed to interest, to inform, and to add to their understanding. (The report has to be readable to be responsive: academic journals are *not* the model.) The approach is *heuristic* – with the research design undergoing continuous redefinition as the knowledge base increases: it is not a preordinate design, with all the questions formulated at the start. Rather, a study evolves, with 'leads' being followed up and new questions coming to the fore. The evaluator starts with intensive familiarization, and then at each stage chooses what next to concentrate upon, in order to build the comprehensive understanding required. And it is *interpretive* – building up, through tightly woven descriptions with examples, with significant facts and figures, an overall depiction of a program that does justice to the inherent complexity and which throws light (hence 'illuminative') on little-known or previously taken-for-granted features of the program that are crucial to its life and character. The illuminative evaluator is not cast in the role of a technician (administering instruments), or an inspector (assessing how well 'they' are doing), or an anthropologist (exhaustively documenting the entire system) but as an interpreter – interpreting the program for those outside, or helping to re-interpret it for those inside it. Thus, he or she orchestrates and sums up points of view, gathers informative facts and documents, identifies critical themes of concern, establishes the historical and other contexts, summarizes solutions and proposals for how to deal with the principal problems (often to do with costs), and attempts to capture in mainly narrative form the life, the human quality, the ethos of the program so that others can partially experience it themselves.

The present book, by demonstrating these features in action, is a healthy addition to the growing body of literature on illuminative evaluation and its relatives – naturalistic, responsive, ethnographic, transactional and democratic evaluation approaches (a family that, like all families, has different degrees of closeness between its members, a natural tendency for members to regard themselves each as the family's centre, and despite overlapping concerns, is not without its own disputes).

Howard Richards formulates a set of definitions, intended to reflect a great deal of contemporary thinking in evaluation and in the social sciences generally, and names the set of definitions 'the systems approach'. Then he moves away from the frame of reference constituted by the set of definitions. In the course of doing so, he makes a number of theoretical contributions through reflections on meanings as causes, hermeneutics and conflict.

In following the suggestion that illuminative evaluators should choose methods to fit the problems studied (rather than definitions of problems to fit preferred methods of enquiry), Howard Richards develops an innovative strategy worth attention: the 'Verbal Image', a composite summary – enabling him to gather and compile information and comment on a large scale, drawing on input from many different peasant communities, and building in (as illuminative evaluators have to do) a means of validation, checking his organization of the substance of the Verbal Image with those who had originally contributed to it. By drawing the staff and peasants into the study, so that they were actively contributing to it almost as co-researchers, he demonstrates another fundamental tenet of the approach – that the study should be a welcome learning experience; that the evaluation is done not *on* a program but, wherever possible, *with* its members; that participants should end up feeling enhanced, rather than diminished, by having taken part. He also lays to rest the assertion that 'this kind of study can be done only on very small scale programs' – manifestly untrue here.

And this brings us to the project itself, the Parents and Children Program: in the final analysis it would be a nonsense if an evaluation methodology imposed demands on a program in a manner that ran altogether counter to the values and purposes that embody that program. One can be certain that the evaluation would be in trouble. Crude and insensitive some evaluations undoubtedly are – but not this one. Howard Richards is unfailingly consistent in reflecting and upholding the essential political and moral values upon which the program is founded. He begins, he continues throughout, he ends without once breaking the thread of his deep respect for the aspirations of the program, the passionate concern for peasants, their lives, their freedom, and their communal self-respect. He is objective – in the sense that a historian is objective – namely, he can stand outside the program and see it in a wider perspective, and is conscious of his own position and the limits to his own understanding. But being objective in this sense does not prevent his being involved in the project; concerned for its cause and its future; respectful of its underlying strategy; and sympathetic to its problems and troubling dilemmas.

Evaluators are human: any philosophy of research that discredits or disparages the full engagement and the political and personal commitment of evaluators is inviting them to deny their own humanity and, with it, the capacity to be authentic, personally honest, and constructive of greater understanding between people. Again, Dr Richards reminds us of what we know already but which easily we can forget: the circumstances of present-day Chilean life do not permit a woolly and weak neutralism paraded as a required scientific detachment.

There is no doubt about it – this account would not be as arresting or as important if it were about a less radical and less ambitious program. But what *is* the Parents and Children Program – or PPH, as it is always referred to? The answer, in the form of a succinct and definitive summary, is not so easy to provide. Insiders (people who have worked with PPH, studied it in detail, and visited it and seen how it works) know that PPH is more than simply a program – it is also a mystique, a style, a way of working with the poor instead of for the poor.

Initially, outsiders are unlikely to believe that the PPH mystique is all that widespread or that it is part of the program's impact; and if they understood and believed the claim, they might not approve. So, instead of pointing out that peasants compose poems and songs praising PPH (an example appears in Chapter 2) or that professional people seem to be converted by the spirit of PPH, giving up deep-seated bureaucratic and technocratic attitudes in the process, the insider resorts tentatively to finding out which words the outsider knows that might provide bridges over the gap between PPH and the outsider's background and experience.

Howard Richards describes the process (in part of his report not included in this book) as follows. 'For example, the insider may try "non-formal adult education". If the outsider's eyes light up, showing that he can relate to the concept of non-formal adult education, then the insider can say, "That is what PPH is. It is a non-formal adult education program." If the outsider's eyes remain dull and glassy, then the insider can try "community development", "pre-school education", "rural education", "*educacion popular*" (a phrase not adequately translated by any

English phrase), "family education", "the psychosocial method", "Paulo Freire", "participatory research", or "*animation rurale*".' All of these phrases are 'true' descriptors and help to communicate to the outsider the nature of PPH – that is, of course, providing that the two parties involved – the imaginary insider and the imaginary outsider – know how the phrases in question are normally used outside PPH, which is not always the case.

Howard Richards continues as follows. 'The insider must be careful not to make too many statements of the form "PPH is . . .", because if he does he will suggest by his readiness to give multiple descriptions of the program that the program itself is an amorphous one that does not know what it is doing, or an inefficient one that is trying to do a great many different things and therefore necessarily doing some or all of them badly. . . . Or he may think that the peasants find the program confusing because he, the outsider, finds the explanation the insider is trying to give him confusing. Therefore, the typical insider will choose his words carefully and not use too many of them, and when the outsider has formed an image in his mind of what PPH is, nodding his head as a signal that the insider has given an acceptable answer to his question, then the insider will stop talking.'

The writer of this Foreword is not deterred by such scruples and, drawing on his own understanding of the program (based partly on a brief visit) and a description supplied by Dr Richards, he offers a capsule summary for those who are encountering the program for the first time.

The initials PPH stand for *Programa Padres e Hijos*, which means Parents and Children Program. The general objectives of the program are: (i) child development; (ii) the personal growth of adults; and (iii) community organization. The combining of three general objectives is deliberate – a hoped-for synergy of pre-school education, adult education and community development, yielding together more benefits than would derive from three separate programs. Thus child development activities for children will be enhanced because they are combined with lessons in parenting for adults; adult learning will be enhanced because community participation is pursued; community solidarity will be furthered because the community is organized around a goal everyone shares and approves, namely a better life for the children, and, through the basic kinship unit, the family.

The weekly meetings in each locality are led by two coordinators elected by the participants from among their own number. The meetings have three constituent parts: *first*, discussions of basic topics to do with living and bringing up children. These discussions are stimulated by pictures and by questions asked by the coordinators (with the help of manuals). The topics concern how to help children to learn to talk, to read, and to count; sex education; human relations in the family; alcohol abuse; nutrition; how to make the best use of available food supplies; and food preservation.

Second, there are pre-school exercises for the children, in the form of worksheets which prescribe activities similar to kindergarten work. The parents go over the material in their meeting, and then take it home for the children. The children (or, depending on the activity, the parents and children together) complete the worksheets, and the parents hand in the completed work at the next weekly meeting.

Third, there are conclusions. These are the results of group discussions; once articulated, they lead to whatever sort of community action the group decides to undertake, for example, organizing healthy recreation activities to draw young people away from alcohol abuse.

PPH is sponsored and organized by CIDE, *Centro de Investigacion y Desarrollo de la Educacion* (Centre for Research and Development in Education), Santiago, Chile. The PPH 'package', developed by CIDE, consists of a set of elements that can be moved from one place to another, and can be applied in one or another situation, with the cooperation of a local sponsoring organization. The elements are formed from the three kinds of software:

(i) the manuals for adult education, with the accompanying pictures, both of which need to be revised in every application to suit local conditions; as do

(ii) the worksheets for children, known as *folletos*;

(iii) the experience, skills and ideas of CIDE staff members, known as *la metodologia*, which permit one to speak of a method, repeatable in its general outlines, for inviting the poor people of an area to participate (*la motivacion*); the training of coordinators (*la capacitacion*); constant in-service training (*la auto-capacitacion*); and the coordination of weekly meetings and other activities of peasants in several dozen localities out of one of the regional field offices (located in San Felipe, Linares, Curico, and other cities). This report is of the application of PPH in (i.e. around) a town named Osorno.

This is obviously only the briefest of introductions. Readers who read the subsequent account will meet people, learn facts, sympathize with feelings, wrestle with numerical data, appreciate viewpoints, and restructure their mental images of PPH, according to a series of theoretical frameworks. In the process they will, to an extent, themselves become insiders, and will find any summary of the kind offered here somewhat misleading by its being incomplete.

The program and the evaluation exercise have been introduced. I am tempted also to try to introduce Howard Richards. But the task of doing so – as his colleagues and friends will immediately understand – is, frankly, too daunting, and he would be acutely embarrassed by any such attempt. This many-sided man cannot be summed up in a few sentences. He will, anyway, reveal a lot of himself in the report that follows. The reader will discover the scholar, sense the moral outrage, and witness the playfulness. The reader will realize much else in the course of reading the account. The writer hides behind no camouflage of impersonal prose: the reader will get to know Howard Richards well, and that, as many of us have discovered, is a privilege.

London   MALCOLM PARLETT

1 Prologue on the Thirty-second Floor

I do not always understand everything. For example, I do not understand why the word 'evaluation' is so widely used and why it appears to be so widely understood. Nowadays everything is evaluated. Children are evaluated in school. Adults are evaluated at work. Obstetrical forceps, insecticides, textbooks, cathedral organs and nuclear missiles are evaluated. People who are mystified if you ask them what 'good' or 'bad' means, appear to know what 'evaluation' means, even though one would have thought that when one evaluates something one must give reasons for judging it to be good, or bad, or partly good and partly bad. People who modestly deny that they know how to think, nevertheless feel authorized to evaluate, even though one would have thought that in order to evaluate something it is necessary, at least, to think about it.

There is even a special field called 'Metaevaluation Research', devoted to the evaluation of evaluations. The study of meta-evaluation, along with the reading of a great many books and articles on the evaluation of educational and social programs, helped to prepare the ground for the evaluation of the Parents and Children Program – for Parents and Children is a third world development programme, and third world development programs, like everything else, must be evaluated.

Let me tell you something about the Parents and Children Program, or, rather, about the portion of the program that is the subject of this study. It was a project in and near Osorno, a town famous for its long periods of uninterrupted rainfall, in rural Chile, sponsored by church and international agencies, in a land ruled by Pinochet's junta, in 1979 and 1980. The general aims of Parents and Children, in Osorno in 1979–80, and in other places

1

where it has been, are, and hopefully will be, child development, the personal growth of adults, and community organization. The combining of three general aims seeks to achieve a synergic effect in which pre-school education, adult education, and community development together yield extra benefits that three separate programs would not yield (as bronze, an alloy of copper and tin, has a synergic strength greater than that of either copper or tin alone). Thus child development activities for children are to be enhanced because they are combined with lessons in parenting for adults; adult learning is to be enhanced because community participation is pursued; community solidarity is furthered because the community is organized around a goal everyone shares and approves, namely a better life for the children. The program builds community through the basic kinship unit, the family.

As I have said, the Parents and Children Program, like everything else, must be evaluated. But evaluations are rarely pleasing to everyone, or anyone. The people evaluated (in the cases where people or people's activities are the objects under study) often feel that they have not been properly understood. The managers, sponsors or administrators who initiate and fund evaluations usually feel that they have paid too much money and have obtained too little useful information. After the evaluation is over, it is regularly concluded that the evaluator troubled his head unduly to find the answer to a question that seemed very important to him at the time, but which turned out not to be, after all, the question that anybody else perceived as the focus that would bring sharply into view (as when you get a micro-scope adjusted just right) the essential form and true crux of the reality which was to be assessed.

Whatever else evaluation is, it is communication. It is a form of communication because an evaluation sends messages from somebody to somebody. It is not too early to say that while we take it to be a general truth about any evaluation whatsoever that it communicates some message to some audience, this particular study adheres to the school of thought known as 'illuminative evaluation', which holds, as its name implies, that an evaluation should make its subject stand in the light and be visible. The receiver of the evaluation should be able to see the Parents and Children Program illuminated, whether the receiver is an officer of the funding agency which sponsors Parents and

Children, a policy analyst for an agency that might sponsor programs somewhat like it, a village worker in India, a community organizer in Sheffield who is on the prowl for useful ideas, an unlettered peasant woman in Bolivia who might decide to start a Parents and Children centre in her own community, or an innocent bystander in München who is generally curious about what is happening in this wonderful world around us. In the light of this illumination, the receiver of the communication should see what PPH is and should see what lessons can be learned from it.

Before departing for South America to evaluate the Parents and Children Program, I interviewed in North America nine members of one of the identifiable sets of receivers of communication about PPH, a group of people who rank, relatively speaking, among the great and powerful of this world. They were executives or staff advisors to major funding agencies. You are about to read an account of a typical interview. It is not a real interview but a *pastiche*, based on notes from nine interviews, and designed to reveal the contours of a prevalent concept of rational decision-making that I found in my interviews and in much of my reading. This is a concept of rational decision-making which I shall call 'cost-effectiveness', or 'the systems approach', or even 'bureaucratic' – without meaning to imply that societies ought not have bureaucracies, nor even that they ought not have large bureaucracies. In making my *pastiche*, I found I had made a personality, who I have called the Reasonable Social Scientist. She and I have become friends, and our dialogues will occur frequently throughout this study.

Her office is in New York City at the United Nations Plaza, on the 32nd floor. As I waited downstairs and went up in the lift, I noticed that the surroundings were not elegant. Any private bank permits itself more luxury in its carpets and furnishings than does a specialized agency of the United Nations. I was, in a sense, at the Capitol of the World, in the buildings where the representatives of the world's peoples deliberated, and where the Secretariat and the Agencies implemented the conclusions of their deliberations by taking steps to assure, among other things, that no child shall be abandoned, hungry, without medical attention, or ignorant. Yet this World Capitol was austere, not at all like the palaces of the emperors of ancient China and Rome, which in their days were also World Capitols, in the sense that their rulers thought of themselves as governing every place known and civilized.

'We really have very little power, you know,' said the Reasonable Social Scientist a few moments after my arrival at her office. 'Oil barons have power. Military commanders have power. Transnational corporations have power. Whether civilian governments have much power is not clear.' As she spoke, she gazed out the window of her office, perhaps with a certain amount of pride, since junior trainees are given offices facing the inner walls and it is a symbol of status in the organization to have a window with a view of the city. Far below us, through a haze composed of specks of dry snow blown about by a cold wind, we could discern the flags of 157 nations fluttering at the United Nations pavilion. The Reasonable Social Scientist continued. 'We in this office are only social scientists who work for the United Nations, an organization with little power, composed of governments whose power in their own homelands is itself questionable. Our budgets are pitiful. UNICEF, for example, in 1978 spent 208 million dollars to help all the world's children – less than is spent on armaments every 5 hours. Somehow we must convince those who exert control over resources that children are important, and that programs to serve children can be effective. As social scientists our role is to convince policy-makers by presenting them with accurate and reliable information.'

'You perceive your special role in the system to be that of a producer of knowledge,' I suggested.

'Our agency tries to channel its extremely limited funds into projects that will have a demonstration effect, showing what could be done if the international community were willing to commit sizable sums to meeting the basic needs of children. In a sense, all the projects we fund are experiments; we are trying to learn the best ways to use scarce resources.'

'As you know,' I said, 'I helped to develop an initial version of the Parents and Children Program in Chile in the years 1972–4. Now, six years later, I am about to return to Chile to take part in an evaluative study of a later version of the same program. I am here to ask you what you believe to be the main questions we ought to try to answer about Parents and Children.'

'What we want to know,' said the Reasonable Social Scientist, 'is whether the program is cost-effective.'

'What do you mean by "cost-effective"?'

'Essentially, it is simply a matter of making a rational decision. Unfortunately, in this office we have seen a number of programs, in Peru for example, launched on what might be called a tide of ideological enthusiasm, but without the slightest regard for economics. Sooner or later, enthusiasm collides with reality, and it becomes manifest that a program costs too much and achieves too little, To be more specific, a program is not cost-effective when there is a less expensive way to achieve the same objectives.'

'But what do you take a cost-effectiveness study to be?'

'Will you agree,' she said, 'that it is better to have more good than less good? Or, in other words, more benefit than less benefit?'

'That must be true,' I said.

'And will you agree that every good has a cost?'

'Why?' I asked.

'Because every time one chooses to invest resources in something, say for example PPH, one sacrifices the opportunity to invest those same resources in something else. The money put into PPH, for instance, cannot be put into a family planning program. The cost of something is, in a broad sense, the opportunities that are foregone by the choice to do it instead of doing an alternative.'

'That must be true too,' I said.

'Now you understand the essence of the cost-effectiveness approach,' she said, 'which is sometimes known as the systems approach. For every system, say PPH, you measure the benefits and you measure the costs. If system A achieves the same objectives (i.e. yields the same benefits) as system B, but at a lower cost, then system A is more cost-effective, or, as we often say, more efficient. Or if at the same cost system A produces greater benefits (i.e. achieves the same objectives to a greater degree) then system A is more efficient.'

At this point, certain thoughts flashed rapidly through my mind. I kept them to myself at the time, because I did not want to lose my opportunity to listen to the Reasonable Social Scientist, and I did not want to offend her by offering an interpretation of her mentality which crystallized her thoughts in such a rigid fashion that she would not recognize in them her reasonable, flexible, open-minded self. Secretly, I was thinking to myself that I was trapped like a fly in a spider web; I had flown into the web when I agreed with certain propositions that seemed to be self-evidently true, namely that it is better to have more good than less good, and that every choice has a cost, but it turned out that these propositions were linked to others as the strands of a spider web are linked to each other, so that I soon found myself committed to a vocabulary in which all the terms are defined by reference to each other. I found myself recalling old definitions from textbooks, and soon I was seeing the world from the Reasonable Social Scientist's point of view; travelling up and down in her web but never escaping it; I was inhabiting the inner structure of her mind. Rapidly, I reviewed in my mind the way the key terms of the systems approach relate to one another.

A SYSTEM is a set of elements which work together to perform a function. For example, one might say that PPH is a SYSTEM whose function is to teach parents how to educate their pre-school children in the home. It is a system in the private, i.e. non-governmental, sector.

The ELEMENTS of a system are its parts which work together to perform the function. For example, one might say that the ELEMENTS of PPH are: (i) the main office in Santiago (located at CIDE, a private Roman Catholic church-related charitable foundation), where the instructional materials are prepared; (ii) the Osorno office, which administers work in the country-side; (iii) the general coordinators (one for each of ten sectors), who deliver the instructional materials and supervise their use; (iv) the volunteer base-coordinators, who teach the parents; (v) the parents, who educate their pre-school children in the home; (vi) the children, who are taught.

The ELEMENTS of systems are often portrayed as boxes on charts. When an ELEMENT can be regarded in terms of the sub-functions it performs (and in terms of its own elements that make it up), it is sometimes called a SUBSYSTEM.

The STATE OF THE SYSTEM is the set of values of the variables that describe a system at a given time. For example, PPH (like any system) might be described by many variables. (It is some-times said that a system can be described 'along many dimensions'.) Let us define, for the purposes of this example, the variables.

S = number of employees at the Santiago office
O = number of employees at the Osorno office
G = number of general coordinators
B = number of volunteer base-coordinators
P = number of parents enrolled (one per family)
C = number of pre-school children enrolled

The STATE OF THE SYSTEM on 1 November, 1979 was:
$S = 3$, $O = 3$, $G = 10$, $B = 114$, $P = 839$, $C = 1190$.

MEASUREMENT is the assignment of values to variables according to rules.

For example, counting rules were used to determine the values given above (e.g. children under 4 were not counted, since they were considered too young to be 'pre-school').

If we were to measure the element children on the dimension 'reading readiness', we would need rules to assign values to the variable R_n = reading readiness of child n.

OBJECTIVES are the desired values of the variables, which represent the successful performance of the system's function. For example, it was an OBJECTIVE of PPH to enrol 2000 pre-school children, or $C = 2000$.

RESOURCES are the inputs into (and the features of the elements of) the system that can be put to use to achieve the objectives. For example, in 1979 PPH could use US$69,500 granted to it by CEBEMO (a private, church-related Dutch foundation), and the instructional materials on hand at the Santiago office, to achieve its objectives.

DEPENDENT VARIABLES are variables whose values depend on those of other variables; for example, in the equation $y = 2x$, y is a dependent variable because its value depends on the value of x. For example, some of the research that led to the founding of PPH showed that the value of the dependent variable 'achievement in school' depended to a high degree on the value of another variable, namely 'attitude of parents toward education'.

INDEPENDENT VARIABLES are the ones on which the others depend. We take them to be to some extent under our control; and we do research to discover how to manipulate them so that an objective is achieved. Hence independent variables represent RESOURCES and dependent variables OBJECTIVES. The former IMPACT the latter. In the equation $y = 2x$, x is an independent variable because the value of *y* depends on its value. For example, money is a resource (independent variable), and the extent to which objectives are achieved often depends on the amount of money spent.

A HYPOTHESIS asserts tentatively that there is a significant relationship between two variables, sometimes called an IMPACT. For example, it is a HYPOTHESIS that a child's enrolment in PPH is positively related to his success in the first year of school. A more ambitious hypothesis would venture to quantify how much more success will result from how much participation in PPH.

An INSTRUMENT is a tool used to measure the value of a variable. Tests and surveys are called instruments. For example, a test might be used to measure the value of the variable R_n (reading readiness of child *n*), or a survey might be used to measure the values of the variables *S*, *O*, *G*, *B*, *P* and *C* defined under STATE OF THE SYSTEM, above.

COSTS are expenditures of resources, and in general anything undesirable or bad. One does not incur a COST for its own sake, but for the sake of some good purchased by it. For example, with respect to PPH, when we consider the program from the point of view of a funding agency, we are interested in expenditures of money. We want to know what objectives can be achieved with a given sum, or how much it COSTS to achieve an objective.

BUDGETS allocate money according to functions and subfunctions. (Here we are concerned with program BUDGETS, i.e. BUDGETS which relate expenditures to objectives.) One can also BUDGET other resources, such as time or personnel. For example, PPH BUDGETED in 1979 $33,500 for preparation of instructional materials, $14,500 for administering work in the countryside, and $21,500 for delivery of instructional materials and supervision of their use.

COST-EFFECTIVENESS refers to the extent to which objectives are achieved with a minimum expenditure of resources. A system is said to be COST-EFFECTIVE when, compared to the available alternatives, it achieves the same objectives at a lesser cost. Or when, compared to the alternatives, for the same amount of money it achieves the objectives to a higher degree. For example, PPH would be COST-EFFECTIVE if it educated preschool children better than did kindergartens (or other alternatives) at the same cost, or as well as did kindergartens (etc.) at a smaller cost.

EFFICIENCY means the same as COST-EFFECTIVENESS.

EVALUATION refers to the measurement of the degree to which the objectives of the system are achieved. EVALUATION serves to suggest new patterns of resource use (i.e. revised budgets, different manipulations of independent variables) in order to improve the system's performance. For example, PPH could be evaluated by defining and measuring variables that indicate (i) how many, (ii) how well, and (iii) at what cost, pre-school children were educated.

The Reasonable Social Scientist noticed that I was staring at the window, intensely examining the occasional flakes of snow blown against the pane.

'I hope you are not getting the wrong impression of me,' she said. 'I am, after all, a fiction specially invented to illustrate a prevalent model of rational decision-making. It would be out of character, contrary to my essence, for me to be unreasonable. I do not, for example, hold the unreasonable belief that all benefits can be quantified; nor do I unreasonably believe that narrowly economic criteria should govern the overall assessment of a project; social goals, such as justice and equality, must not be forgotten.'

As I continued to stare at the window, the Reasonable Social Scientist was provoked to ask a rather rude question.

'What are you thinking about?' she demanded.

'Paulo Freire,' I said. My answer was not false, for although I had reserved for my private meditations my analysis of the systems approach, thinking the Reasonable Social Scientist would find my brief and crude summary of her mentality disturbing and unfair, my thoughts had in fact drifted from there to the educational philosophy of the great Brazilian author of *The Pedagogy of the Oppressed* and other indispensable, epoch-making works.

'Personally, I have the greatest admiration for Freire,' said the Reasonable Social Scientist. 'I would send him a fan letter if I were not convinced that the man has such a sincere passion for humility that praise would only embarrass him. Unfortunatly, however, in our agency Freire has acquired a reputation for being a nice man.'

'A nice man?' I asked.

'When I was reading *On Cultural Action*,' continued the Reasonable Social Scientist, 'I was so excited that I read passages aloud to my boss at coffee break. "Listen to this, Max," I said to my boss. "This is great stuff:

Nobody educates anybody; no one is educated alone; people educate each other together, in interaction with the world."

My boss looked up from his coffee and said "He's a nice man".'

'Your boss meant to say that Freire expresses fine sentiments but presents no evidence that his methods work,' I said.

'Exactly,' said the Reasonable Social Scientist. 'We have nothing against Paulo Freire. All we want are some data showing the benefits achieved through the use of his methods, and the cost of achieving them. Is that too much to ask? Am I being unreasonable?'

'You are the essence of rationality,' I said, 'or at least the essence of one historically-determined species of rationality. Far be it from me to say that you are unreasonable. You employ, as some French philosophers say, a certain *problematique*, i.e. a certain frame of reference. A set of key terms determines how you describe a situation, what you see in it, what questions you ask about it. Within your own frame of reference, you are surely reasonable; whether or not it will be possible to transform the *problematique* to achieve a more adequate grasp of reality is another question.'

I do not think the Reasonable Social Scientist was ready for the preceding remark. Judging by what she said next, her frame of reference was such that she was not prepared to hear what I was saying; it passed over her head, or, as Jean Piaget would say, she neither assimilated it nor accommodated her mental structures to it. But I am not worried about the Reasonable Social Scientist – in the following chapters, practical experience itself (*praxis*) will take the lead in transforming her *problematique*; in due course, she will come to see cost-effectiveness in a more adequate perspective. Meanwhile, I must be careful not to spend too much time attending to the concerns of the Reasonable Social Scientist, for if I do, I shall lose all my friends among the advanced thinkers who perceive her as not worthy of attention because she is *passé*, an unreformed positivist, a part of the ideological apparatus of the bourgeoisie, a focalist (i.e. one who focuses on small problems in order to conceal broader political issues), etc.

'Promise me this,' said the Reasonable Social Scientist. 'I know PPH is inspired by the philosophy of Paulo Freire. But please do a useful evaluation. Don't write an essay on the dignity of the peasantry. Don't do a whitewash. Give us some information we can use in our decision-making process.'

I do not know whether I chickened out for fear of offending someone who might have influence with the funding agencies supporting my own and my friends' work, or whether I was persuaded that human solidarity required that one deal patiently with the Reasonable Social Scientists of this world by accepting their viewpoint and then gradually moving beyond it, or whether my own thinking is not yet so advanced that I am able to reject the systems approach *problematique* out of hand without further examination. In any case, I made the promise the Reasonable Social Scientist asked of me.

NOTES AND REFERENCES

The following quotations from prominent authors are evidence that the formulation of the systems approach given here is not an arbitrary construction, but is an interpretation of the thinking of important sectors of the managerial élite of our civilization.

'To decide whether this particular project should be replicated, one would need to know ... whether the project represented the least cost alternative' (Roger Grawe of the World Bank, in C. U. Weber *et al.*, *An Economic Analysis of the Ypsilanti Perry Preschool Project* (Ypsilanti, Mich.: High/Scope, 1978) p. 65).

'It is essential for the manager to look at costs *before* he is committed to a course of action. This ... enables him to determine whether it is worth pursuing what may initially have looked like a good objective. It also helps him develop and evaluate alternative ways to reach the objective ... This step reflects the "budgeting" aspects of action planning. As such, it provides a logical link between the MBO (management by objectives) system and the organization's budgeting process' (Anthony Raia, *Managing By Objectives* (Glenview, Ill: Scott, Foresman, 1974) p. 73).

'Objectives are often identified with desired outputs, which in turn are treated as dependent variables' (William Alexander, Course 1715F Methodology for Policy Research, Ontario Institute for Studies in Education, 1979).

For an example of an attempt to classify the kinds of educational research, which implies that they all contribute directly or indirectly to efficiency, see Carlos Muñoz Izquierdo, 'Consideraciones para Determinar las Prioridades de Investigacion Educativa en América Latina', *Revista del CEE*, vol. II, no. 4 (1972) pp. 15–44. The author proposes 'Identificación de los factores determinantes del rendimiento del sistema y de las causas por las cuales cada factor genera el efecto que se le atribuye' (p. 37).

'Objectives and evaluation should, in essence, be identical; that is, test items should be drawn from the class of behavior specified in the objectives' (James W. Popham and Eva L. Baker, *Systematic Instruction* (Englewood Cliffs, N.J.: Prentice-Hall, 1970) p. 16).

'Measurement is the assignment of numerals to events or objects according to a rule' (S. S. Stevens, in C. W. Churchman and P. Ratoosh (eds), *Measurement Definition and Theories* (New York: Wiley, 1959) p. 25).

In defining systems design, C. West Churchman says: 'It tries to estimate in thought how well each alternative set of behavior patterns will serve a specified set of goals' (*The Design of Inquiring Systems: Basic Concepts of Systems and Organization* (New York: Basic Books, 1971) p. 5).

'. . . the opportunity costs of choosing a commodity, service, or activity "A" (or of already having chosen A) are what the individual, or group or society gives up (or gave up) in making this choice' (Mary Jean Bowman, 'A Generalized Concept of Costs and Its Dimensions', in *Textes Choisis*, p. 787).

Textes Choisis is a bilingual French–English selection of documents on the economics of education, published by UNESCO in Paris in 1968, for the benefit of third-world development planners.

It should be mentioned that whereas the systems approach as outlined here is part of the family of doctrines Richard Bernstein calls 'the positivist temper', (Richard Bernstein, *The Restructuring of Social and Political Theory* (New York and London: Harcourt Brace Jovanovitch, 1976)), the word 'systems' is often used to mark definite departures from positivism, as in the works of Ludwig von Bertallanfy.

The notion of '*problematique*' used here is adapted from Louis Althusser, *Pour Marx* (Paris: F. Maspero, 1965) p. 64, n. 30. Similar notions are found in works by other recent French writers, sometimes under other names, such as 'symbolic order', or '*système d'interpretation*'. For the latter, see Maurice Merleau-Ponty, *La Prose du Monde* (Paris: Gallimard, 1969) p. 201. See also Jacques Lacan, *Ecrits*, and Roland Barthes, *Systeme de la Mode*, both published in Paris by Editions du Seuil in 1967. Another way to make the same point is to use the notion of 'semantic field', i.e. to point out that to understand one word, one must examine the *ensemble* or field of words it relates to. Paulo Freire thus examines the word 'extension' in *Extension o Comunicacion* (Buenos Aires and Mexico: Siglo XXI, 1977).

'*Problematique*' is similar in some ways to the notion of 'paradigm' used by Thomas Kuhn in *The Structure of Scientific Revolutions* (Chicago: University of Chicago Press, 1962). '*Problematique*' is easier to work with than 'paradigm', because the former is tied more closely to the meaning of a set of words, while the latter relies on the more diffuse concept of the concrete historical achievements of a great scientist, such as Sir Isaac Newton, which become an example of how to do science taken as a guide and standard by other scientists. One could perhaps consider the systems approach as a paradigm, and refer to the Coleman Report – James S. Coleman *et al.*, *Equality of Educational Opportunity* (Washington, DC: US Government Printing Office, 1966) – as a study taken to be an example of how to do social science by many Latin American researchers.

2 Prologue in the Mud

The Holy Spirit gives different gifts at different places and times. At Osorno in the rainy south of Chile in the year 1980 it gave a priest the form of a leprechaun, for no other image so fairly describes the slight, short figure, the red beard and hair, and the inquisitive blue eyes of Father Winfredo van den Berg, a missionary from Holland, the head of the Radio School for Rural Development Foundation (FREDER, *Fundacion de Radio Escuelas para el Desarrollo Rural*). Father Winfredo directs The Voice of the Coast, the station on which the radio school broadcasts its lessons. Upon him, the Spirit also bestowed unusual gifts of joy and courage, which are manifested in the enthusiasm with which he dances the mambo at peasant gatherings, and his persistence in working for justice in spite of persecution.

Persecution is not new to Father Winfredo; in 1942, when he was a boy, his father was a leader of the Dutch resistance; his family lived for years with 18 Jews hidden in the attic of their house. In Chile he has been beaten and jailed. In 1976, an order was issued expelling him from the country, but he managed to persuade General Gustavo Leigh, who was then a member of the ruling junta, to countermand the order. General Leigh was impressed by Father Winfredo's assertion that he personally had buried more than 1400 Chilean children who had died from causes directly or indirectly traceable to malnutrition.

Father Winfredo has a very democractic way of making decisions: he gives the people what they ask for whenever he can. That is how PPH came to 60 communities in the region surrounding Osorno. A United Nations agency selected 16 communities for a pilot PPH program conducted in the first three months of 1977. The people who take radio school courses, 'the FREDER family' as Winfredo likes to say, are accustomed to writing their own tickets. In the past, they had asked for courses on rabbit-raising, beekeeping, cattle diseases, weaving, managing cooperatives, and sewing, and that is what they were

14

given. When they had had a taste of PPH, they told Winfredo they wanted more. Winfredo authorized a two-year program, to run from January 1979 to December 1980, to reach 60 peasant communities. It was to be financed by CEBEMO and other church-related aid agencies, and was implemented by Jorge Zuleta, a staff member borrowed from the Centre for Research and Development in Education (*Centro de Investigacion y Desarrollo de la Educacion* – CIDE). CIDE already had six years' experience in building PPH programs in other places.

That, in brief, is how PPH came to the region surrounding Osorno, a region as far south of the equator as the coastal redwoods of California are north, where the winter lasts from May until September, and the rains last from March until October. Almost 100,000 people live in the city of Osorno; some of them own large cattle ranches, drive Mercedes Benzes, and dress elegantly to attend chamber music concerts at the Municipal Auditorium on the European-style town square – but most of them do not. The surrounding countryside is, for the most part, very poor and sparsely populated; 25,000 people are scattered through the country districts where PPH chiefly operates.

One might ask, of course, why in 1977 the UN happened to pick Osorno for a one-month pilot study of PPH, or why in 1978 CIDE happened to be ready to provide FREDER with instructional materials and experienced personnel. Or why in July 1980 a professor of philosophy and education from Earlham College in Indiana, USA, arrived to do an evaluative study of PPH-Osorno. But those are other stories. People who want to hear those stories may be comforted to know that their desires deceive them; they think they want to know, but they do not. If I should proceed to tell them, they would wish they had not asked.

The professor soon found himself in the back of a Landrover jeep making its way through steady rain along a poor excuse for a road, jolting over ruts and gullies, splashing through rivers of mud, going from Osorno to Los Hualles, one of the rural communities where a PPH centre had been established. The leprechaun had taken a very empirical approach to evaluation: if you want to know what PPH is and how it works, go and look! Tito Barrientos, the driver, said that it had begun to rain in March and had rained every day for five months. He shifted the jeep into four-wheel drive in order to get past a previously deceased North-American school bus which had been resurrected here in western Patagonia to serve as cheap transport but which was now ingloriously stationary, axle-deep in mud. The passengers were outside it in the rain, cutting branches to put under its wheels. The bus, known as a *micro*, is the lifeline of the peasants. There is a *micro* from Los Hualles to Osorno every morning, and a *micro* back the same afternoon. The peasant-woman (and it is mostly women who do the gardening and marketing in these communities) loads her produce onto the *micro* and sells it at the fair at Osorno to a middleman, colloquially known as a *buitre* (buzzard or vulture), who later resells it at a substantial profit; then she buys her supplies at the same fair and loads them onto the *micro* for the return trip. When the winter mud becomes so deep that the *micro* cannot get through, the peasants are totally isolated. Except, of course, for The Voice of the Coast, the peasants' radio station.

At that very moment, The Voice of the Coast informed us through the jeep's radio of our own expected arrival at Los Hualles – not, of course, of my arrival or Tito's, but the arrival of the distinguished passengers who shared the metal floor in the back of the vehicle: Uncle José, the MC of the program 'Children's World', Sparky and Squirrel, two child stars of the same program, and Father Winfredo. It was announced that Los Hualles was holding a feast to inaugurate its community building, built by the members of the PPH centre, and that visitors were coming on foot and on horseback from Cuinco, Dollinco and Trosco, and by Landrover from Osorno.

The green hills around us began to remind me of pictures in story books. There were crests suitable for castles, and river valleys that could be kingdoms, rainbows in the distance where the sky was clearing, trees similar to pines and oaks but sufficiently different from pines and oaks to be imaginary species, bushes with red flowers similar to fuchsias. My mind wandered to Mother Goose. It was from her that I had first heard of buying and selling at fairs. In the peasants we passed along the road, I saw Cinderella dressed in her rags; Simple Simon with his gnarled walking stick; the old woman who lived in a shoe, walking barefoot with her barefoot tribe; Jack, with his mother's emaciated cow; the emaciated face of Peter Pumpkin Eater. The King rode by on an 85 horsepower John Deere, dressed in a Sears Roebuck yellow raincoat and a felt hat. I asked Tito whether the peasants realize that they live in a land as beautiful as Bavaria, or whether, since they have never been anywhere else, they suppose that all the world looks like this. Tito reminded me that I was a dumb foreigner by saying: 'In the winter no peasant thinks the countryside is beautiful.'

We ascended a muddy slope and at the top found a fork in the road and, near it, our destination. In Canada, it would have been the toolshed of a careless farmer, who had neglected to paint it and to close the cracks between the boards. This was the community building of Los Hualles, which is not a town, but rather a locality. The scattered dwellings there are small and crowded, built of unpainted wood tinted green by lichen, so warped by wind and rain that one can travel for miles without seeing a corner that makes a true right angle or a wall that is flush into the ground. The people here eke out a living on hilly, wooded plots of about 20 hectares per family. They are Spanish-speaking people of Indian ancestry. Their ancestors were driven off the rich land in the valleys by the Spanish in the 18th century. They live now mainly by selling *carbon*, a charcoal fuel they make by burning wood, and *leña*, firewood. The *carbon* is transported to the fair at Osorno in sacks tied to the luggage rack on the *micro*'s roof, beside pigs and other merchandise, while the owners of the *carbon* and the owners of the other merchandise ride to the fair inside the *micro*. The *leña*, a much bulkier product, is bought up at minimal prices by *camioneros* (men who own trucks). For subsistence, and for occasional sale, the *campesinos* of Los Hualles sow peas, oats, potatoes and garden vegetables; and they raise a few animals – pigs, chickens, goats, sheep.

The new community building was not identified by a sign – there are no signs in Los Hualles. It was 15 feet wide and 21 feet long, too small to hold the 50 people, counting children and visitors, who had gathered to inaugurate it. Between the small, crowded building and the muddy road there stood a wooden fence, but there was no gate, it being assumed that anyone who was likely to come here was used to climbing fences. A few feet away, down a wet embankment, two members of the PPH centre were roasting a pig over a fire protected from the drizzle by a makeshift shelter of branches and boards. Each of the twelve households that constitute the Los Hualles PPH centre had contributed 100 pesos, slightly more than the proceeds of the sale of one sack of *carbon*, to raise the 1200 pesos needed to purchase the pig for the feast. All the other food was donated.

As many people as were able crowded into the building, taking care to avoid pushing a child into the brazier of burning coals placed in the centre of the room to provide heat. I worried that the floor would collapse. Uncle José, the MC, disc jockey, and announcer of The Voice of the Coast, performed gymnastics with his portly body and portable tape recorder, edging through the crowd, extending his arm and tilting his torso to place the recorder near the mouth of each speaker in turn. Each visitor was introduced and duly applauded. A young man in a tattered blue suit led a rendition of the national anthem, lagging, off-key.

> Pure Chile, to you we pledge
> Either you will be the tomb of the dead,
> Or else a refuge against oppression
> Or else a refuge against oppression!

The last verse, recently added by the armed forces in praise of themselves, was omitted. It was explained with some embarrassment that the people had not yet learned it.

The minutes were read, consisting mainly of a list of the sacrifices the members had made in order to construct the building.

Eduardo Fuica	donated the land
José Naguil	gave 25 boards and one kilo of roof nails
Sra Maria Garcés	2 kilos of nails
Elva Hernandez	3 kilos of nails
Florencio Nilian	3 logs
Pedro Catriyao	4 logs
José Tremihual	3 kilos of nails
Eduardo Fuica	all the necessary 2 × 4s and roof beams

Francisco Periguel loaned the centre 1000 pesos, without interest, for having the wood cut at a sawmill, the sum to be repaid from the proceeds of the next benefit.

The roof was purchased from the proceeds of a raffle, for which the members donated the prizes. (Some of the prizes were three bowls, a butter dish, a chicken....)

Sr José Felipe Naguil, a participant, spoke, concluding as follows:

Nothing remains for me to say except to thank the community repeatedly, to thank the group that is working with iron unity. May we continue with this idea of united effort, because unity, as they say, makes strength, and we shall continue forward. May this not be the enthusiasm of a day or a couple of months, but let us continue from here on. Let this be the beginning of our organization, the beginning of our union as people and as neighbours, in order to show our children that we are people. We have duties and we also have something to give, something to contribute, because each person, no matter how small, no matter how humble, has a grain of sand to contribute for his own welfare and that of the community, and that is all I am able to say to you at this time.

As soon as Sr Naguil was properly applauded, Sr Florencio Nilian proceeded to read a poem, which was also properly applauded.

El Fervor Campesino	*The Ardour of the Peasant*
Presente coordinadores!	We are present, coordinators!
Debemos felicitar	We must congratulate
que nos muestran el progreso	those who show us progress
que debemos apechiguar.	that we should take to heart.
Con amistad y cariño exigo	With friendship and affection I say
sigamos el camino	we must continue on the path
del estudio padres e hijos.	of PPH studies.
Aquí van mis preferencias	Here are my opinions,
con dignidad doy a conocer	with dignity I make them known,
para el campesino el progreso	for the peasant progress
lleva por nombre FREDER.	is named FREDER.
Sus enseñanzas nos dan valor	Its teachings give us courage
y alegria para vivir mejor.	and joy for a better life.

Then it was Father Winfredo's turn to speak. He told the people that Los Hualles had always been a combative community. He reminded them of why they had built the building; it was because PPH was not allowed to meet in the school. Years ago, in the days of democratic governments, the people had built the school with their own hands; it was intended to be a place to hold meetings of all kinds. Winfredo had gone to the provincial education director to protest against the exclusion of PPH from the school, accompanied by Margarita Mellao, the teenage girl who serves as one of the volunteer coordinators (every centre has two) for PPH-Los Hualles. They got nowhere. It was then that Margarita, with the courage of youth, had exclaimed: 'Los Hualles will go forward even if we have to meet in my father's chicken coop!'

The crowd resisted the urge to burst into applause. (Some confessed later that they were worried that Winfredo would go too far and get them all arrested.) A foreign priest, under the protection of the Dutch ambassador and the bishop, can take risks that a Chilean peasant cannot afford.

Father Winfredo ended his speech by not saying goodbye. 'FREDER never says goodbye, ever, because our people, our equipment, our vehicles, our microphones, are always and at all times at the service of the *campesino*.'

The last person invited to speak was Don Eduardo Fuica himself, the man who had given the land, the 2 × 4s, and the roof beams; a grey-haired senior citizen whose teeth were yellow-brown and few. 'What can I say?' he asked. 'Nothing,' he answered. Instead he sang a song. The old man's song was so utterly frivolous that I am reluctant to waste the time of the important decision-makers who may read this report by writing down the words, for they are surely the least important of all the words uttered there that day, although they were the most applauded.

O gran señores	Ladies and gentlemen,
de mis amores	from my love life
una aventura voy a cantar	I shall tell you of an adventure,
que me ha pasado	something that happened
en una noche oscura	on a dark night
cuando a una rubia fui a conquistar.	when I went to conquer a blonde.
Salí de casa muy presuroso	I left my house in a hurry,
muy orgulloso y muy formal	very proud and very formal,
bien afeitado mi terno nuevo	well-shaved, in a new suit and
mi buen sombrero rico galan.	my best hat, a rich gallant.

Como la noche fué tan copiosa	Since the night was so wet,
que dejo el suelo como un jabon	it left the earth like soap,
yo sin pensarlo caí sentado	and I fell, sitting
sobre me tongo de un resbalon	on my fancy hat,
con mi tonguito todo agollado	my hat flattened
de un fuerte golpe que le atraqué.	by the force of my fall.
Fui a casa de mi adorada	I went to the house of my adored, but
por desgracia no le encontré	unfortunately she was not there;
me hizo el turno y a carcajadas	she played me false and mocked me, and
y esta manana ya se te fué.	in the morning she had gone away.

Pedro Catriyao, whose surname, like Tremihual, Nilian, Naguil, is Mapuche Indian, not Spanish, in his capacity as volunteer coordinator, used Uncle José's gracefully proffered tape recorder microphone to speak on the radio to his neighbours who were not present:

I ask those people who today are not in this program, I call on them to come close to us here, and we can work with greater unity, for in this area of Los Hualles there are 25 households, and we are only 12 families participating here in this program. Not everyone has joined us yet, but I make a call that they come close, and we will work together united, and thus our community will advance much more, and also I ask the young people to come here to this little house to a new life.

After the speeches, we devoted ourselves to trying to keep warm while the cooks finished preparing the feast. I huddled in the north-west corner with some men in ponchos, approximately my own age, who kept their hands in their pockets and their shoulders hunched as they sniffled and coughed. In view of the abundance of virus in my immediate vicinity, I drew from my pocket a plastic bottle containing vitamin C, and took 100 milligrams. The sniffler next to me had noticed me taking the pill, so I politely offered him one. Somewhat to my surprise, he eagerly accepted it. Since several people in the north-west corner had seen me giving the pill, I thought it best to offer one to each of them, by asking whether anyone else had a cold. They all had colds. Everyone along the north wall had a cold. Whether the rest of the members of PPH-Los Hualles had colds I do not know, because by the time I got to the north-east corner I had no more pills to give.

The peasants had a better idea – *chicha*, a rustic alcoholic beverage made of whatever fruit is available, in this case apples. Taken in moderation, it is compatible with the new life to which Pedro Catriyao called the young people. It was awful-tasting stuff, but I had to down mine rapidly because there were only two glasses, and I had to empty the glass so that the next drinker could use it. After a few drinks, the men in the north-west corner began to mutter against one 'Don Transito', a neighbour. Their opinion was that he had made a profit in the past by acting as middleman in the sale of building materials to community organizations, but that when he found that there was no money to be made from PPH, he decided to oppose it.

Meanwhile, in the south-east corner, Uncle José, waist deep in urchins, was taping a show for 'Children's World'. He and his assistants encouraged each child to sing a song or to recite a verse. Uncle José commanded the audience to applaud enthusiastically, no matter how badly the child performed, even – as was usually the case – if the child did not perform at all, and especially if she broke into tears. Children who failed the first time were given a second and sometimes a third chance. The assistants were Sparky, a 12-year-old boy, small for his age, and Squirrel, a pretty 13-year-old girl. Sparky and Squirrel were the encouragers. They chatted amiably with the children, bringing greetings from the city children, and telling them that they too had been scared the first time they were on the air. Sparky began his part of the broadcast by saying: 'It's very cold today in Los Hualles, but we are warm inside because of the *cariño* (love, affection, warmth) in our hearts.' After the show Sparky and Squirrel played and made jokes, while the country children stood quietly, in a group in the corner, staring straight ahead – thinking, no doubt, of food.

The promised feast finally arrived: enormous quantities of roast pig, boiled potatoes, carrot and potato salad, chicken stew, homemade bread, homemade butter, homemade quince jelly, honey biscuits, cake and *chicha*. Jorge Zuleta, the CIDE staff member who coordinates PPH-Osorno, in a characteristic stroke of genius, found a way to make the meal a symbol of solidarity. First, we all held each other's hands and raised them into the air. Second, the parents served the children. Third, the children served the parents.

Back in Osorno the next day, I listened to the news on The Voice of the Coast. The staccato voice of the announcer was interspersed with excerpts from 'Seventy-six Trombones'.

Cairo: The ex-Shah of Iran died today in a military hospital near Cairo. Egyptian president Anwar Sadat announced that the Shah will be given a state funeral.
(Seventy-six Trombones)
Los Hualles: The PPH centre of Los Hualles inaugurated yesterday its new meeting place, built by the labour of the people of the community.
(Seventy-six Trombones)
On the occasion, don José Felipe Naguil, speaking for the members of the Centre, declared (tape recording): 'with iron unity . . . we shall continue forward . . . to show our children that we are people'.

3   The Candle

Having seen the opening of the community building at Los Hualles, which represented a notable achievement of Parents and Children, we need to see a regular weekly meeting of a centre in order to form a preliminary image of the program's ordinary mode of operation.

Los Parrones (literally 'The Grape Arbours') was the name of one of the places where Tito and I went in a jeep, on another rainy day, to visit a regular weekly meeting. Los Parrones is a locality where subsistence farming is relatively less important than commercial cattle-raising, where the members of PPH tend to be wage-labourers on other people's land rather than tillers of their own mini-farms, although here too they have garden plots and a few animals. In general, about two-thirds of the Parents and Children centres in the Osorno region are in the hilly coastal lands, where Indian surnames predominate and people subsist by gathering wood and raising poor crops on poor soil, while about one-third are in the flatter, richer central valley areas, where commercial agriculture is feasible, where PPH members are more likely to have Spanish surnames and to be employed as labourers, or to be chronically unemployed. Overall, the numbers of indigenous and European surnames are roughly equal – a fact which is worth mentioning because the high proportion of Mapuche or Huilluche names is evidence that PPH reaches the poorest strata of the population. But, from another point of view, it is a fact that should not be mentioned, since it suggests that the members are consciously aware that they are in a biracial program, which is misleading because (except in 6 centres in an area where the Mapuche language is still spoken, called San Juan de la Costa, where PPH deliberately promotes the preservation of Indian music) in Parents and Children, race is not noticed.

The meeting at Los Parrones was held in a private home, a

two-room structure made of unpainted boards whose bent and irregular shapes made it impossible properly to close all the cracks, set a hundred yards back from a sort of road, in a grove of trees. The windowpanes were pieced together from transparent or translucent scraps of plastic that had once been sacks for powdered milk, or shelters for seedlings on one of the area's large farms.

It was not clear to me whether the house and its immediately adjoining land were owned by the hosts, Guillermo Mujica and his wife, Señora Ofelia, or whether the place formed part of a large farm on which, as is not uncommon, the landowner allows his employees to occupy or erect rustic dwellings and to cultivate small gardens. Six families had sent representatives, in each case the mother, which meant that official attendance was seven (six plus the Mujica family itself), a lower-than-average figure for which several explanations were suggested to us, including the miserable weather, the long distances people had to walk in the rain on muddy roads and trails, and the fact that this meeting was the fourth and last of a unit. Every fourth meeting is devoted to review and evaluation; these last meetings of units are consistently less attractive than the first three. There was also the inconvenient hour (3 o'clock on a weekday afternoon), necessitated by the circumstance that the coordinator, Señorita Anita, who worked as a maid, could get *salida* (permission to leave the house where she works) only at that hour of that day. Guillermo Mujica was a coordinator too, but it was clear that Anita was the driving force of the centre, Guillermo being accorded the honour of the office due to his status as host, as a man, and as the owner of a handsome imitation leather jacket. He stood up wearing his jacket during the entire meeting, as if he were a sentinel or sergeant-at-arms, although his intention may have been only to show respect for his guests by remaining standing, or to reduce by one the number of boxes and other somewhat incongruous objects pressed into service as chairs.

The number of warm bodies in the room considerably exceeded the official attendance. There were two ladies who came 'just to come', who had not joined PPH because they had no young children. There was a young man, short in stature, with longish hair, large, deep-set fever-ravaged eyes, muddy boots, dirty clothes and smelling of *chicha*; he took no part whatever in the meeting, except for occupying a space, and occasionally expressing exaggerated politeness, mainly by saying *gracias*. There were also Anita, the coordinator; Tito, the driver; myself, the foreign visitor; Maria Catriyao, the sector-coordinator, who had come in the jeep with Tito and me; and assorted children, who for the most part remained in the other room with the *abuelita* (little grandmother), since the meeting was supposed to be for adults only.

Anita conducted the meeting with the help of a coordinator's manual, asking the people to recall conclusions they had drawn in the three previous meetings of the same unit. The home should be a place of *cariño* (warmth, affection) and *unidad* (unity). People should talk over their problems and express how they feel; in particular, women should not be afraid to talk to their husbands. Anita was particularly interested in pursuing a question that apparently had been discussed in previous meetings but had not been satisfactorily answered: 'Should we hit our children?'

'*El niño no tiene que crecer humillado* (the child should not grow up humiliated),' said Sra Ofelia. Her statement seemed to be a reminder of a conclusion of a previous meeting, which was relevant to the question of whether children should be hit. However, Sra Ofelia did not go so far as to declare baldly that children should never be hit, although one had the impression that such was the conclusion the coordinator wanted the group to draw.

Senora Fresia spoke next. She was middle-aged, tense, dressed in a jumble of recycled hand-me-down materials – a manner of dress that spoke of exigency rather than style or tradition. She described a case, which might have been her own, where the children ran wild and the mother's attempts to *enderezarlos* (straighten them out) were futile because she had no support from her husband. One of the children got into trouble (she did not say what kind), and the woman said to the man: 'Now you see what happens when you don't pay any attention to the children!' After that, *los dos vieron* (the two of them saw to it), and the children straightened out.

Anita wanted a clear answer to the question, 'Should we hit our children?' But Maria, the sector-coordinator, who acted as Anita's supervisor and trainer, gently led her to move the conversation in the direction of encouraging people to share their personal experiences. The discussion turned to the problem of don Rosendo, a topic the participants evidently found deeply disturbing, for the conversation became disjointed, interrupted by long pauses, composed largely of elliptical remarks pregnant with hidden meanings. Left to my own devices, I would have understood nothing, no doubt partly because it was a subject which the group could allude to only obscurely in the presence of a visitor. Maria explained the gist of it to me later. Several years ago, Manuelito, a son of a family inscribed in PPH, tried to steal a baby pig from a neighbour named Rosendo. Rosendo caught the child with the pig and *se pasó* (went too far), not just repossessing the pig but also beating the child on the spot, sending Manuelito home bruised, bleeding and terrified. How Manuelito's father reacted, neither Maria nor anyone else wanted to tell me.

The conclusion of the discussion, or of this series of discussions (for it seemed that the group had been strengthening its commitment to its conclusion over the course of several meetings), was that reconciliation was needed. The rift in the community stemming from the Manuelito incident and its aftermath had gone on too long.

As one of the women put it, 'the important thing is for everybody to go forward united'. Guillermo said: 'Things are much better in Los Parrones now that we have the PPH centre and we can talk over our problems.' This last remark may have been an effort on Guillermo's part to let me hear what I wanted to hear, but in any case I found his assertion plausible.

It is well known that any top-down system of development planning throws away enormous amounts of available information because it ignores the expertise of the peasants concerning their own problems. A program such as PPH, on the other hand, because it empowers people to analyse and solve their own problems, uses local information better; at the same time, it shifts downward the locus of control of the planning process. Only a methodology like PPH's can bring it to light that what is stopping progress in Los Parrones is a petty feud stemming from the attempt of a child to steal a pig; in the course of coping with the obstacle they have identified as holding their community back, the people of the locality become better organized, and because better organized, more influential.

After concluding that a reconciliation among certain neighbours was needed, the expectation was that the group would act to solve the problem it had analysed, but in fact the process went no further at this particular meeting because Anita decided that because it was getting late, it was time to move on to the worksheets; she passed out lithographed sheets of pre-reading exercises for the parents to take home to their children. The children do the exercises at home with help from the parents, and then the parents return the completed work to the coordinators at the next meeting of the centre. After distributing the material, Anita carefully drilled the parents by asking them detailed questions, until it was very clear that someone from each family understood the exercises thoroughly; in reality, some of the mothers and fathers were learning to read themselves, under the guise of helping their children.

Anita had to go, her *salida* was over. The others began the third phase of their meeting, which consisted of sewing. The ladies tear up outgrown children's clothes and use the material to make new clothes, exchanging material with each other so that the children will not recognize their new clothes as made out of their siblings' old clothes – an idea that began in one PPH centre and spread to several others.

I found myself more or less alone on a rainy evening, sitting on a bench in a rustic two-room wooden house in Los Parrones, while the women neglected me to devote themselves to their sewing, and the jeep and its driver left to take Anita and Maria home, intending to come back for me later. I decided to review some recent World Bank publications on the economics of education, which I was carrying in my briefcase, not so much because I had to read those particular books at that particular moment as because I wanted to relieve my hosts of the obligation to entertain me. As time passed, the guests departed by ones and twos. The alcoholic young man was among the first to leave. Guillermo assured me that he was harmless, 'not like those who make trouble'. He had come just to be with people for a while.

I was provided with great quantities of home-baked bread and *café au lait*, which I did not deserve and which the Mujicas could not afford to give me, and when darkness fell, with a candle. The peasants spend their evenings in the dark; even if they have a candle or two for emergencies, they ordinarily cannot afford to burn them. This kindess was embarrassing, because I, a moderately prosperous citizen of an industrialized democracy in the northern hemisphere, should not be receiving a burning candle from Guillermo Mujica, and I felt a need to give Guillermo something, even though my research budget did not include a line item for giving gifts to the subjects under study.

I did not, at that point, compose a letter to the Reasonable Social Scientist, and I hesitate to share my speculations on what I should have said to her if I had written to her then, without first marking a line between fiction and fact. The Reasonable Social Scientist is a fiction introduced to facilitate the discussion of methodological issues. By contrast, Winfredo, Guillermo, Maria, Anita, and all the people, events and statements reported from the field, are facts; I have rearranged my notes and added commentary to facilitate presentation, but nothing is imaginary. Whether the anecdotes reported are typical is another question; we shall have to deal later with issues concerning moves from descriptions of single events to statements about what PPH-Osorno is in general, or to lessons people elsewhere might learn from PPH's experience.

Now, here is what, with the benefit of hindsight, I think I should have written to her then.

Los Parrones, Region 10
Chile

25 July 1980

Dear Reasonable Social Scientist

The time has come when we must clarify certain aspects of our relationship. You will recall that we agreed on certain tautologies – that it is better to have more benefit, that every choice that commits resources puts the resources somewhere instead of somewhere else, that evaluation should provide data useful for making decisions. You may think that a sound systems management research methodology is simply a matter of following the logical consequnces of these self-evident propositions. Since I want there to be no misunderstanding between us, I need to assert that certain standard doctrines are not consequences of self-evident propositions, and are not valid, as is the case, for instance, with the doctrine of preordinate objectives.

Until recently, the doctrine had no name because the validity of its precepts was tacitly assumed. It was not necessary to give the doctrine a name, because it was not necessary to talk about it. It was a blind commitment; it lay beyond the horizon of consciousness.

The doctrine of preordinate objectives permits the evaluator, if he is lucky, to pocket his fee without doing much work. He begins by reviewing documents and consulting the staff in order to determine the objectives of the project, or program, or curriculum, or whatever. If the whatever has no clear objectives, then the evaluation can be a short one – the whatever fails. The premises of this brief evaluation can be left implicit if the audience to which the evaluation is addressed accepts them tacitly, or, if necessary, the premises can be spelled out in some such terms as the following: you cannot go anywhere if you do not know where you are going, because if you travel without a destination you will never know whether or not you have arrived. You cannot achieve your objectives if you do not know what they are. Every whatever should be efficient, but efficiency is measured as cost per desired outcome; hence if the desired outcomes are not known, a whatever cannot be efficient. A whatever is, or ought to be, a system, but a system, by definition, has objectives; so if a whatever has no objectives, it is not a system, and therefore it does not exist, or if it does exist it should not. An evaluator is supposed to measure outcomes, but cannot be expected to measure outcomes if it is not known what outcomes are desired; hence a progam without clear objectives cannot be evaluated, but every program ought to be evaluated. Therefore, a programme without clear objectives is a bad program QED.

If the program does have clear objectives, then the evaluator who believes in preordinate objectives will have more work to do, starting with the selection of instruments to measure the outcomes.

PPH lends itself to evaluation by the short method, because its objectives are not clear. To be sure, the evaluator may not realize at first that the short method applies, because a cursory review of the project documents will show that the two-year program is divided into 12 units, that each unit has a manual for the coordinators, that each unit is divided into 4 meetings, that each meeting is divided into 4 parts, and that each of the 192 parts ($12 \times 4 \times 4 = 192$) has one or more clearly stated objectives. For example, the manual for Unit 8 says for Meeting 1, Part 2:

We must achieve	that the group airs its opinions on alcohol and discusses the extreme opinions (good–bad) that exist in the group.

There are 35 sets of worksheets for children; the parents use them in helping the children to learn at home. They all have clear objectives too, and the psychologists who prepared the worksheets took the trouble to make most of the objectives clear to the parents. For example, Worksheet 25, Activity 3, provides a cartoon of a father asking his pre-school children to compare two saucepans, saying how they are alike and how they are different. An explanation for parents reads: 'with these games, the child learns to concentrate and to pay attention'. There are approximately 660 objectives. (The figure 660 is derived by estimating an average of 8 objectives per worksheet and 2 per part of a meeting: $8 \times 35 + 2 \times 192 \doteqdot 660$.)

However, the evaluator who attempts to discern the master plan behind the approximately 660 clearly stated or clearly implied objectives, by relating them upward to the goals and philosophy stated in program documents, and downward to the actions of project staff, coordinators and participants, will soon find himself confused.

The evaluation of PPH-Osorno cannot be saved from unseemly brevity by an ingenious method for deducing the true main overall objectives from a mass of inconsistent evidence, but it can be saved by shifting the focus. One such shift of focus, which will be discussed later, would be to consider the inspiration which PPH has drawn from Paulo Freire, who holds that in good education we all become more human in dialogue, sharing in truth and in common projects – on this view, PPH can be perceived to have (if one wishes to keep the word 'objective') a peculiar sort of objective, a second-order objective, in which it becomes an objective that the peasants participate in the setting of objectives not previously set by the staff. Another shift of focus, to be discussed briefly now, can be achieved by heeding the wise counsel of Michael Scriven.

Scriven and others have denounced a logical error in the doctrine of preordinate objectives. The benefits achieved may or may not be those intended at the time the objectives were set. Since evaluation determines the worth of a thing, it is properly concerned with the thing itself, not with the intentions that were in the minds of its creators and managers. One can even argue that the evaluator works best when she does not know the objective of the thing she studies, since she can best ascertain the real effects if her mind is not clouded by knowledge of intents. A diagram which I have produced, somewhat under the influence of Scrivenism, classifies the real effects as follows:

	Good	*Bad*
Expected	Objectives achieved	Bad objectives achieved
Unexpected	Unexpected benefits	Unexpected harm

The doctrine of preordinate objectives invites us to focus on the upper left-hand corner of the diagram, and even there it tempts us to over-simplify, because it calls for a focus on stated objectives, whereas real objectives are likely to be unstated. It is irresponsible, because it judges the worth of a thing on the basis of an arbitrary subset of its effects.

Robert Stake has affixed the label 'responsive evaluation' to studies that attribute no special importance to preordinate objectives, but instead estimate the value of the benefits a program has actually produced.

Since I take the view that in embracing the doctrine of preordinate objectives you, the Reasonable Social Scientist, err (or, if I have persuaded you, used to err), I should, for the sake of candour, mention an issue where the argument you would probably make would probably be correct. You would probably say that the same Professor Scriven who has driven home the point that to evaluate, that is to say, to determine the worth of a thing, and to find out whether the stated objectives were achieved, are two separate and distinct activities, has also emphasized that for us to see a thing as it truly is, rather than as we wish it were, or as we expect it to be, or as we fear it might be, what we must above all control is bias. Bias is, however, you would probably say, an unwanted commodity with which I am abundantly supplied, since I admire the peasants too much, since I have no end of philosophical and political axes to grind, mostly of an anti-establishment and leftist sort, and mainly because I am an insider, having led the initial planning of an earlier version of PPH conducted a thousand kilometres to the north of Osorno in the years 1972–4.

By way of mitigation rather than exoneration, it should be entered as evidence that, considering my absence from Chile between 1974 and 1980 insufficient to make me an authentic outside evaluator, a panel of true outsiders, specialists in evaluation and social science methodology with no previous knowledge of Chile or of PPH, Messrs Malcolm Parlett, Joel Weiss and Edmund Sullivan, supervised the design and methods of the study. Parlett spent a week in Osorno in July 1980, and visited the PPH centre at El Monte. I am also tempted to defend myself further by saying that certain attitudes, such as the appreciation of Senor Mujica's kindess in providing me with a candle to a degree that some observers might regard as admiring Senor Mujica too much, are, from the point of view of a cultural activist, an accenting of the admirable in order to find generative themes which can lead to a heightening of awareness and to the growth of solidarity, even though from another point of view the same accenting of the admirable may look like an idealization of peasant virtue, to the detriment of a sober and balanced assessment of the main features of the mentality of an oppressed class. But this remark does not belong here – by referring to cultural action, I am using a frame of reference for which you (the Reasonable Social Scientist) are not yet prepared.

> Yours truly,
> The Borrower of the Candle

NOTES AND REFERENCES

The views of Scriven and Stake, and the use and abuse of objectives in evaluation in general, are discussed by Elliot Eisner and other contributors to David Hamilton and Malcolm Parlett *et al.* (eds), *Beyond the Numbers Game* (London: Macmillan, 1977).

Among the summaries of recent trends in evaluation are *Effective Evaluation: Improving the Usefulness of Evaluation Results Through Responsive and Naturalistic Approaches*, by Egon Guba and Y. S. Lincoln (San Francisco: Jossey–Bass, 1981) and 'Educational Evaluation: Trends Towards More Participatory

Approaches', by Steven Klees, Paulo Esmanhoto and Jorge Werthein (August 1982), available from CIDE, Casilla 13608, Santiago, Chile. Both have extensive bibliographies.

'The thing is not created in its objective, but in its realization. Nor is the result the true whole; rather the true whole is the result together with the process. The objective by itself, as the guiding tendency of the process, is a lifeless generality; by itself it is unreal. The naked result is the corpse which the process leaves behind' (G. W. F. Hegel, *Phänomenologie des Geistes* (Bamberg und Würzburg: Goebhardt, 1807) paragraph 3; my translation).

4 Some Definitions of Efficiency

Evaluation, as Daniel Stufflebeam and my friend the Reasonable Social Scientist have emphasized, should provide decision-makers with information that is useful for making decisions. In this respect, efficiency is a particularly important concept, because it is closely linked to an important definition of rational decision-making; namely, a decision is rational if it accords with the maxim: among several means to a given end, choose the most efficient.

Efficiency epitomizes the systems approach – so much so that from a systems point of view, research that does not culminate in a judgment about efficiency is not complete. In the end comes the decision. The decision, if it is rational, selects the most efficient system for achieving the benefits. Research provides information that helps the decision-maker to make the decision.

The ideal reader, who remembers everything and forgets nothing, will remember that in Chapter 1, efficiency was defined as cost-effectiveness.

COST-EFFECTIVENESS studies compare the cost of achieving the same benefits by different means.

COSTS are the resources that must be spent to attain the objectives.

An INSTRUMENT is a tool used to measure the values of variables, for example to measure costs, or to measure benefits (a benefit being equivalent to the attainment of an objective).

A HYPOTHESIS proposes for testing a relationship or impact between two variables, e.g. that where PPH methods (or a specific method) are used, children learn more (or score significantly higher on a specific test).

The DEPENDENT VARIABLE and the INDEPENDENT VARIABLE are

related by the HYPOTHESIS. The INDEPENDENT VARIABLE is the one the manager controls, e.g. how much of RESOURCES to BUDGET for a given program, while the DEPENDENT VARIABLE corresponds to the desired outcome, i.e. the benefits.

MEASUREMENT keeps track of how much a system is costing and how effective it is, by providing numerical information that reflects COSTS and benefits.

A SYSTEM is a set of ELEMENTS that work together to perform a function. Some systems are more COST-EFFECTIVE, i.e. more EFFICIENT than others. For example, PPH may be more or less EFFICIENT than another SYSTEM for organizing communities, or another SYSTEM for teaching pre-reading skills.

It follows from these definitions that efficiency is desirable. It could not possibly be undesirable. Nobody needs to say, 'I have tried efficiency, and on the basis of my own personal experience I assure you that it is good', because it is good by definition. The efficiency of a system is the sum of all the good things (benefits, objectives achieved) minus all the bad things (costs), compared to a similar calculation made for alternative systems.

It follows also that, strictly speaking, efficiency is not a good thing, because it is not an objective or a benefit. It is a proportion that measures benefits against costs.

EFFICIENCY v. EQUITY

Some people who consider themselves friends of efficiency will resist the logic of my analysis at this juncture. In particular, people who are accustomed to speak of 'efficiency v. equity', as if equity, i.e. justice, were by definition inefficient, will drag their feet and rack their brains in search of counter-arguments when they are made to realize that the usual definition of efficiency implies that to speak of 'efficiency v. equity' or 'efficiency v. X' is nonsense because efficiency is not a goal; it is a summary of our success in reaching any and all goals.

Equity, or any other good, counts as a benefit. It is therefore included in efficiency. The staff members of PPH and other people who do *educacion popular* will smile when they read this, because they are people who work for equity (justice), who are constantly told by people who consider themselves to be at a higher level of sophistication in the field of economics: 'It is nice that you are in favour of justice, but you are naive if you do not realize that the only way to get justice is to sacrifice efficiency.' They smile because they are reassured that whatever sophisticated critics of this type may mean to say, what they do say is a misuse of the word 'efficiency'. If the sophisticated critic goes on to say that in the long run it would be better if PPH did not exist, because such programs are bound to lead to levels of justice incompatible with efficiency, the critic only compounds his error.

If, as Michael Scriven says, the role of evaluation is to determine the worth of a thing, then from a true systems viewpoint (as distinct from a perturbed systems viewpoint that allows talk about the trade-off between efficiency and equity), the role of evaluation is to determine the efficiency of a thing, in this case the efficiency of PPH.

But perhaps this discussion is becoming too complex. Using a dialectic method, this study begins with a cost-effectiveness or systems frame of reference, and then edges away from it gradually as the realities we encounter impose upon us a transformation of our concepts. This method imposes a burden on the reader who is accustomed to executive summaries, because dialectic logic by its nature resists summary.

The table of contents provides a sort of general outline of the text of this report, but it is unable to deliver the instant grasp of the logic of the report that readers of executive summaries are accustomed to demanding and getting. Such a summary would have to show how the transition from one viewpoint to another is achieved, but the transition cannot be briefly summarized at the beginning.

It is not that the transition is hard to grasp – this text is not profound or mysterious – it is simply that the reader must first get used to thinking in terms of the particular version of the systems approach used here, before the idea of moving beyond it will make any sense to him.

Unfortunately, the reader, who may be in a rather grumpy mood because of the postponement of the gratification that comes with understanding, who may not be ready to believe that understanding this text is, although necessarily a little slow, not difficult, and who is also aware that even after he understands it, he may conclude that it is wrong, may be inclined to complain about what he may consider a bothersome ambiguity. Remembering that some tenets of the systems *problematique* were already questioned in the last chapter's letter to the Reasonable Social Scientist, he may legitimately raise the question of whether the rejection of the doctrine of preordinate objectives, so that we speak of real benefits with no special regard for intentions, is or is not the first of a series of dialectic transformations of the systems approach. The reader may charge in all fairness, and without the writer being in the least able to defend himself against the charge, that the writer did not say either that responsive evaluation is part of the antithesis or that it is part of the thesis. My conscience permits me to believe that the puzzle just mentioned constitutes a pardonable, even desirable, ambiguity. It adds suspense to the story; the reader needs to read the following episodes to answer the questions: Which side is the writer on? Will the concepts be transformed?

Unfortunately, however, on top of the considerable strain introduced into the already not necessarily amiable relations between the reader and the writer by the ambiguity just mentioned, we are now beginning to discuss some definitions of 'efficiency' that do not figure in this study, at the beginning, or in the middle, or at the end, which must be mentioned in order to make clear by contrast the premises of the cost study of PPH-Osorno. Since I felt, as I still feel, inadequate to the task of exorcising certain alien concepts of efficiency from this text, to prevent them from haunting it by ringing seductive bells in the mind of the reader, calling to mind common definitions of 'efficiency' that pass themselves off as being, but are not, the simple concept of searching for effective ways to do good that this study takes as its initial standpoint, I invented a pretext for leaving The Voice of the Coast office in Osorno, where I was writing this, to take a short walk.

I walked to the telephone company to make a long distance call, passing several beggars along the way. At the door of the telephone company, two boys, apparently about 14 and 5, asked me for money to buy bread. Child beggars make me angry because they whine and plead while they are begging, or while they are trying to sell you some useless thing at an inflated price, which amounts to the same thing as begging; and then they laugh at you and fight among themselves as soon as your back is turned. The adult beggars have developed more consistent personalities. I did not make a deliberate decision about the two boys, but I soon found myself listening to myself tell them that I would not give them money, but if they would wait for me to make my telephone call, I would give them bread. As I made the telephone call, I rationalized my attitude by saying to myself that however little they deserve a piece of bread, they deserve it at least as much as I do. When I emerged from the telephone company, I found that the two boys had gone away; either they did not want bread, or they did not believe I would keep my promise. But since I was brought up to believe that a promise is a promise, I bought some bread anyway in case the boys should turn up: 10 pieces, each piece the size of a doughnut, for 38 pesos (US $1). In the short journey from the bakery to the office, I met 6 beggars – 2 adults, 3 large children, and 1 small child – to each of whom I gave one piece, distributing all told six-tenths of my supply. One of the two adults, a blind man seated on the sidewalk with a cup held in both hands, put the bread under his poncho for future consumption. The other five beggars began to eat the bread immediately.

I do not know which is most useless: theorizing about evaluation, giving away bread, or evaluating PPH-Osorno. However, I have decided to continue all three activities.

Three doctrines relating to efficiency, the libertarian, lifetime-earnings and count-all-costs doctrines, will be discussed in the following paragraphs. The libertarian provides a reminder that the systems approach has many virtues because it opposes it for reasons the present writer thinks are the wrong reasons.

LIBERTARIAN EFFICIENCY

The libertarian viewpoint identifies efficiency with the decisions made by a perfect market. It permits, as does the previously-discussed doctrine of preordinate objectives, a short and negative evaluation of PPH. From such a viewpoint, no social program is efficient. The holders of such views have become well-known for advocating that public services like hospitals and schools should be privatized, and that individuals should be provided with funds with which to purchase the services they want in a market. Although libertarian arguments are usually made against social programs financed by taxes, in principle they apply also to programs like PPH paid for by the contributions of European churchgoers. If no social program is good, then PPH is not good; aid to the peasants should take the form of cash grants to individuals or to households.

The doctrine in question is deduced in the following way: efficiency is defined as a social optimum; that is to say, a maximum of good and a minimum of bad for everyone in the society (given the constraints imposed by available resources and technology). But good and bad are adjectives standing for judgments each person must make for himself; no one should make a judgment about what is good for someone else. Hence instead of 'good', we should say 'preferred', and define the social optimum as the state where most people get most of what they most prefer, and least of what they prefer to avoid. Now, it can be shown mathematically that (given equality of property and income) if each person chooses what he prefers, i.e. uses money to buy the things preferred in a perfect market, then the result will be an optimum, a maximum of good (preferences satisfied) and a minimum of bad (preferences frustrated) for the society as a whole.

On the systems approach, one might adopt as an objective, for example, that every peasant parent in the Osorno region should know which combinations of foods will provide balanced nutrition for his or her children. (Indeed, that is one of the objectives of Units 10, 11 and 12 of PPH.) One would then measure efficiency by how cheaply the objective is achieved compared to other ways of achieving the same objective; or by how well it is achieved compared to other ways of spending the same amount of money in pursuit of the same objective. The libertarian view, on the other hand, implies that such objectives are illicit, and measures efficiency in another way, namely by the extent to which markets are used to allocate resources.

A cost-effectiveness study of PPH must use a concept of efficiency suitable for evaluating social programs. This study will be closer to the systems approach than to the libertarian approach, even though it will be a critique of the former.

Since I am dismissing two rejections of the systems approach (namely, the previously-discussed view that opposes efficiency to equity, and the first of the three distracting definitions of efficiency, which is the libertarian definition), it is evident that, even though I spend a good many of my waking hours fretting about its inadequacy and fuming about the seductive air of self-evidence surrounding its specious claim to be the paradigm of rational decision-making, I do not consider it to be the worst of all possible approaches. The two distractions which will be considered next can be regarded as two bad interpretations of the systems approach, and the flaws in them that will be pointed out can be regarded as showing that systems thinking, which is neither as bad as libertarianism nor as good as cultural action, itself admits of degrees of merit, so that certain interpretations of it are worse than others.

LIFETIME-EARNINGS AS A MEASURE OF EFFICIENCY

The lifetime-earnings approach is the next distraction; that is to say, another definition of efficiency that we shall not use, but which we need to mention in order to distinguish our cost-effectiveness study from others.

Any definition of efficiency relates inputs (costs) to outputs (benefits); the distinctive feature of lifetime-earnings studies is the way they measure benefits. They measure the value of education by the increased earnings of graduates. (The word 'benefit' is sometimes reserved to designate desirable outcomes measured in terms of money. Where the word is used according to this convention, the cost–benefit study is defined as one where the values of the outcomes are expressed in money, while the cost-effectiveness study is one where the values of the outcomes are expressed by comparing the real state of the system with a desired state of the system.)

When one tries to imagine a lifetime-earnings cost–benefit study of PPH-Osorno, one thinks of estimates of how many children will succeed in school because of PPH, of how many years they will prolong their schooling, and of how much money they will make in life that they would not have made if they had not been qualified for relatively high-paying jobs, because they went to advanced schools, because they succeeded in elementary schools, because their parents enrolled themselves and their children in PPH when the children were four. Letting one's imagination run in a slightly different direction, one thinks of existing studies of the economic value of pre-school education, and then of estimating what fraction of the knowledge and good habits delivered by a kindergarten is delivered by PPH, hoping that nobody will doubt the inference that a fraction of achievement of kindergarten learning goals produces some fraction of the earning power associated with further education.

Cost–benefit studies may sometimes be far-fetched because they depend on long, unverifiable chains of cause–effect relationships, asking us to attribute some part of the surgeon's income to the high quality of his playpen. But the causal links between early learning and adult income are not so vague that they cannot be traced. It really is the case that PPH is giving some children a headstart that will produce elementary school graduates, where in its absence these would have been early drop-outs, and that some of these children will become *micro*-drivers and waitresses instead of being unemployed. The increased earnings to be expected are not, in principle, unestimable. The reason why we do not define the benefits of PPH in this way is not reluctance to commit ourselves to far-fetched inferences, but rather the conviction that increased earnings are not the principal benefit of PPH. Furthermore, if the principal benefit of a program for peasants were that it increased the earnings of individuals, we would for that reason lower, not raise, our assessment of the program's merits. Lamentably, many educational studies do take the earnings of graduates as a measure of efficiency, or, similarly, as an index of the 'rate of return on investment in education' – thereby lending academic and scholarly prestige to the assumption that cash in the pockets of graduates is the proper aim of education.

Martin Carnoy has shown with data from several Latin-American countries that the main effect of increased schooling for the poor is to increase the number of years of school required for one to be selected for a job. The number of unemployed does not change, and the general level of wages rises only slightly; the main reason why higher qualifications are required to do the same job is not that more highly-schooled people do the job better, but that large numbers of highly-schooled people are trying to sell their services in the labour market.

We may put it down as a vice of the lifetime-earnings approach that it lends itself to promoting the illusion that the children of the peasantry will escape from poverty if, in the future, large numbers of them attain the 'educational' (i.e. school) levels that at the present time would cause them to be selected for jobs that pay relatively high salaries.

Another vice of the lifetime-earnings approach is that it contradicts the values PPH is trying to promote. Church-related schools and educational programs, and programs that respect the values of Latin-American workers and peasants, ordinarily assume that a well educated person is *una persona útil* (a useful person), not necessarily an earner of high wages. The evaluator can identify being well-educated with high earnings only if he accepts an apologetic and outmoded economic theory, which holds that in labour markets, rewards for services correspond to the social usefulness of the services. In fact, where the distributions of wealth and income are very unequal, and a market is used to allocated rewards for services, those who dedicate themselves to meeting the basic needs of people who have little or no money will work for low pay (in fact, in some cases they will be unpaid volunteers), while those who provide luxuries for people who have large incomes may receive high pay.

The Osorno region is a typical example of the very unequal distribution of wealth and income found in many parts of the third world. Visitors are impressed by the abundance of fine automobiles, yet the region figures prominently on the *Map of Extreme Poverty* issued in 1975 by the planning office of the Chilean government. A recent study of poverty in the area, by Dario Menanteau-Horta, states that all of the four provinces of the tenth region, where Osorno is located, have an infant mortality rate greater than 135 deaths per 1000 births. Textbook discussions of how the labour market would operate to reward those who work to satisfy other people's needs if income were equally distributed are not relevant.

The assumption that the only or main aim of rural education is to increase peasant income by qualifying them for higher-paying jobs or for the use of more profitable techniques is not relevant either. Indeed, if my friend Guillermo Mujica were told that the solution to the problems of the peasants in the region is for their children to go to school longer, to qualify themselves for employment in high-paying jobs, he would rightly dismiss the idea as *cosa que no va a pasar nunca* (something that will never happen). Earning more money by learning appropriate skills and technologies is a more realistic option, one that in a

balanced picture of benefits to peasants has its place; nevertheless, it is sometimes a benefit to learn to participate less rather
than more in the money economy – as many North Americans
are learning by reading the *Mother Earth News*, and as the
participants in PPH learn in Unit 12, *Aprovechamos lo que Tenemos*
(Let's Use What We Have), where the high nutritive value of the
grains and legumes the peasants produce or can obtain by barter
is contrasted with the low nutritive value of the soft drinks, teas,
prepared soups, gelatin desserts and refined flours that they buy
with cash.

To summarize the discussion so far of definitions of educational efficiency that we shall not use, not even as a point of
departure, we reject the misunderstanding that considers justice
an obstacle to the achievement of efficiency, the libertarian view
that identifies efficiency with the allocation of resources by the
market, and the lifetime-earnings view that measures benefit
through increments in individual incomes due to education. The
libertarian distraction objects to setting social objectives. The
lifetime-earnings distraction assumes the false premise that the
amount of money that finds its way into the pockets of adults
who as children used PPH worksheets is a good indicator of the
worth of the program.

COUNTING ALL COSTS

In addition to the libertarian and lifetime-earnings distractions,
one more distraction threatens to confuse our very young and
still innocent cost-effectiveness study of PPH. This distracter is
an interpretation of the systems concept of 'cost'. It is the
doctrine that the essence of a cost-effectiveness study is to count
all costs to anybody. An example of a study counting all costs to
anybody would be a study of a proposed dam in Oregon that
counts costs to farmers, fishermen, tourists, hunters, taxpayers,
and so on, and, of course, on the other hand also counts all
benefits to anybody. If the study does not attempt to count all
costs, it is not (according to this viewpoint) a cost-effectiveness
study. It is often said that a common defect of cost studies of
third-world development projects is that the shadow price of
volunteer labour time is left out or undervalued.

From the count-all-costs distraction, it follows that PPH is very expensive. Indeed, the more it succeeds in mobilizing volunteer support, the more expensive it becomes. If it were completely successful, its cost would be stratospheric. Let us estimate that the wages of a kindergarten teacher are roughly twice those of a paid PPH sector-coordinator, and that the time of the paid coordinator is twice as valuable as that of a volunteer coordinator and three times as valuable as that of a mother. The imputed values of the time of volunteer coordinators and mothers are estimates of the cash value of the lost opportunities to garden, launder or cook that the mother or other volunteer foregoes when she devotes an hour to helping her child learn or to another PPH activity. (We hope that the low values assigned to the time of mothers will not be taken as an insult to motherhood. It would be easier to draw the conclusions that will appear below if the values were high; we are using low estimates in order to show that the conclusions remain valid even where low estimates are used.) Rounding off actual PPH figures for the sake of ease of calculation, and estimating where necessary, we assume:

1000 children,
  500 mothers with 1 child each in the programme,
  250 mothers with 2 children each in the programme,
  100 volunteer coordinators,
   10 paid PPH coordinators;
1 hour spent in meetings (counted here as training) for each 3
    hours mother spends working with child;
value of an hour of a kindergarten teacher's time: $2 per hour;
average size of kindergarten class: 25.

On this basis, counting only labour costs, the cost of PPH for 1000 children for 1 hour is:

(mother-contact-hours × value of mother's time)
+ (mother-training-hours × value of mother's time)
+ (mother-training-hours × value of volunteer coordinator's
    time)
    ÷ number of mothers per volunteer coordinator)
+ (mother-training-hours × value of paid coordinator's time)
    ÷ number of mothers per paid coordinator)

$$= 750 \times 0.33 + 250 \times 0.33 + (250 \times 0.50) \div 7.5 + (250 \times 1)$$
$$\div 15*$$
$$= \$363.33$$

Making a similar calculation, counting only the value of labour as measured in money, the cost of 1 hour of kindergarten for 1000 children is:

number of children ÷ number of children per teacher × value of teacher's time = $1000 \div 25 \times 2 = \$80$.

On these assumptions, PPH costs approximately four and a half times as much per hour as kindergarten.

If, on the other hand, we make the same assumptions but do not impute a shadow price to the time of mothers and other volunteers, then the cost of PPH for 1000 children for 1 hour is:

(mother-training-hours × value of paid coordinator's time)
   ÷ number of mothers per paid coordinator
$$= (250 \times 1) \div 15 = \$16.67.$$

Making the same assumptions, except for disregarding the money value of the time of volunteers, kindergartens cost nearly five times as much as PPH.

It is evident that we stand in the presence of yet another way to abbreviate the evaluation of PPH. Even without obtaining more precise and reliable figures than the estimates used in the preceding calculations, one can deduce that it is highly probable that when a shadow price is imputed to donated time, PPH is not cost-effective. Fortunately for PPH, but unfortunately for the evaluator who wishes to complete this work quickly in order to do some sightseeing in South America before returning to Indiana, we believe that there are good reasons for counting as costs only the money actually spent.

Before continuing the argument, that is to say, before moving ahead to give reasons for not counting voluntary donations as

---

* The number of mothers per paid coordinator is set at 15 instead of 75 to account for the fact that the paid coordinators travel from place to place, regularly attending 5 different meetings, thus attending to 15 at a time instead of 75 at a time.

costs of the program, I shall give a concrete example of a successful volunteer effort.

Tremaico, a village not much different from Los Hualles or Los Parrones, suffered severe repression after the *coup* of 1973. For years afterwards, the people there were intimidated and disorganized. A PPH centre was organized in Tremaico in March 1979. In January 1980, the members of the centre, many of them illiterate and all of them poor, decided that what they and their children needed was to see a bit of the world. They organized a series of fund-raising events, all held on the same Sunday – a bazaar, a soccer game, a raffle, a *rayuela* tournament (*rayuela* is a local game similar to quoits), and a dance, selling refreshments at all of them. With the proceeds (about US $700), they bought bus tickets for themselves and their children, 75 people in all, to take a three-day tour of southern Chile. The tickets were the only expense of the trip, because the people contributed the food and packed it in advance for the trip. For Tremaico, the trip became a symbol of what the people could do working together; as one participant said: 'We worked together, and together we were strong.'

Two young women of Tremaico were the vital forces (the 'generators' as Jorge Zuleta would say) behind the bus tour of southern Chile. They were the volunteer coordinators who infected the others with their energy and enthusiasm. I can speak of only one of them because she is the only one I know; she was not employed at the time she helped organize the Tremaico bus tour, but is employed now. At work, she is a live-in maid, expected to be available to wait on the family seven days a week. If you see her at work, you will find that the expression in her eyes is dull, she speaks rarely, she moves slowly, and never talks back to her employers; I am inclined to guess, although I have not seen enough of her to prove it to myself, that she is evasive and resentful. On her prized and rarely-granted time off, she is still a volunteer PPH coordinator. It turns out that she can lead a group discussion, persuade the police to grant a permit to hold a meeting, and speak on the radio. She regards her volunteer hours as the time when she plays the role that gives meaning to her life.

An advocate of the count-all-costs doctrine could respond to this example by saying that 'cost' and 'benefit' are quite flexible concepts, which can be adjusted to describe this reality, and which, moreover, play a constructive role in describing it because they remind us to include information which we might otherwise omit. Surely, the opportunity the maid gives up to be a PPH coordinator in her time off is worth something to her, however little, so let us assign a small value to it, say, for the sake of argument 10 cents per hour. Then, on the benefit side, one could assign a high value to her activity as PPH coordinator – her new sense of her own worth, her *joie de vivre* and her dignity, say, for the sake of argument, $100 per hour. One has thus preserved the conceptual scheme, and done it in such a way that avoids treating the sacrifices made by volunteers in order to participate in a program like PPH as if they did not exist.

In reply, we note that the artificiality of assigning two numbers to the same hour, one to show its costs and the other to show its benefits, is not a mere coincidence due to the fact that we are writing our opponent's argument for him and are prejudiced against it, but is a necessary consequence of following the broad systems approach category 'cost' in a way that requires one to describe everything in Heaven and on Earth in terms of its money value.

Also in reply, we must say that we were misunderstood if we were taken to mean that the aim of rejecting the count-all-costs doctrine is to suppress information. If the mothers neglect their gardens to help their children learn to read, that neglect and the mothers' unhappiness about the size of the weeds in their cabbage patches, and the consequent shortage of cabbages, must be registered somewhere in the study. Our claim is that there are better and worse ways to describe, and that one of the worst, most abstract and most misleading ways to describe is to add apples and oranges: for example, by associating the activity of a peasant-woman attending a PPH meeting with a number representing the cost to her of being there instead of scrubbing the dirty clothes that are soaking at home, and then to take another number representing the cash provided by a church-related foundation in Holland, and to add the two numbers.

Here are some reasons why, in a program like PPH, the actual money spent is best left sole and undiluted as the definition of cost, provided that budget expenses are supplemented by descriptions of various disadvantages of the program, sacrifices people make, reasons for not funding it, etc.

1. The decision a funding agency makes is whether or not to approve a certain budget. The clearest way to provide useful

information is to answer the question of what happens if certain actual money expenditures are approved.

2. The cost-effectiveness study should throw into relief the fact that mobilizing volunteers is primarily a sign of a program's success. From the point of view of a funding agency, voluntary cooperation validates the decision of the agency, because it shows that its perception of a need is shared by the peasants themselves. It shows further that the agency was able to use the contributions of the European churchgoers who finance PPH through charitable agencies that represent them, as seed money, as a catalyst that mobilized resources far beyond the amounts of time and goods that the agency itself could afford to pay for with the money at its disposal.

3. Counting volunteer time as a cost constitutes a systematic bias aganist grassroots mobilization of local resources, but the bias of the decision-maker ought to be in the opposite direction. The decision-maker (that is to say, the one in New York, Toronto, Amsterdam, etc.) should favour volunteers because the amounts of aid that can come from outside are small compared to what is needed, hence the peasants must inevitably rely to a large extent on their own efforts; and because of democratic values – programs that rely for their existence on grassroots support are likely to be, to a large extent, under grassroots control.

Since a responsive approach to the study of PPH-Osorno requires that one become thoroughly acquainted with the program as a whole before trying to assess its main effects, one will postpone benefits at this point, and take up costs. The following chapter will be a cost study, to be completed by information on effectiveness later when one has presented a portrait of the program sufficiently complete to warrant judgments about its benefits.

NOTES AND REFERENCES

Joan Robinson and John Eatwell point out a fallacy similar to the one involved in speaking of a trade-off between equity and efficiency in a context where the word 'growth' is used where I use 'efficiency', i.e. where 'growth' means success in achieving society's objectives. 'Now the cry is raised that growth causes destruction and ought to be stopped. A better argument for the antipollutionists would be that, if the true costs of production were included in the calculation of GNP, growth might very well be negative, so that it is really they who are in favour of positive growth' (*An Introduction to Modern Economics*. (Maidenhead, Berks.: McGraw-Hill, 1973) pp. 310–11).

PPH is, in many ways, a so-called 'flexitime' program, which helps people to find ways to use their time at hours when they would otherwise have little to do, and to find ways to combine activities, e.g. talking with children while shelling peas. The use of time by peasant-women has been studied by Eleonora Cebotareve (*Mujer Rural y Desarrollo* (Bogota: CIID, 1979)).

The data on poverty in the Osorno region are found in *Mapa de la Extrema Pobreza en Chile* (Santiago: ODEPLAN, 1975) and in Dario Menanteau-Horta, 'Algunos Indicadores del Nivel de Vida en la X Region' (Valdivia: Universidad Austral (mimeo), 1976).

On the relationship between education and employment, see Martin Carnoy, *Education and Employment: A Critical Appraisal* (Paris: UNESCO (IIEP), 1977) and Francisco Vio Grossi, 'Adult Education and Rural Development', *Convergence*, vol. XII, no. 3 (1980) pp. 30–8.

Mark Blaug claims that, in spite of its theoretical difficulties, neo-classical economics is overwhelmingly superior in such applied fields as cost–benefit analysis (Mark Blaug, *The Cambridge Revolution: Success or Failure?* (London: Institute of Economic Affairs, 1974) pp. 85–6). On the contrary, it is precisely in applied fields that neo-classical assumptions lead to misleading results.

5   The Cost-effectiveness of the Parents and Children Program

The cost per pre-school child per month of **PPH** is considerably less than the cost of the other programs for which we have been able to obtain information. The comparative costs, expressed in US dollars, are as follows.

PPH cost per pre-school child, Osorno 1979	$ 6.83 per month
Cost per child of a high-quality kindergarten in Osorno, 1980	$37.50 per month
Cost per child of kindergartens run by the national kindergarten system (*Junta Nacional de Jardines Infantiles*), 1979	$28.15 per month
Cost per child of the '*Plaza Escolar*' programme (an experimental approach to intellectual stimulation of infants), 1979	$25.60 per month
Cost per child of a low-quality day-care centre in Osorno, 1980	$12.50 per month
Cost per child of German Foundation for Aid to Children (minimal program), 1979	$10.00 per month

The foregoing information is, of course, insufficient to justify the conclusion that **PPH** is cost-effective. To decide whether or not it is, we need to know not only its costs but also its benefits, and we need to compare its benefits with those of alternative programs. Furthermore, from a certain kind of systems point of view, we still have more costs to count, since for reasons given in the preceding chapter we count here as 'costs' only actual money costs.

Unfortunately, we are able to include in this study only incidental remarks concerning benefits of other programs. People who want to know about the achievements of other prgrams, not only the five just mentioned for which we have cost data, but for many others in Latin America and around the world, will find at the end of this chapter a set of interesting references.

With respect to our method for assessing the benefits of PPH itself, since our study will be responsive (i.e. one that sees what is actually accomplished instead of looking exclusively at achievement of preordinate objectives), we necessarily limit ourselves to costs in this chapter. It will take us several chapters to prepare our responsive measures.

Nevertheless, the preceding figures may be regarded as laying the foundations for a study of the benefits of PPH. Suppose that we think of total benefits as the number of children served times the average benefit per child:

$$B = Nb,$$

where

B = total benefit,
N = number of pre-school children served,
b = average benefit per child.

Then it follows (if we think of the problem in this way) that benefit can be increased either by increasing the number of children or by increasing the benefit per child. Since cost per child is lowest for PPH among the programs considered, it is the most cost-effective (i.e. has the greatest benefit for a given cost) among them – unless the benefit per child of the other programs is so much greater than that of PPH that it outweighs PPH's ability to reach more children.

The comparative cost figures may be looked upon as a 'sensitivity test of benefits', by which we mean a measure of how sensitive to variations in benefits the cost-effectiveness of PPH is. For example, if we suppose that the benefits per child of all the programs listed are of equal value, then PPH is the most cost-effective, because it achieves more benefit for the same cost. If, however, the benefit per child provided by the minimal program of the German Foundation for Aid to Children is judged to be twice that of PPH, then the GFAC is more cost-effective than PPH, since although it reaches fewer children per dollar, it helps each child so much more that the greater benefit per child justifies serving fewer children.

The ratio of the cost per child of one program to the cost per child of another program can be looked on as a break-even point. We form the break-even point ratio (i.e. the cost ratio) by placing the cost of the more expensive program over the cost of the cheaper one. We form the benefit ratio by placing a number representing the value of the benefits of the more expensive programme over a similar number for the cheaper one. For example:

cost of GFAC = \$10.00 per child per month,
cost of PPH = \$ 6.83 per child per month,

break-even ratio: $\dfrac{10}{6.83}$

hypothetical benefit ratio: $\dfrac{2}{1}$.

This is, of course, a purely hypothetical example. We do not know the benefits of GFAC, and in the sequel we study only the benefits of PPH. In the example, GFAC is more cost-effective than PPH because

$$\frac{2}{1} > \frac{10}{6.83}.$$

If and only if the benefit ratio exceeds the break-even point (the cost ratio), the more expensive program is cost-effective. Thus, in order for it to be the case that the high-quality kindergarten for which we know the price is more cost-effective than PPH, it would have to be true that:

$$\frac{\text{benefits of high-quality kindergarten}}{\text{benefits of PPH}} > \frac{37.50}{6.83}.$$

In other words, to justify the kindergarten, we must say that its benefits are so great that it is better to put 1 child in kindergarten, leaving 4 with no attention, or with whatever attention they would get in the absence of the work of the agency making the decision, than to enrol 5 children in PPH $(37.50 \, / \, 6.83 \doteq 5/1)$.

We say that the cost ratios provide a sensitivity test of benefits because they tell us what the benefit ratios have to be in order to warrant the judgment that one program is more efficient than another.

The figures we have given overestimate the cost of PPH. One important reason why \$6.83 per month is much too high is that PPH is not only, and not even primarily, a child-development program for children between the ages of 4 and 6. It promotes family life, the personal development of adults, and community organization. Therefore, we consider it more accurate to count as beneficiaries of the prgram not only the members of the family between 4 and 6 years of age, but all the members of the participating families. At an estimated average of 6 beneficiaries per family, the cost per person per month in Osorno in 1979 was \$1.62.

There are other programs in contemporary Chile that seek to integrate entire families into community organizations; to put the same thing in another way, they seek to organize entire communities by dealing with problems that concern community-members in their roles as family-members. They include the work of the Catholic Church's Vicarate for Solidarity (known as the *Vicaria*) in organizing the relatives of people who have been executed or who have disappeared; the Mapuche Cultural Centres, working to preserve the language and music of indigenous peoples; the community-based projects assisted by the American Friends Service Committee (AFSC); and the government-sponsored mothers' clubs, known as CEMA-Chile. There are some villages where evangelical protestantism has become so pervasive an influence that it can be described as bringing whole families into a community organization. However, we have found it difficult to get cost data for such programs and movements; we have information on costs only for one American Friends Service Committee-sponsored family project, working in urban slums in Chile's capital city, Santiago. The project in question attends, in the first instance, to the needs of pregnant mothers, extending its scope from that initial focus to facilitate dialogue and mutual support concerning all the felt needs of the family and the neighborhood, at an estimated cost of $15.84 per mother per month.

When we compare the cost-effectiveness of one program to that of another we assume that the value of the benefits of the first can be compared to the value of the benefits of the second. Strictly speaking, such comparisons can be quantitative only when the benefits are of the same kind, but in practice it is rare to find two programs delivering the same kinds of benefits. For example, PPH and the AFSC program mentioned both organize, but PPH-Osorno organizes peasants, while the AFSC program organizes urban slum-dwellers; both educate mothers, but the AFSC program provides help for mothers who are pregnant that PPH does not provide. Consequently, in terms of its support of pregnant mothers, the AFSC project is superior to PPH, even though it is more expensive per person per month.

Cost-effectiveness studies rarely show unequivocally that one social prgram is more efficient than another. In principle, they can do so only when:

(i)   the two programs have the same benefits; and
(ii)   one of them is superior to the other on all dimensions (i.e. for all benefits); and
(iii) the superior program costs the same or less.

Furthermore, the benefit ratios of social programmes do not correspond exactly to anything real. Social benefits virtually never lend themselves to ratio scale measurement such that one can say objectively that program A does twice, or 3 times, or 1.72 times as much good as program B. The exception to this rule would be the case where the same benefit reaches equally needy people under similar circumstances, and program A reaches 1000 people while program B reaches 100. Then the benefit ratio of A to B would be 10/1. But there are no cases where identical benefits reach equally needy people in similar circumstances. Consequently, the comparison of cost ratios to benefit ratios is not a factual comparison; it is a form of mental discipline that helps one to be aware of the magnitudes that are in question when one makes value judgments. It says, for example, how many people in program A are left out in the cold if the decision-maker is so impressed by the benefits of a small but expensive program B that she funds B instead of A.

SOME OF THE ASSUMPTIONS MADE IN CALCULATING THE COST OF PPH PER PERSON PER MONTH

We have announced that PPH in Osorno in 1979 cost $1.62 per person per month, or $6.83 per pre-school child per month, with considerable aplomb; as if we expected our readers to accept our figures as complacently as they would accept the information that General Bernardo O'Higgins, the liberator of Chile, was born on 20 August 1778, and on no other day; as if we did not recognize that sooner or later someone is bound to challenge the way we arrived at our conclusions, and to draw our attention to plausible reasons for arriving at cost figures higher or lower than ours, depending on what one counts as costs, who count as pre-school children, whom one takes to be persons benefited, and which months count as months. It would have been more honest, although also more tedious, to give our raw data first, the assumptions second, and the conclusions last, but out of kindness to the reader who wishes first to see whether he finds our conclusions sufficiently interesting to justify a detailed study of their premises, we have placed our conclusions first.

We shall now state our most important assumptions, but, to save ink, instead of printing our raw data we can post it to persons who request it.

1. The figure of $1.62 per month was derived by dividing the yearly budget by 12 months, to obtain the cost per month PPH-Osorno, and then dividing the cost per month by the number of persons benefited in a typical month. Since PPH is a flexitime program, which holds meetings only during the 9 months when peasants can afford to take time off from farming to attend them, the reader may consider it outrageous to assume that the benefits accrue during all 12 months even though meetings are held only during 9. The outraged reader will wish to change the divisor from 12 to 9, which amounts to multiplying the cost per person per month by 4/3.

2. The calculation for cost per pre-school child is similar. We counted all children enrolled, without checking that they were in the 4 to 6 age group for which the materials were designed.

3. When a family enrols in PPH with one, more than one, or no pre-school children, all the members of the family are counted as benefited. We multiplied the number of the families by 6,

assuming the average family size to be 6 persons. A larger cost per person could be derived by assuming smaller families, or by assuming that not all members of the family participate in the activities that take place in the home. A smaller cost per person could be produced by assuming larger families, or by counting as beneficiaries people outside the enrolled families who benefit in one way or another – such as the estimated 20,000 listeners who enjoy 'PPH Radio Theatre' on The Voice of the Coast.

4. Home office costs at CIDE headquarters in Santiago, including administrative overheads, are part of the budget and are counted. They are substantial – about a third of total costs.

5. The start-up costs of motivating the peasants, organizing the centres, printing materials and training coordinators are counted.

6. The research and development done by CIDE to perfect the instructional method, which the staff calls its 'methodology', is treated as a sunk cost, i.e. not counted. The rationale for counting it as sunk is that it represents decisions made in the past, which cannot now be changed. The 'methodology' is an existing asset that it costs CIDE nothing to use, now that it has it.

7. The amount actually spent to change previously-created manuals, worksheets, etc. to tailor-fit them to the Osorno region, is included in the costs. About 30 per cent of the instructional material was changed.

8. The powdered milk, flour and lard donated to volunteer base coordinators by *Caritas* (see Chapters 11 and 14) are not counted as costs. The rationale for not counting them is that *Caritas* was going to provide nutritional aid anyway, and it does so more efficiently by using the PPH organization to distribute it; hence instead of sacrificing other objectives to help PPH, *Caritas* is itself helped to accomplish its own objectives better – a symbiotic relationship.

9. The air time on The Voice of the Coast occupied by PPH is not counted as a cost. PPH paid for its radio time by creating *teatros* and other programs that The Voice of the Coast used, and by dotting the countryside with what amount to Voice of the Coast fan clubs. The station manager, Celedino Fierro (who personally is strongly in favour of PPH), said: The radio station has been more than compensated (*compensado con creces*). The time invested in promoting PPH at first has more than paid for itself

by giving the radio station a network of contacts with the people (*bases*) and a set of programs.' (See Chapter 16.) Both in the case of *Caritas* and in the case of The Voice of the Coast we treat the relationship as one where the other organization advanced its objectives efficiently by cooperating with PPH. In another situation, or in the future, a joint-cost treatment might be appropriate, e.g. if a Dutch charity sends a new transmitter partly to support PPH and partly to support other aspects of The Voice of the Coast, then a proportion of the cost of the transmitter would be a cost of PPH.

10.   Where possible, figures are given for 1979 instead of 1980 because the US dollar was closer to its world market value in 1979. The exchange rates fixed by the Chilean government make Chilean prices high when quoted in dollars, more so in 1980 than in 1979.

SENSITIVITY OF PPH COSTS TO CHANGES IN KEY COST ITEMS

We can make another kind of sensitivity test of PPH costs. Instead of comparing one program with another in terms of their respective costs and benefits, we can ask what the costs of PPH would have been if prices and other key variables had been different than they were. This kind of sensitivity test is especially useful for the Rest of the World, because the Rest of the World does not want to run a program in 1979 in Osorno, but somebody out there in it may wish to run some such program at some other time, somewhere else. Since the costs somewhere else at some other time will be different from those of Osorno in 1979, it is worthwhile to speculate on the costs of this sort of thing under conditions that did not exist but might have, and might in the future.

Our results are as follows.

1. Cost per person per month for PPH-Osorno in 1979 $1.62
2. The same as in case (1) but substituting Peruvian prices for Chilean prices, i.e. what it would have cost on the basis of the purchasing

power of foreign hard currency in Peru in 1979	$1.08
3. The same as (1) using Bolivian prices in 1980	$0.97
4. The same as (1) assuming PPH had purchased portable slide projectors and used slides instead of plain pictures and charts	$1.65
5. The same as (1) but adding slides (as in (4)) and assuming that the excitement of slides augments participation by 20 per cent	$1.38
6. The same as (1) increasing the salaries of paid sector-coordinators by 50 per cent	$1.85
7. The same as (1) counting as beneficiaries 3 people per family instead of 6	$3.24
8. The same as (1) assuming 8 people per family, as would be appropriate in areas where families are known to be of that size	$1.22
9. The same as (1) but assuming that instead of revising 30 per cent of the material to conform to local conditions, 50 per cent is revised	$1.67
10. The same as (1) but revising 50 per cent of the material (as in case (9)), and thereby increasing peasant participation by 20 per cent	$1.39

The formula used for making the preceding calculations was:

$$\text{cost per person per month} = \frac{(69{,}548 + X)\ P}{12\ I\ (3576)},$$

where

69,548 = actual cost of PPH-Osorno in 1979 in US dollars,
X = additional cost incurred with the objective of improving the program.
  (In cases (4) and (5), X represents the cost of slides and projectors, and was estimated at $1457. (The price is low because the slides needed already exist, and only copies of existing slides plus projectors and batteries would be needed.) In cases (9) and (10), X represents the estimated cost of revising additional material to add local colour, and is set at $2115. In the other cases, X is zero.)
12 = the number of months in a year.
3576 = mean number of beneficiaries of PPH in a month of

1979, i.e. the number of peasants who participate in the program.

I = a coefficient designed to express increased participation. When we suppose a 20 per cent increase, we set I at 1.2. Otherwise, I is 1.

P = the general price level. It is ordinarily 1, but to represent the lower price levels of Peru and Bolivia, we set P at 2/3 and 3/5 for cases (2) and (3) respectively.

The formula disregards the small increase in costs, about $0.03 per person per month, that occurs when peasant participation increases slightly. PPH meetings in Osorno in 1979 averaged 12.16 adults plus an estimated quarter as many children (children are not counted on the attendance records); if attendance had gone up to 22 adults, the only increases in cost would have been a longer print run for worksheets distributed, plus the price of additional pencils and scissors for the pre-school children of new participants.

One can play with the formula by introducing revisions, ramifications, refinements and replacements. A revision could be introduced by setting $I = 2$ for a hypothetical program where, unlike Osorno, the government and PPH love each other, provided that the person making the calculations is willing to entertain the supposition, which, as will be seen, is not an unreasonable one, that such mutual admiration would increase participation by a sizable magnitude, like 2. A ramification is practised by changing more than one variable at once, as by considering Peru with slides, setting P at 2/3 and I at 1.2. A refinement incorporates variables we have disregarded, such as cost increases when participation goes up, or research and development costs where, unlike our happy case, they cannot be treated as over and done with. Replacements can be done by people who know more than we do, i.e. by anybody. For example, if you know the actual prices at place X and time Y of the inputs to a program like PPH, then you can replace with specific sums our expedient of using a variable P to compare average Chilean 1980 prices to Peruvian or Country X prices.

We omit to remind the reader to consider inflation, because these days no one ever forgets it.

NOTES AND REFERENCES

For studies of programs that can in one sense or another be considered alternatives to PPH see the following.

CIDE, Resumenes Analiticos en Education (Santiago: 1972–). This is an abstract service that provides summaries of research on education in Latin America.

Peter Bachrach, 'Evaluating Development Programmes: a Synthesis of Recent Experience' (Paris: OECD Development Centre, 94 rue Chardon Lagache, Paris 75016, 1977).

Patricio Cariola, 'Educacion y Participacion en América Latina' (Santiago: UN Economic Commission for Latin America, 1980) CEAL document E/CEPAL/ILPES/R.26. – this paper includes an annotated bibliography of studies on participatory education in Latin America. The annotated reports it lists can be obtained from the CIDE documentation service, Casilla 13608, Santiago, Chile.

High/Scope Educational Research Foundation, 600 North River Street, Ypsilanti, Michigan 48197, USA, has published a number of studies of its own pre-school programmes and of other programs, including Robert Halpern, 'Cuidado Diario en el Vecindario, una Revision de la Literatura', sponsored jointly by High/Scope, UNICEF and the Venezuelan Fundacion del Nino.

Jeremiah O'Sullivan-Ryan and Mario Kaplun, *Communication Methods to Promote Grass-roots Participation* (Paris: UNESCO, no date) – Number 6 of UNESCO's Communication and Society series; includes an annotated bibliography.

Ernesto Pollitt, *Early Childhood Intervention Programs in Latin America: A Selective Review* (a report presented to the Office of Latin American and the Caribbean, Ford Foundation, 1979).

Daniela Sanchez, 'La Vicaria de la Solidaridad: Una Experiencia de Educacion para la Justicia' mimeo (Santiago: Vicaria de la Solidaridad, 1979).

A wealth of material is available from UNICEF, including: Sonia Bralic *et al.*, *Experiencias de Educacion Inicial no Escolarizada en América Latina* (Lima: UNICEF, 1979); Manuel Tejado Cano, 'From the Child to Community Participation, the Peruvian Experience' (United Nations document E/ICEF/LATAM-79/6); Lia de Mejia *et al.* (Panama), 'Participacion de la Comunidad en la Education Inicial: Centros de Orientacion Infantil y Familiar Comunitario' (Guatemala: UNICEF, 1978).

Periodicals in which accounts of relevant programs are regularly found include: *Cultura Popular*, a quarterly review of popular education, available from CELADEC, Av. General Garzon 2267, Lima 11, Peru; *Revista Latinoamericana de Educacion*, Centro de Estudios Educativos, Avenida Revolucion 1290, Mexico 20, DF.; *UNICEF News*, UNICEF, New York 10017, NY; *High/Scope Report*; *World Education Reports*, 1414 Sixth Avenue, New York 10019, NY; *Development Communication Report*, 1414 22nd St NW, Washington DC 20037; *The NFE Exchange*, Institute for International Studies in Education, Michigan State University, East Lansing, Michigan 48824; *Pespectives, Revue Trimestrielle de l'Education* (UNESCO), 7 Place de Fontenoy, Paris 75700, France.

It should also be mentioned that PPH has the characteristics that are usually associated with cost-effective programs, according to the set of features that a study by Ahmed and Coombs found to be characteristic of efficient programs. Those features are: (i) in general, PPH uses existing buildings to meet in; (ii) the community helps to create the necessary installations; (iii) the participants consider making the installations a part of their community activity; (iv) the paid sector-coordinators are part-time; (v) most work is voluntary; (vi) material for self-instruction is used; (vii) the project concerns a permanent interest of the community, i.e. the welfare and development of children. See UNICEF document E/ICEF/L.1304 (27 March 1974) p. 164. See also Philip Coombs *et al.*, *New Paths to Learning for Rural Children and Youth* (New York: International Council for Educational Development, 1973).

Further, it should also be mentioned that very poor children are often too undeveloped to learn much in a kindergarten. It is typical to find that kindergartens benefit children from relatively culturally advantaged homes more than their poor classmates. Hence something like PPH may be needed in addition to (rather than as an alternative to) kindergartens in order to prepare poor children to take advantage of the opportunities a kindergarten offers. However, it is also clear that slum children are not hopeless; sufficiently intensive and expensive intervention can bring them up to nearly normal standards. See on this latter point Harrison McKay *et al.*, 'Improving Cognitive Ability in Chronically Deprived Children', *Science* (1978) vol. 200, pp. 270–8.

6 A Systematic Analysis of Error

As our last chapter ended, the reader was invited to enter a world of fantasy where the cost of PPH per person per month could be made to approach zero by assuming favourable exchange rates, large families, slides, and good government. Experienced international educators – I have some wise old codgers in mind but I shall not mention their names – no doubt noticed the gross features of the cost model, but declined the invitation to speculate on the hypothetical costs of hypothetical replicas of PPH. Experience breeds scepticism. Even those of us, of whom I am one, who cannot resist the temptation to try out equations on a pocket calculator, must admit that if one has a certain amount of money to spend to help the poor of the third world, and one must decide how much of it, if any, to spend on programs like PPH, then after five chapters, during which some of the sentences have been longer than the average sentence, one still is a long way from possessing the information that would be required to make a rational decision. Between the numbers on the calculator and the peasant-woman sloshing 8 kilometres in the rain to attend a meeting, there is an immeasurable distance.

Let us try to be systematic. First, we shall analyse what we were doing in the last chapter. Then we shall make a catalogue of all the types of error one might possibly make when doing that sort of thing, which one hopes will not be too pretentious, but which one fears will be. Then we shall make a reasonable choice – summoning the available human wisdom to our aid, but without pretending to achieve the wisdom predicable only of the All-knowing – concerning which errors it is most important to reduce.

First, the analysis. We were pricing a product. We derived a price, a certain sum of money, from certain variables describing the process: the prices of inputs (based mainly on the sums actually spent in Osorno), the number of participants, and certain factors assumed to determine the number of participants. Our *metaphor de base* was the following: for the money we spend on inputs (the independent variables) we obtain as outputs numbers of peasants benefited (dependent variables) and also, eventually, degrees and kinds of benefit (more dependent variables). The crucial assumption is what, in systems theory, is called systems stability. A system is said to be stable when the same inputs always yield the same outputs. For example, an electronic guidance system for a space vehicle is said to be stable when the same input signals always guide the rocketship in the same direction.

There are only four possible types of error: data errors, variable errors, form errors and metaphysical errors.

A data error occurs when we do not know the correct value of a variable. We are estimating, for example that when slides are used instead of flip charts, participation will rise by 20 per cent. But our data may be incorrect, or insufficient to generalize to the population for which a given program like PPH is being planned. When we think in terms of data error we assume, in terms of the same example, that there exists some coefficient X that describes the relationship between participation in a given program without and with slides, and that our problem is that our data are not good enough to make a reliable estimate of the value of X.

A variable error occurs when we do not know the factors on which the answers to our questions depend. The most conspicuous *lacunae* so far in our efforts to determine the efficiency of PPH concern participation and benefits. The cost study serves mainly to make it obvious that everything depends on the peasants; if they choose to participate, then cost per person is low; if not, it is not. It looks very much as though we have an enormous source of variable error: our ignorance of the factors that determine motivation; and a promise to keep: to assess the benefits.

Form errors occur when the data and the variables are not treated with the most convenient or appropriate mathematical techniques. In our cost study, we could, no doubt, improve our model by adding a step function to indicate that when increases in peasant participation pass a certain point, it is necessary to hire and train more coordinators, and therefore costs go up. A simple linear coefficient like 1.2 might be replaced by a function that considers, for example that increases become small or zero as participation approaches 100 per cent of the population of a village.

A metaphysical error occurs when reality stubbornly refuses to conform to our research procedures and root metaphors. The procedures used to find values for variables and to fit them into a suitable form may not be the best way to learn what needs to be learned. PPH is not a stable system; there are no circumstances in which the same inputs will yield the same outputs. It is not even a replicable system: it is not possible to use the same inputs twice, and it is not desirable to try – hence the question of what would happen with identical inputs cannot arise.

In the classification of types of error adopted here, 'metaphysical' serves as a grab-bag or residual category. Data, variable and form errors are the kinds one is likely to recognize when working within the systems problematic; 'metaphysics' is a category used to file 'all other errors', and it includes the kind that sets the world spinning and prepares the way for a new focus, a destroy-and-reconstruct cycle. The important part, no doubt, is the reconstruction, since there is no shortage of people who, in moments of self-criticism, are ready to convict themselves of a metaphysical error. They are people who have set out to identify all the variables relevant to the explanation of a phenomenon, who have come to realize that the number of relevant variables is very large, and that most of the variables will never be measured to any tolerable degree of accuracy; they have gone on to wonder whether their faith that all those variables exist out there in the world somewhere, waiting for someone to measure them, is misplaced. The important question is what happens next.

This brief attempt at a systematic analysis of error has led us to the point where we see some gaps in the systems approach. To fill the gaps, however, we shall not invent a new hypothesis or imagine a new theory. Instead, we shall turn to the experience of people who have worked and are working in the slums of Lima, Caracas and Mexico City, and in the remote rural misery of Bolivia, Botswana, Chad and Niger. The procedure set out in the first paragraph of this chapter calls for making a reasonable choice concerning which errors it is most important to reduce. The analysis has proposed a way to classify the errors. It becomes clear, in this way, that what is needed is an exercise of good judgment that draws on experience. In order to assist us in making good judgments, we assembled a panel of experienced people – or, to be more exact, we telephoned them, wrote letters to them, and talked to them in person when we could – whom we called 'interlocutors of the evaluation'. What they had to say will be discussed in the next chapter.

7 Attitude Change

We began the evaluation of PPH by thinking of it as communication among a set of interlocutors; the job of the evaluator was to facilitate communication among peasants, program staff-members, officers of funding agencies, and others with an interest in PPH and in the kind of thing PPH is. The first problem was to decide who the interlocutors were, and what they wanted to know. Hence we began our investigation of PPH by seeking the advice of people who are in a position to judge what aspects of PPH's experience are most likely to shed light on those things the interested portion of the public needs to know. Those with practical experience working with poor people in third-world rural and urban slums urged us to concentrate on 'attitude change.' The phrase is in quotation marks because it is a tag for several intimately related concerns.

It is easy to cast 'attitude change' in a tragicomic light, as when one imagines a poor South American saying: 'I have no shoes, no bread, no job. The police beat me up because I voted for the wrong candidate in the election – the last time we had an election, which was ten years ago. They broke my leg and it didn't heal right. It's freezing cold and I've got no coat. What I've got is the 'flu, and I'm soaking wet, and the roof leaks, and some jerk comes down here from North America and tells me my problem is my attitude. He says I have to change my attitude, raise my consciousness, learn to speak up and demand my rights. If he were really a nice guy, he would give me something to lower my consciousness – like some *coca* leaves to chew, or a bottle of *chicha*, or a ticket for the cinema.'

It turns out to be the case, however, that what our interlocutors mean by 'attitude change' stems from their legitimate work to make things better, not from a patronizing attitude that blames the victim.

From the point of view of costs, the main concern identified by the advisors we consulted is motivation to participate. From the point of view of benefits, the main concern is to overcome an attitude that many observers have perceived as a decisive obstacle to social change, often called 'discouragement', the 'dominated consciousness' or 'apathy', described and analysed by Paulo Freire as 'the internalization of the oppressor'. From a practical point of view, people want to know how the staff did it – they want to know, to use the staff's own magic word, 'the methodology'. Although it may not be obvious at first that 'the methodology' belongs in the 'attitude change' cluster together with the key to costs and the heart of benefits, it will become obvious soon.

The advice given to us by our interlocutors converged. Some of our advisors asked for a cost-effectiveness study, while other advisors asked us to study those attitude changes which are simultaneously the key to the study of costs and the heart of benefits. Attitude changes are the key to the study of costs because they determine how many peasants participate, and therefore cost per person per month; they are the heart of benefits because they conquer apathy.

Our inside advisors, the PPH staff, concurred in our choice of priorities. Father Gerry Whelan, CSC, who directs PPH's main office in Santiago, with overall responsibility not just for Osorno but also for 16 other places in Chile, 8 in Bolivia, and one each in Peru, Argentina and Colombia, told us that the main and most important objective of the program was to instil an attitude of desire for lifelong self-education. (Something is lost in translation here: *auto-educacion* as it is used in PPH does not mean self-education in an individualistic sense, but cooperating in a group in which the members help each other to organize courses and to learn.) Father Gerry also said that he does not think 'attitude change' is as important as 'change of values' – a problem which I solve by adding 'change of values' to the cluster of intimately-related concerns to which I affix the tag 'attitude change', and by hoping that the ensuing study will respond to what Gerry had in mind. Cecilia Yañez, who led the training sessions (*capacitacion*) for the ten sector-coordinators of PPH-Osorno, suggested a specific meaning for the phrase 'attitude change', as follows: the criterion for evaluating PPH should be whether the poor acquire a capacity to plan and carry out activities that were not programmed by the staff.

THE CONCEPT OF ATTITUDE

We shall now discuss the concept of 'attitude'. The less philosophical reader should omit this section and go directly to 'The Interviews'.

The word 'attitude', in both English and Spanish, is derived from the Italian *attitudo*. It came into use in the 18th century to designate a posture or dramatic pose, especially in paintings and plays where figures were posed in a way that represented their sentiments. Later, in the USA, 'attitude', like much else in American culture, was run through the mill of the testing movement. 'Everything that exists, exists in some degree and therefore can be measured', was the motto. Attitude scales were invented, designed to express attitudes in terms of the values of variables, i.e. to put them into a form that could be assimilated to the prevailing view of how to design an experiment; and how to organize cost-effective treatment, therapy and social intervention. Among Chilean educators, the Spanish word *actitud* has a meaning dependent on its use to translate the English word 'attitude'. This sense of *actitud* is a token whose meaning is identical to that of the English word 'attitude', not because the cultural evolution expressed in the Spanish and English languages has led by parallel paths to the same terminus, but because North-American technical aid missions and graduate schools have come to set the tone for Latin-American psychology and educational research. On the other hand, the older Spanish sense, derived from the Italian, still exists in Chile, as when one speaks of *la actitud asumida* (the attitude assumed) in describing the position or posture of a person, or the face he puts on (*la cara que pone*).

Recent philosophical and methodological work on the concept 'attitude' in English-speaking countries has rescued some of the common-sense and traditional uses of the term from the rigid identification of 'attitude studies' with devising techniques for assigning numbers to variables. It has stressed that:

(i)   the term properly refers to an inclination to act, and that actions are evidence of the existence of the attitude;
(ii) the beliefs of the actor are inseparable from his attitudes, and that both must therefore be studied from his point of view;

(iii) individual attitudes and group norms are so closely inter-
      twined that it makes no sense to talk about or study one
      apart from the other;
(iv) the component of attitudes known as 'affect', 'emotion' or
      'sentiment' has proven to be elusive and to lack meaning
      when separated from acts, beliefs and social relations.

Father Gerry will be pleased to see that, in my account of the
strong doses of common-sense injected into the concept 'attitude'
by recent methodological discussions, it coincides very nearly
with 'values'. Intellectuals who never thought much of the
testing movement will be similarly pleased.

Meanwhile, the concept of explanation that interfaces with
attitude scales has been crumbling. The point of expressing an
attitude in the form of a number (or an index or scale) was to
treat that number as the measure of a variable. And the point of
that was to explain the values of dependent variables as due to
the action of independent variables. However, recent work in the
philosophy and history of science has shown that it is not, in
general, true that scientific explanation is achieved by stating the
law (or function) that relates one variable to another. There is no
universal 'scientific method' equally applicable to physics,
chemistry, biology, economics, sociology, psychology, and the
evaluation of adult education programs, and in particular the
interaction of variables approach does not constitute the *mathesis
universalis*. To explain something, it is necessary to become
acquainted with the thing itself, to become acquainted with the
mechanism by which it works. In educational evaluation, which
is increasingly affected by the winds of change blowing in the
social sciences generally, the analogue to what a biologist might
call 'becoming acquainted with the mechanism by which it
works' is often styled 'looking at process'.

My strategy will be to begin by looking at process – to become
acquainted with the mechanism by which attitude change in
PPH is achieved. It is essential (see point (ii), three paragraphs
above) to view the process from the point of view of the people
who are changing their attitudes, the peasants, and for that
reason I shall use a method that, as much as any other, has
succeeded in providing insight into the workings of human
groups whose culture is different from that of the investigator,
the ethnographic interview. Later, the results will be checked by
using a variety of methods.

From each of the ten sectors of PPH-Osorno, I chose a PPH centre at random, and obtained from it an informant – one each from Huampatué, Huilma Grande, Anchiquemo, Costa Rio Blanco, Mashué, El Monte, Los Hualles, Dollinco, La Poza, and Ex-Estacion. The process for obtaining the informant included a feature not mentioned in textbooks on cultural anthropology – the informants were legitimated by election. The centres were sent (via the sector-coordinators) a summary of the qualifications for a good informant, adapted from Spradley's text, *The Ethnographic Interview*, and asked to elect a person of their confidence from among those who met the qualifications. The qualifications do not amount to much – the main points are that the informant should be thoroughly enculturated, i.e. be a regular PPH attender for over a year, and have time to talk.

Legitimation by election made sense to the informants. The FREDER family is accustomed to elections: the peasants elect from among themselves the monitors for their radio-school courses, and they elect their volunteer PPH coordinators. The paid sector-coordinators are nearly all people who were entrusted with some responsibility by their peers at some earlier point in time. The elected informants were playing a role they could understand.

THE INTERVIEWS

Except for a few reports from informants collected during my visits to the country, most of the interviewing took place in a rambling, old, pink stucco house on Los Carrera Street, that serves as the home away from home for members of the FREDER family who visit the city, although several informants said that their trip to see me was the first time they saw Osorno.

The informant would get out of bed at a ridiculously early hour, on a cold morning; walk several kilometres to the road; wait in the rain for the *micro*; pay the fare with funds previously advanced for the purpose by the sector-coordinator; bump along among the pigs, other agricultural products, and owners of same for several hours; and arrive at the *feria* (fair). If she had brought something to sell with her, she sold it then, shrewdly taking advantage of funds provided for scientific research to make a market trip without paying her own fare. Then she made her

way to the FREDER office in Los Carrera Street, with the help of
a guide if it had been anticipated that she might have difficulty
finding her way, where her arrival caused a considerable com-
motion – the word was passed from front rooms to back rooms
and from downstairs to upstairs: 'Señora Eduvina, the informant
from Huampatué, has arrived!'

A welcoming committee of five or so people assembled to greet
her, including several who knew her because they had attended
PPH meetings in Huampatué, and a foreigner, who looked
rather like one of the Chileans of German ancestry who tend to
own large tracts of land and hold high ranks in the armed forces,
who was not entirely unknown because he had made a few
remarks on The Voice of the Coast about what good work the
peasants in Chile are doing, with whom she knew she was
destined to have a conversation when the two of them got up
enough courage to talk to one another. She was taken immediately to a kitchen, similar in its general mode of functioning
to peasant kitchens in the country, where she stood by the wood
fire and warmed herself while Isabel made coffee and set the
table, Noelia went across the street to buy bread, butter and
sausages, and the foreigner washed dishes. Next came the
delicious breakfast, with Isabel constantly urging her to put
more butter on her bread and take more sausage – butter and
sausage seemed to be in limitless supply – after which the
foreigner (more exactly: the *afuerino*, the person from outside,
from elsewhere) explained who he was, who was paying him,
and what he wanted.

He said that he was a foreigner, which was no surprise; that in
other places there was interest in learning about PPH with a
view to doing something similar; and that he wanted information
from people who have first-hand experience. The part about who
paid him was unintelligible, but at least he did not keep it a
secret. Then he carefully wrote down everything the informant
said, asking her to pause every now and then so that his
handwriting could catch up with her voice, reading back every
page to be sure it was correct. If she had nothing to say, he asked
her to begin with a 'grand tour' of a PPH meeting, beginning
with what happens first, then telling what happens next, and so
on until what happens last. After the informant's initial statement (if there was one), or the grand tour (if, as happened about
half the time, the informant initially said nothing), all the

questions were requests for clarification or elaboration, to make clearer to the *afuerino* points the informant had already raised. No new words were used; the requests for clarification used the vocabulary the informant had already introduced. (Spradley calls these 'native language questions' because they are questions posed in the language of the informant. The purpose of them is to get inside the point of view of the informant by minimizing the intrusion of the frame of reference of the interviewer.)

By this method, 10 informants, 7 women and 3 men, were interviewed, from 1 to 7 times each.

The mechanism through which PPH changes attitudes became quite clear. It is participation combined with public commitment.

Participation is achieved by posing problems for discussion. The content of the instructional material is so slight that instead of 'instructional materials', they might be named 'conversation starters' – Jorge Zuleta has suggested that they be called '*material de apoyo*' ('supporting material', i.e. material to facilitate the process). In the ensuing discussion, each person is asked to offer an opinion, sometimes contributing a piece of the story of his life. By participating in the conversation, the person takes a stand, becomes identified with a view of the problem, becomes for the others a part of the process of searching for the correct view of the problem.

'Public commitment' is a phrase that needs some explanation. The Spanish expression *compromiso con los demás* (literally, 'promising-together with the others'), is closer to the meaning intended, but it has no convenient English equivalent. It is not that the public makes a commitment, but that you make a commitment in public. You are in public not because there is a large crowd, but because you are in a small group of people who know you, somewhat as Dylan Thomas as a child could be 'famous among the barns', or as one can be 'world-famous in Weyburn, Saskatchewan'.

At some point in the discussion, not very well marked, the group begins to *sacar conclusiones*, i.e. to draw conclusions. The *conclusiones* represent the consensus of the group about what they should do. They become *consejos*, precepts, that the group formulates through discussion and legitimates by consensus – norms that the participants are committed to respecting because they prescribed them for themselves. (There is a difference between the staff's view of the method and the peasants' view. For the staff, the word *consejos* is a suspect term because it is associated with authoritarian instruction; the peasants nevertheless regard the *conclusiones* generated by the process as *consejos*.) The *consejos* are often implicit in the coordinator's manual, and the legitimacy of the conclusion is enhanced by the prestige of the volunteer coordinator and that of the sector-coordinator – but the mark of a good coordinator, the essence of the 'methodology', is not to *dar consejos* (give advice), but always to return the problem to the group for it to solve, and to *sacar las conclusiones del grupo* (to draw the conclusions out of the group). The *conclusiones* lead to and imply actions, what the peasants sometimes call the *realizaciones* (implementation) or *cambio de vida* (change of life) – the actions can be looked on both as the product of attitude change and as a further part of the process that produces attitude change. (The latter aspect, action producing attitude change, is emphasized by Darryl Bem, an author who has had a certain amount of influence on PPH's ideology.) Further, the same process that can be called 'attitude change' can also be called 'community-building', since it is the process by which the group achieves unity.

It can also be called 'value change'. Participating in PPH is not just a matter of going to a meeting to hear a talk or take a lesson. It leads to a change in values. The constant struggle of the coordinators to keep up attendance can be explained in part by the fact that many people do not want to change their values, as in the case of the heavy drinker who told his wife: 'I don't want to go to PPH and listen to talk about why I shouldn't drink.' Public commitment grants other people a licence to criticize one's behaviour, as in the case of the mother who was told by her child: 'You are not supposed to hit me. You yourself said so in PPH.'

Four of the informants composed *teatros* (plays) for me. They were familiar with the idea of *teatro* because The Voice of the Coast broadcasts *radio-teatros* to accompany each unit of PPH. I asked them to tell me a *teatro* that represented what happens at a typical PPH meeting.

One might have thought peasants would be embarrassed to compose plays, or that they would fall silent waiting to be inspired before responding, but as it turned out they readily dictated scripts to me, occasionally with a tinge of emotion in the voice when the informant warmed to a part – but without making the kitchen of the rambling pink stucco house on Los Carrera Street into a stage. I wrote down the *teatros* in the same way that I wrote down everything else, and I am afraid I have translated them into English in a literal and unimaginative way that lacks the charm of my informants' picturesque Spanish, but *qué querís*? (*qué querís*? is a charming and picturesque way to say *qué quieres*? which means 'what do you want?'.) Here is a sample.

'PPH Teatro' by Ema Rosales

Scene: the PPH meeting.

Srta Juanita (the sector-coordinator): Is it right to teach the children to know how chickens lay eggs?

Everybody together: Of course!

Sra Juanita (a volunteer base-coordinator): Have you taught your children how eggs are laid? How do you teach your children?

Sra Adriana: I tell my children that the rooster makes the egg, because my baby daughter asked me if the chicken laid eggs just because it was sitting on the ground, and I told her that the rooster makes the egg and the chicken lays it. My baby daughter asked me, 'Where, mummy?' Then I said the chicken laid eggs just because it was sitting on the ground.

Sra Juanita (base-coordinator): You do not teach the children correctly. For example, when you are pregnant, your children ask you, 'Why are you so fat, mummy?' 'Are you going to have a baby?' What do you answer?

Sra Adriana: I answer that I have swelled up because I have been cold.

Sra Juanita (base-coordinator): You have to be clear. We are not supposed to bring up our children to be ignorant, because if we do, the children will not trust the mother. Sometimes we lie to the children and they converse with another child who has more experience. Then our children come home and tell their mother that it is not true that mothers walk around swelled up because of the cold.

Sra Ana: It is not good to teach the children. I do not agree with teaching my child those things. Afterwards he will talk with someone else, and he will say something ugly, and then someone else will tell him off.

Sra Graciela: It is good, so that the children will not grow up ignorant. We have to give trust to the children, because if we do not, the children will learn to lie because we lie to them.

Sra Juanita (base-coordinator): Is this good?

Sra Malena: No. It is not good. Because the children will grow up acting too old for their age.

Other mothers: It is good because we have to give the child trust, so that there will not be ignorant children, with some children knowing more and others less.

Sra Elisa: Yes. It is good because when I am going to have a baby, I am big because the baby is coming, and my children know the baby is coming because they have to do the work because there is no one else to help.

Sra Juanita (base-coordinator): Is it good to teach the children about these things?

Some said Yes and *others* said No.

Sra Malena: Yes, it is good. Otherwise we wait until the teachers explain it in school, because when I was in school the teachers asked me and I did not know how to answer because my parents raised me ignorant. So I shall agree that the children should know, and that I shall talk to my children.

Sra Graciela: Yes, I am also in agreement, because we have to give trust to the children, so that they will trust their mothers. Since we come to the PPH Centre to learn, we also have to teach them so that some day, when they are older, things will not happen that should not happen. Sometimes those things that should not happen occur because of the ignorance of the children, and then we ourselves, the parents, are to blame.

Sra Juanita (base-coordinator): How do we conclude? Are all the mothers in agreement?

We said we were. It was important that the children know. Then Srta Juanita (the sector-coordinator) said that was good, that every day we have to have trust with the children.

Then the session ended.

The previous *teatro* shows the structure of a typical meeting, starting with posing a problem and ending with agreeing on a practical conclusion, but it is atypical in the respect that the coordinators are unusually directive. Although it is an illusion to believe that coordinators are as non-directive as the PPH ideology prescribes, the reader will get a more balanced picture

from another *teatro*, in which the coordinators, Celinda and
Albertina, are somewhat less directive. It is from a *centro* that has
elected a board of directors, and plans to continue to function as
best it can even if the program ends.

'PPH Teatro' by Clara Manaos

Scene: the PPH meeting.
Celinda: We want to raise money.
Rosamel: How can we do it?
Samuel: We will have a *rayuela* tournament, because there is no
  other way we can do it because we are poor people.
Albertina: It is a good idea to do a tournament, in order to raise
  the money that is lacking to finish our first-aid kit.
Clara: How much better it would be to solve this problem of the
  first-aid kit if we had a *posta* (a branch clinic operated by the
  government health service – HR) to solve this whole problem.
  We have to walk ten kilometres to be able to find a few pills.
Celinda: The only thing we can do is be more closely united so we
  can go forward together.
Albertina: We have to make the effort. Let us all be united.
Rosamel: If we are united, we shall go forward, with a great
  sacrifice.
Samuel: We have to be all united.
Florentino: The most necessary thing is the *posta*. We have had so
  many problems. We shall never abandon our PPH Centre.
Clara: Because the centre is educational. But what will we do
  when the program ends this year?
Then some others spoke, backing the centre and giving their
  support.
That is all.

In PPH, people create meanings together. They come to share
words, to be guided by the same *logoi*. At the beginning of the
discussion, each person has his own words – and some do not
have even that. At the end, the conclusions belong to everyone.
The group made them together; they belong to each and every
person, and they are intended to guide each person's action.

NOTES AND REFERENCES

The process observed in PPH is similar to some processes James Redfield finds at work in Homer's *Iliad*. For example, a hero fights to show that he is what he claims to be (James Redfield, *Nature and Culture in the Iliad* (Chicago and London: University of Chicago Press, 1975) p. 129).

The word 'apathetic' is not one the peasants use to describe themselves. They may say that they are 'disorganized', that some people are concerned with their own family problems too much to take an interest in community problems, that there is too much *egoismo* (selfishness), or that some people are *amedrentado* (intimidated). We use the term as a shorthand expression, and because 'apathy' is a word readily understood by outsiders who speak of the attitudes of a discouraged peasantry. Unfortunately, some of the connotations of the term are bad ones. Intellectually, it lends itself to reification – to supposing that there is a thing in the world named apathy. Politically, it lends itself to blaming the victim – to supposing that the suffering of the oppressed could be overcome if only they would shake off their apathy. See William Ryan, *Blaming the Victim* (New York: Random House, 1976).

The information on the history of the word 'attitude' comes from the *Oxford English Dictionary* and the *Diccionario de la Real Academia Espanola*.

The ethnographic procedures followed were those recommended by James P. Spradley in *The Ethnographic Interview* (New York: Holt, Rinehart & Winston, 1979).

A classic discussion of the concept of attitude is Donald T. Campbell's 'The Indirect Assessment of Social Attitudes', *Psychological Bulletin*, vol. 47 (1950) p. 15.

For more recent discussions, see the essays in Rom Harré (ed.), *Personality* (Oxford: Blackwell, 1976); see also Robert Audi, 'On the Conception and Measurement of Attitudes in Contemporary Anglo–American Psychology', *Journal for the Theory of Social Behaviour*, vol. 2 (1972) p. 179; Rom Harré and Paul Secord, *The Explanation of Social Behaviour* (Oxford: Blackwell, 1972), especially Chapter 10 and pp. 302–13.

Darryl Bem has shown that self-conscious action changes attitudes; actions produce attitudes as well as being produced by them (Darryl J. Bem, 'Self-perception . . .', *Psychological Review*, vol. 74 (1967) p. 183).

Roger Scruton argues that attitudes are expressed in directed behaviour, and that they change when a person changes pertinent beliefs (Roger Scruton, 'Attitudes, Beliefs and Reasons', in John Casey, *Morality and Moral Reasoning* (London: Methuen, 1971)).

8 The Verbal Image

In the preceding chapter, ethnographic interviews and the study of scripts composed by the *campesinos* proved to be suitable methods for learning about their attitudes. They enabled us to see the process of attitude change at work. The essential mechanism of attitude change in PPH consists of people talking about problems, reaching agreement, and acting on the conclusions.

What the peasants like about the program is the opportunity to do things that they themselves plan and carry out. This is attitude change because it is a change from attitude A (apathy) to attitude B (disposition to participate in constructive activities). PPH's strong points with respect to motivation are the sense of self-worth people gain from participation, and the flexibility that makes it not so much a program trying to accomplish something as a set of resources for helping poor people to accomplish whatever they deem it wise to try to accomplish.

Consider, for example, the motivation, or rather the re-motivation, of Ruth Cofré, a mother in her early twenties who belongs to the PPH centre in a wretched little town perched on the rocks above the Pacific Ocean, named *Bahia Mansa* (Tranquil Bay), a name no doubt invented to conceal the truth because neither the winter storms that come in from the sea nor the inhabitants are tranquil. The people there are fishermen who have at best old-fashioned rowboats, and at worst only a licence that authorizes them to call themselves fishermen and to catch what they can while standing on the shore; unemployed workmen who eke out less-than-a-living (the equivalent of $33 a month in a country where prices are higher than in Canada) in the government's minimum employment public works program; and women without men who eke out less-than-a-living God knows how.

Sra Ruth loved the first year of PPH, but during the second year she became discouraged. 'Why don't we do something?' she said. 'Our children cover the holes in their clothes with old milk sacks.' (In Chile, milk is sold in plastic sacks.) Ruth proposed to take apart old clothes, and use the material to make winter wraps for the children. Her plan was accepted, and Ruth became, to use one of Jorge Zuleta's favourite terms, a *generadora* (generator), that is to say, a leader. PPH gained a new activity, the group gained unity, Sra Ruth got a new role, and the children got coats.

Defining and measuring variables do not help us to explain attitude change in PPH, because trying to explain, for example, Sra Ruth's re-motivation as due to the impact of some independent variable X on some dependent variable Y, would only be to try to explain the known in terms of the hypothetical. Nevertheless, I regret the absence of a measurable variable because measuring a variable gives a ready answer to the question, 'How much?'

Sra Ruth proposed that the PPH centre sew clothes for the children; the group agreed that it was a good idea and did it. We have a good explanation of the ladies' action without X or Y, but we are left with the question of whether this was an isolated incident that happened once in one PPH centre, or whether it represents a sort of thing that happens frequently, and is therefore typical of what went on in PPH-Osorno generally, and consequently is the sort of phenomenon one may expect to occur if one undertakes to implement a similar program in the Yukon or in Madagascar. We need an answer to the question 'how much?' analogous to the answer we would get by measuring a variable if we had a variable to measure.

A lot depends on what one means by 'sort of thing' or 'sort of phenomenon', that is, on what names one gives to what classes of the phenomena under study. If the experience of PPH-Osorno is to be of any use to the people of Madagascar, it will have to be transmitted in categories that are pretty nearly universal. If we expect to communicate with the people of the southern Chilean countryside, we shall have to use their language – not mine, not yours, not that of social science, not the Spanish of the local élite, not the code of the PPH staff. The 'instrument' – which is not an instrument, because it does not measure variables – should depict the reality of PPH-Osorno in the language of the peasants, and, in a second phase, the results must be put into a somewhat more universal language, and some background that the speakers take for granted must be mentioned so that the information can be understood (and its significance recognized) by outsiders. The reason why the language of the actors (in this case, the peasants) is essential in social research is that the objects of social research, such as PPH, are constituted by mutual expectations; hence the language that describes a social reality is not independent of the social reality's existence. The peasants own their PPH centres; without the speech-guided mutual expectations of the members, the PPH centre would not exist at all. Among all the languages in which PPH may be described, the language of the participants themselves has a certain priority, because it is PPH's working language. It is the language that does things in Bahia Mansa. It functions in Los Hualles; in it promises are made and expectations created in Los Parrones and in Dollinco.

But if we admit that the peasants own their social reality, then it is outrageous to suggest that we already know what is important about PPH, even if the priorities of the evaluative study have been rigorously deduced from the requirements of the systems approach, and even if distinguished advisors in the slums of Lima and the offices of New York concur. What is really important is what is important to the peasants. However, the choice of attitude change as a research priority gives an opportunity for a last minute change of priorities to adjust them to peasants' perceptions of the program.

A verbal image of PPH is constructed by using the series of non-directed interviews (the ones described in the previous chapter), in which participants told about the significant features of PPH as they perceived them. The verbal image consists of a series of quotations, arranged in a sequence that the interviewer considers plausible, reflecting the main points made by ten informants in thirty-one interviews. In the verbal image, the picture of the mechanism at work, problem-posing discussion leading to action, remains quite clear, and the high points of the process are those perceived by ten participants as described in their own words. The verbal-image document was read to every PPH centre by a sector-coordinator or volunteer base-coordinator, with the request that the group reach consensus on whether each sentence describes PPH as they see it, and with the invitation to change the text where the group considers that something needs to be added or corrected.

The verbal image is a method that helps us to begin to answer the question 'how much?' and to see what is salient in the peasants' perception of their project.

The first part of the verbal image is presented in the statements below, together with:

(a) number of centres agreeing with the statement;
(b) number of centres disagreeing;
(c) amendments and additions made by various centres;
(d) interpretive comments. (In the English-language version there are actually two interpretive moments, one in translating from the peasants' Spanish to my English, and one in part (d).)

Peasant Report

A. How we run the centre.
  (a) Ordinarily under (a), we put the number of centres agreeing, but since 'Peasant Report' and 'How we run the centre' were a title and a heading, the centres did not deliberate on whether they agreed with them.
  (b) Number of centres disagreeing: for the reason given in (a), no centre disagreed.
  (c) Amendments and additions: for the reason given in (a), to which an allusion was made in (b), there were no amendments or additions.
  (d) Interpretive comments: Jorge Zuleta saved us from using the phrase 'verbal image', which no peasant would have understood, by proposing the title 'peasant report'. Ema Rosales, the informant from Ex-Estacion (so-called because there used to be a railway station there), used the phrase 'How we run the centre' in the first sentence of her interview. It must be significant that 7 of 10 informants used the first person plural in their first sentences.

  1. The people who participate are, in the majority, people who know how to read very little; some do not know how at all. They are all people of scarce resources.

(a) Agree: 43
(b) Disagree: 0
(c) Amendments: none
(d) It was anticipated that some centres might have difficulty reaching consensus on some items, and it was suggested that in such a situation they should vote. As it turned out, no such situations arose, and there were no votes.

2. In the first place, we discussed the undernourished child, and there the people asked: 'How can this be prevented?'
   (a) 39
   (b) 4
   (c) None
   (d) Hunger among children stands out in the memories of many participants as the first major discussion.

3. There they asked us how to answer children if they ask why the rooster stands on the chicken, and all those things like that.
   (a) 35
   (b) 4
   (c) None
   (d) (i) 'There' means 'in the PPH meeting'.
       (ii) The statement refers to the unit on sex education.
       (iii) A unit is designed to be done in a month, in four weekly meetings.

4. Each unit has a sign. The coordinator says, 'read it.' 'Read it,' he says. And we read it, although reading is hard work for some of us, and from there the conversation is built.
   (a) 43
   (b) 0
   (c) None
   (d) (i) Each unit has 10 or 12 pictures. For example, sex education features a boy putting a finger on a woman's enlarged tummy.
       (ii) The things that need to be read are printed questions. The pictures themselves are *sans* print.
       (iii) The coordinator is equipped with a manual that gives additional questions for each picture. His aim

is to draw people out, to get them to tell their experiences and ideas.

5. Then the coordinator asks us if we find it good or if it is bad. And we, since everything is there to see, what we find good we say is good, and what is not correct we say is bad.

   (a) 44

   (b) 0

   (c) None

   (d) (i) The volunteer base-coordinator leads the discussion and the sector-coordinator backs him up.

        (ii) Most of the conversations are about what is good and what is bad, and most of the conclusions prescribe norms. Such heavy moralizing puts the coordinator in the position of the minister's daughter, who is expected to embody the congregation's ideals. Several wayward coordinators had been obliged to resign when their flocks said, in effect: 'If you don't walk the walk, don't talk the talk.' One coordinator reportedly persuaded her husband to join the local priest's Teetotalers' Club by saying: 'I have to be a model for others because I am a PPH coordinator, and you have to help me be a model because you are my husband.'

6. There in the worksheets it tells about, for example, when a boy asks his father something, for example a colour, then whether the father answers well, or says to him: 'Don't bother me kid, I'm tired.' And the people answer. Some say the boy should not bother his father, and other people say the father should explain then to his children.

   (a) 41

   (b) 2

   (c) None

   (d) (i) Sets of worksheets are distributed in the 2nd, 3rd, and 4th weeks of each unit.

        (ii) The coordinators use points in the worksheets as opportunities to provoke discussions. The coordinator's passion for problematizing all themes comes not from the worksheets themselves, or from the manuals, but from the spirit of PPH the coordinators acquire in training (*capacitacion*) and in constant in-service training.

7. And there in the meeting they asked what to do if the man came home drunk to his wife. Some said you do not have to let yourself be hit, and others said you should let yourself be humiliated to not give problems to the children. That is the way it goes in all the meetings – they review the worksheets, they draw conclusions.
   (a) 40
   (b) 2
   (c) None
   (d) (i) When the agreements and disagreements do not add up to the expected sum, it is because some centres did not answer or because a page was lost.
   (ii) Drawing conclusions, *sacar conclusiones*, has the sense of deciding what the solution to the problem is, of deciding what should be done.

8. We play a kind of game, a game of making accusations and arguing. We throw the wife out of the house. It is a dispute but it is a game. Afterwards, the coordinator herself asks you, 'How did you feel señora?' or 'How did you feel señor?', if you feel nervous, if you hold a grudge because of something someone said, or something like that.
   (a) 24
   (b) 15
   (c) The centre at Las Quemas reported that their game was different. First they dramatized an argument, then the group discussed who was right.
   (d) (i) The four meetings of a unit form a cycle as follows:
       (1) show the pictures;
       (2) *taller* (workshop) and worksheets;
       (3) *hoja problema* (problem sheet) and worksheets;
       (4) review and worksheets.
   (ii) The pictures and the newness of the topic make the first meeting the best. Some sector-coordinators have promoted the use of group games and play-acting to liven up meetings 2, 3 and 4.
   (iii) We are talking here about meeting 3 of Unit 8, the *hoja problema* on alcohol, which poses the problem

what to do when a man comes home drunk and demands food, but the woman has no food to give him. Some coordinators took off from the *hoja problema* to make it into a psychodrama.

9. Afterwards come the worksheets for the children. The coordinator explains the worksheets to us so that we will be able to teach the children.
   (a) 43
   (b) 0
   (c) None
   (d) (i)   Everybody studies the worksheets together; those who can read take turns reading aloud. There are about 8 pages, consisting mostly of pictures; about 25 sentences need to be read.
        (ii) I think the word 'explains' is to be broadly construed here. In the 14 meetings I analysed, the coordinator played Socrates, asking questions until she got the answer she wanted; she did not, strictly speaking, explain, although, in effect, she did explain.
        (iii) Although the nominal purpose of the worksheets is to help children aged 4–6 to prepare for school, in fact grandma, the neighbour, dad, mum and the older child who is already in school learn from them too.

10. We all comply, because when the day of the next meeting comes we have to bring the worksheets done. This is an assignment they give us. We return the worksheets the other Saturday filled with the work done by the children.
    (a) 39
    (b) 1
    (c) None
    (d) The children colour, draw, cut out, recognize letters, learn new words and do exercises in lower mathematics such as drawing a line from the number 4 to a picture of 4 rabbits.

11. Afterwards, at home with the worksheets, we teach the children; those who have children explain everything to the

children. As one is taught, one teaches the children.
   (a) 43
   (b) 1
   (c) None
   (d) None

12. PPH also distributed coloured pencils and graphite pencils last year, and this year little scissors with round-ended blades.
   (a) 43
   (b) 1
   (c) The centre at Mashué added that in each meeting they review who is sick, and assign someone to take charge of taking food and other things to the sick person and his or her family.
   (d) The pencils and scissors are provided by European churchgoers. The food and other things are provided through the cooperation of the neighbours of Mashué.

13. In the house, one begins to go over the meeting again in the family, now in the form of a conversation. This conversation is joined by children and adults, and, generally speaking, the conversations take place in the evenings, or at night, when the labours of the day are over. All meet who are in the house.
   (a) 43
   (b) 0
   (c) None
   (d) None

14. In the *centro*, we formed a Board of Directors. Now with them we reach agreement about the work we are doing.
   (a) 29
   (b) 13
   (c) The centre at Cumilelfu added that they also name committees to take charge of each type of activity.
   (d) The 13 *centros* answering 'no' are *centros* that did not elect boards of directors. The *directiva* usually consists of a president, a secretary, a treasurer, and the two coordinators. It acquires a rubber stamp with a distinctive seal, such as:

PPH
CENTRE
"THE WINNERS"
Casa de Lata

The verbal image is a description of the project. It is made up of words provided by participant informants, and validated by review by all of the participants. It is a way to learn some of the operative words, *idées forces*, that function in a project, and to check them by review on a fairly large scale, thus avoiding some of the limitations of microsociological techniques that depend on the sensitive analysis of face-to-face interaction, while keeping some of the advantages of such techniques.

NOTES AND REFERENCES

For a review of many of the writers who have stressed the importance of understanding social realities from the point of view of the people whose realities they are, see Ian C. Jarvie, *The Revolution in Anthropology* (London: Routledge & Kegan Paul, 1967).

The PPH process is described by the phrase *energeia kata logon* from the *Nichomachean Ethics* of Aristotle (various editions) vol. I, bk vii, p. 14. St Thomas Aquinas comments on this passage: 'the proper function of a man is activity in accord with reason itself or at least not independent of reason' (*Commentary on the Nichomachean Ethics*, Litzinger trans. (Chicago: Regnery, 1964) p. 54).

Much recent philosophy supports a broadly Aristotelian conception of human action. For example, Alan Donagan, in his presidential address to the western division of the American Philosophical Association, uses the tools of modern logic to defend an Aristotelian–Thomist view of intentions (Alan Donagan, 'Philosophical Progress and the Theory of Action', *Proceedings and Addresses of the American Philosophical Association*, vol. 55 (1981) pp. 25–52). Rom Harré's theory of social psychology is also broadly Aristotelian. See Rom

Harré, *Social Being* (Totowa, NJ: Littlefield, Adams, 1980) pp. 159, 244. Harré is, at the time of writing, the lecturer in philosophy of science at Oxford.

However, for many Latin Americans, the name 'Aristotle' is anathema, partly because he is identified with the 'Greek' theology condemned by liberation theology, and partly because since the days when the Council of the Indies cited Aristotle to attack Bartolomé de las Casas (of blessed memory, Bishop of Oaxaca and defender of the indigenous peoples), using Aristotle to claim that some people are naturally inferior, the name Aristotle has been associated with the claim that slavery is natural. Suffice it to say that Aristotle (and Harré) made more than one statement, and that to agree with one of his statements does not commit one to the general principle that what Aristotle (or Harré) says is correct.

It will be noted that when we say we know why Sra Ruth did something, we are willing to say that we know the cause. This will surprise some people who are used to saying that ethnographic research is 'not causal'.

In our view, a great deal of confusion has been caused by H. M. Blalock, Jr (ed.), *Causal Models in the Social Sciences* (Chicago: Aldine-Atherton, 1971). The models treated in that book are in many cases not properly called causal on a realistic view of the sciences, as is made clear in Rom Harré's works. The popularity of views such as those in Blalock's book leads many people to refer to research that provides insight into processes, mechanisms, *modus operandi*, roles, rules and meanings as 'not causal', and to interpret the notion of 'causal' to mean $y = f(x)$, plus the claim that the direction of influence is from x to y, as Stroth and Wold do in the book cited, on pages 180–1. Compared to Blalock, we find much more convincing the concept of 'cause' delineated by Michael Scriven in 'Maximizing the Power of Causal Investigation: the Modus Operandi Method', in W. J. Popham (ed.), *Evaluation in Education* (Berkeley, Calif.: McCutchan, 1974).

A variety of considerations lead various writers to narrow or to expand the scope of the concept of 'cause'. See, for example, the remarks of Peter Manicas in 'The Concept of Social Structure', *Journal for the Theory of Social Behaviour*, vol. 10 (1980) pp. 65, 76. We prefer to construe 'cause' broadly, glossing over distinctions that might be made between 'cause', 'reason' and 'motive' because we believe our readers will find it convenient to regard as a cause whatever explains an action and provides guidance to those who wish to participate constructively with other people in dialogue, leading to further actions. Our readers would be disappointed if they were told that, whereas other methods claim to be able to ascertain the causes of social phenomena, ours admits that it cannot.

The ambiguity of some responses could have been reduced, at the expense of incurring certain disadvantages, by dividing the text into smaller parts. For example, instead of:

14. In the *centro*, we formed a Board of Directors. Now with them we reach agreement about the work we are doing.

we could have presented two smaller statements:

14a. In the *centro* we formed a Board of Directors.

14b. Now with them we reach agreement about the work we are doing.

The disadvantages that dissuaded us from subdividing the text entirely into 'bits' of information are two: (i) the danger of making the discussion of the text in the *centros* unbearably long, by examining evey detail separately; (ii) the danger of failing to evoke the holistic image expressed in the words of the informant. To make the second point clearer, consider that some people may recognize a 'bite' or clump of statements as true to life, as a recognizable image of how things are, when they would be disoriented if the 'bites' were broken into 'bits'. The balance between 'bits' and 'bites' was worked out by pre-testing the verbal image with a group of coordinators. The same pre-test eliminated a few phrases the coordinators found unintelligible, apparently because they were idiosyncratic wordings or because the informant took for granted a context not widely shared.

9 Actions and Achievements

The previous chapter dealt with one aspect of understanding attitude change – obtaining and validating the peasants' perceptions through the formulation and the first phase of the checking of the verbal image. This chapter deals with another aspect of studying attitude change – ascertaining what actions the peasants performed. It begins with an area in which it is extremely difficult to obtain reliable information, the reform of alcoholics.

When the informant from Anchiquemo, a sparsely-populated locality in a region where many people still speak Mapuche, told me that the men who attend his *centro* (of whom there are 7) had given up excessive drinking, I was inclined to think it was a pardonable exaggeration of some sort; he was telling me what he thought I wanted to hear; or he was trying to enlist my support in the conflict between his friends (the PPH members) and his enemies (the non-members), by dwelling on the virtue of the former and the depravity of the latter; or he had confounded the faculty of intellect with the faculty of will, mistaking drawing the conclusion that one ought to change for the actual changing.

We have good reasons for believing that most of the peasants perceive alcoholism as one of their main problems. For example, Sra Rosa Huenulef from La Poza, Hueyusca, described the members of her *centro* as follows.

Patricia says to her husband Juan: 'Think of your home and your children; don't mis-spend your money so much.'

Juan: 'I still have a little money left. I shall buy the things that are lacking.'

He goes to the store, to the market. He stays there [i.e. at the bar] and does not bring what is lacking in the house. He mis-spends all the money on drink, finally he goes and he doesn't bring anything for the kitchen, and finally he does not accept the *consejos* of his wife.

Fresia lives the same problems with her husband, always misery in the house. She tells her husband to go to the PPH program, and he answers: 'I won't go because there they bug me about alcohol, and I do not want to listen to what they say to me there.' She says to him: 'You don't understand the *consejos*; there they will tell you how we can live better, like other homes where people are happy. In other homes nothing is lacking, and we could live happily like that.'

And that is all about that family.

Araucaria (her husband is Sergio) has a family, a marriage, that is united. They work equally, the two of them, to be able to give education to their children, and to help their children afterwards when they have finished their studies. They talk to each other in the family, because he *avecina*. [I cannot decide how to translate *avecina*; literally, it means 'he comes close'.] They don't live the way we live. In their house nothing is lacking.

That is all.

Olga and Clemente: in their home what is lacking is intelligence on his part. She tells her husband to be a good worker, so that they will not lack so many things to complete the kitchen, and to be able to permit the children to go to school, so that they will not grow up to be illiterate like them. They are illiterate, and so people don't pay him for his work, because he does not know what quantity of money he is supposed to receive, and he continues with his irresponsibility, and what he earns is for drink.

That is all about Olga.

Alicia goes to the meetings to help the families that are lost in alcoholism, and to give them good *consejos*, so that they will not lack food, to give advice to the families. If they do not take *consejos* from their wives, they may accept them from the coordinator. [Alicia is a volunteer base-coordinator.]

Inez also goes for the same reason, to give *consejos* to the family, because they have pity on those families that lack many things, and they invite many families that live in alcoholism, so that they will be able to live a normal life, as they live in their house. Those families don't want to come; they don't want to participate in the meetings, so that no one will speak to them about the life that they live, and she as a coordinator demands according to the programmes of PPH that give these *consejos*.

That is all.

Two of the 12 units of PPH deal with alcoholism, and we know that they incite discussion. A *teatro* by Ema Rosales provides a glimpse of what the discussions are like.

Sra Juanita (the coordinator): Alcohol – the man who is very drunk – does harm to the entire family.

Sra Maria: Not so much to all the family, because it is worst for the child. Worst for the child because he is little, and he suffers more because dad drinks away the money, and there is nothing to give the child to eat.

Sra Graciela: It is not only the child, because it is all the family that is harmed, and even the neighbours, because if the man arrives drunk, when the neighbour looks at him he gets mad in his drunkenness. So it is not only the child who is harmed by the man, but everybody in general. And besides, it is because of alcohol that he leaves the house without the things it needs, and it is a bad example for the children.

Sra Julieta: This is true, because I have seen it in my neighbour. My neighbour makes good money. What is it worth to him when he drinks it all with his friends over there? I see how that family suffers. I myself know, because my husband does not drink. He is an *evangélico* [evangelical protestant].

Sra Graciela: Evangélico? Doesn't he forbid you to come to meetings?

Sra Julieta: Never. He never forbids me to come, because he finds that it is good for our children, and good as well for us ourselves. We have acquired more confidence to talk about our problems since we began to come to the *centro*.

Sra Graciela: My husband drinks, but not very much, and he has never raised problems about me coming to the *centro*. When the centre began, he gave me permission to enrol, because he said it was good to be in any centre; he even wanted the sessions to be held on Sundays, 'so that I could go, because on work days I can't'.

Sra Adriana: I wish my husband were like that, so good, like that man. When he comes home from work the only thing he wants is that you invite him to eat something, and if there isn't anything he gets angry. The first thing he says is: 'Where have you been? In the PPH centre?' And I answer him: 'You gave me permission to go, and now if you don't like it, go stew in your own juice!'

Sra Juanita (coordinator): Well, we have seen that this is a problem, and that some suffer more and others less. Therefore we have to try to understand our husbands, so that we will be able to keep coming to the *centro*, and we can all meet together....

It is evident that alcoholism is widely discussed. My initial scepticism that headway was being made in solving the problem was weakened as reports of reform multiplied. Sra Rosa from La Poza said: 'People are taking *consejos* from PPH who never before took *consejos* from anybody.' Miguel Oyarzun, a sector-coordinator, reported that in Chahuilco, when the PPH centre sponsored a party, they used to order 50 litres of wine for 50 people. This meant 50 litres for 30 drinkers, or $1\frac{2}{3}$ litres per drinker, since Miguel's estimate is that of 25 men and 25 women, all the men and 5 of the women, a total of 30 people, drink. The party consisted of dancing and drinking. If there was no wine, no one would come; and if there was too little wine, when the wine ran out everyone would leave. Now, in the second year of PPH, they order 30 litres of wine for 50 people, one litre per drinker, and they have added some new *recreacion sana* (healthy recreation) to the dancing-cum-drinking format. The main new activity is listening to children sing.

We should not be carried so far by enthusiasm that we conceive of PPH as possessing a power to cure alcoholism equivalent to that of evangelical protestantism. God saves drinkers in southern Chile principally through the instrument of His servants the *evangélicos*; the question about His PPH servants is not whether their success in combating the bottle is equivalent to that of protestantism, but rather whether in their capacity as allies, using a somewhat different method with a somewhat different population, they achieve any considerable success at all.

The sector-coordinators helped me to interpret the reports of informants, by reviewing the transcripts with me. When one of them, Maria Catriyao, came to a transcript which affirmed that what happens next after the *sacar conclusiones* is the *cambio de vida* (change of life), she said that, for the informant, *cambio de vida* meant to adopt a disciplined and cooperative lifestyle, free of drinking bouts. Further, the informant himself was an individual who had made progress in conquering his vice.

The next time I saw the informant in question – who was not the same person as the man from Anchiquemo who had told me about the temperance of himself and his six friends, and who was from a different place – I asked him what he had meant in his previous interview when he had said, '*cambio de vida*'. Either he considered it so obvious that alcohol was the topic that it was unnecessary to say so, or he resisted explicit talk about his drinking problem. In any event, he did not say that alcohol was the problem, but instead referred to it obliquely: 'Of course, you have to notice, you have to understand as *cambio de vida*, when a person with his knowledge [the knowledge learned in PPH] begins to utilize better all the resources that are at his command, then this is what is understood as *cambio de vida*.'

Later, a young volunteer base-coordinator shared part of the story of his life with me as we journeyed together to the *centro* at Caracol. He said that when he left the army he did not know whether alcohol was good or bad. He knew that many people said: '*Tomando se puede hacerse hombre*' (by drinking you can make yourself a man). He found PPH functioning in his home, and became a base-coordinator. After he led the discussions of the unit on alcohol, he began to seek more information on the subject, consulting people in Osorno, *sacando conclusiones* in conversations with people, and forming his ideas. He decided not to become a heavy drinker. Moreover, although he had not noticed it happening, one day he realized that his father, aged 60, who had long been a heavy drinker, had stopped drinking altogether. When we arrived at Caracol, I was able to observe that the young man was beginning to enjoy a form of *recreacion sana*: playing the guitar to accompany hymns. It was a good thing that the group was interested in his welfare as a person, and not just in his services as a guitarist, because he took so long to find the chords that he surely would have been dismissed if he had been a hired musician.

Although I am adopting a wait-and-see attitude on the question of how long the sobriety of the 60-year-old man will last, in general I find these stories plausible. On the other hand,

I despair of making a list of authenticated cases of diminished drinking. Partly for this reason, I am grateful that there are achievements of PPH that are relatively easy to verify: the concrete actions of the centres. We are interested in actions not only because they tell the reader what PPH actually did in Osorno, thereby empowering the reader to draw his or her own conclusions, but also because the actions are evidence of attitude change. The changes in attitude toward alcohol are part of a larger process, in which PPH participants study their problems, draw conclusions, and act. Some of the actions that are part of the larger process lend themselves to confirmation and to quantification; we are interested in them because they lend credibility to the total picture. Confirmation of concrete actions buttresses the reports of the informants in the same way that the testimony of a witness at a trial gains credibility when the parts of it that can be checked turn out to be true. Further, a list of actions gives the reader a sense of the magnitude of the phenomenon, a rough answer to the question 'how much?'

Because what we want to assess is attitude change, we are interested in actions that represent the achievement of non-objectives. The expression 'non-objective' is used here to describe objectives that do not exist from the beginning in the plans of the program staff, but instead emerge during the project from the ideas of the peasants themselves, who analyse their problems and make plans for coping with them. Here, the 660 stated objectives do not count. The change of attitude that we are interested in leads the peasants to affirm themselves and their organizations as generators of their own objectives, which are non-objectives in the sense that they were not previously set as objectives by the project staff. (From time to time, I wonder whether 'attitude change' was the right phrase to choose for PPH's leading benefit; at such times, I meditate on other phrases that might have been chosen, such as 'consciousness-raising', 'community-building', 'people-affirmation', 'confidence', 'humanizing values'.)

We need to consider whether or not to count as evidence of attitude change actions that are proposed by the sector-coordinators. Against counting them, one might argue that the sector-coordinators are on a slightly higher rung of the non-hierarchy (the hierarchy that, according to PPH ideology, has been abolished, but which in practice persists), and that therefore when their ideas are implemented, the only change in attitude is an unwanted one – from apathetic acceptance of grand tyranny to apathetic acceptance of petty tyranny.

On the other hand, all the coordinators are themselves peasants; the sector-coordinators as well as the base-coordinators are neighbours and peers who live in the same localities and run the same kind of semi-subsistence mini-farms. Hence the initiatives generated by sector-coordinators are peasant initiatives. (We use the term 'staff' to refer only to the Santiago and Osorno office staffs; the achievement of an objective set by the staff is, by definition, not evidence of attitude change.)

As it turns out, usually we cannot make a verifiable or even a meaningful distinction between what the sector-coordinator proposes and what the group proposes. When a sector-coordinator such as Maria Catriyao is in action, she is inconspicuous, supportive, encouraging. If it is necessary, she calls people's attention to what other people said; she reminds the group of decisions it made at prevous meetings; realizing that bodies and minds will be cold unless someone brings burning coals to light the fire, she brings them herself; she keeps a list of who volunteered to donate which prizes for a raffle. If it is not necessary, she does none of these things, propitiating autonomy by the opportune withdrawal of the helping hand. By the time an idea reaches the action stage, it is the group's idea, even if it happens that it coincides with a suggestion made by Maria at some earlier time.

It is not an accident that the question of who is setting the objectives is often unanswerable. The methodology is designed to make the *conclusiones* the outcome of a conversation through which reason prevails over pride. The question becomes not who is right but what is right. Further, the sector-coordinators have a different kind of interest, which overshadows any interest they may have in getting their ideas accepted, an interest perhaps classifiable as a third-level interest: not to achieve a preordinate aim (which would be level one), not only for peasants to set their own aims (which would be level two), but to make the process of programming activities produce unity and the capacity for cooperative action. That is what I think Sergio Ramos, a sector-coordinator, meant when he said: 'In Caracol we made a community first-aid kit, but it did not work. We have the first-aid kit, but it didn't work.' He meant that the group set itself an objective and achieved it; the *centro* held a benefit dance and a raffle, thereby succeeding in raising money to buy the components of a first-aid kit, which works perfectly well, but the activity did not produce regularity of attendance at meetings, nor acceptance by individuals of responsibility for performing ongoing tasks in a continuing organization, nor confidance in the group's ability to produce, by united effort, further triumphs in the future.

The verbal image has three parts. Part A, which was reproduced in the previous chapter, is about meetings. Part B is about implementing the conclusions reached at the meetings. Part C, to be discussed in a later chapter, is about problems and difficulties.

Most of Part B of the verbal image is a list of the actions carried out in one centre or another. We considered the peasant-initiated actions so important as evidence of attitude change that we confirmed our information by using several sources to verify the same facts: letters and documents on file at the Osorno office, interviews with coordinators, interviews with participants, site visits, and photographs. One of the results of our effort to check claims and track down rumours has been to find that some of the achievements that have been attributed to PPH-Osorno are imaginary. It is not true that through the program peasants have dug latrines, disinfected wells, repaired bridges, or built roads.

Number of centres where non-objective has been achieved: 47   Onces.
Nature of non-objective: An *once* is a large afternoon snack. To celebrate an *once*, members bring from their homes tea, coffee, bread, butter, jam, cheese; sometimes milk, ham, biscuits, or cakes. This sharing of food means more than it would in Amsterdam, because it happens in places where, as Sra Eduvina Queupan of Huampatué said, 'If a woman has many children, not all will survive, because there is not enough food.' Another informant expressed the charm of the *once* by saying: 'Wednesday we made an *once* to be able to spend time together talking, and to be with Srta Teresa, and so together we all brought the things for the *once*.' (The particular *once* she referred to was one the participants organized as a surprise for the coordinators.)

Number of centres where non-objective has been achieved: 40   Fund-raising events.

Nature of non-objective: These are commonly *rayuela* tournaments, at which refreshments are sold; dances used to raise funds; *onces* organized as benefits; bazaars; and raffles. The most common (in 26 centres) is the raffle. The following is a translation of the announcement for a raffle at Los Parrones, composed by the members and typed (making copies with carbon paper) by Maria at the PPH office in the rambling pink home away from home in Osorno.

Great Raffle

The centre of the Parents and Children Program of Los Parrones has organized a raffle that will be used to benefit the pre-school children. The draw will be held on Friday 22, August at 1600 hours, in the place where the program meets. Tickets: 10 pesos

Prizes

A flashlight and two plates	Two cans of peaches
Four plates	Three cups
A sweater and a pair of stockings	A bottle of *cinzano*
Four cans of salmon	Half dozen small glasses
A pitcher and two glasses	Half dozen wine glasses
A chicken	Two ashtrays
A bottle of *pisco*	A surprise

Some explanatory notes:
(i)   It happens that the place where this *centro* meets is the ramshackle house described in Chapter 3. The meetings there end at sundown, because there is no electric light and it is too expensive to burn candles.
(ii) The prizes are donated by the members.
(iii) *Pisco* is a drink made from grapes in Chile and Peru, similar to *tequila*.

Number of centres where non-objective has been achieved: 39
Participation in radio programs.
Nature of non-objective: The reader has possessed inklings of peasant participation in Voice of the Coast programming since Chapter 2, when he met Sparky, Squirrel, Uncle José, and the singing children of Los Hualles; and since Chapter 4 when he

learned how a coordinator from Tremaico used the radio to announce a football game, a dance, and a bazaar – all organized by the *centro* to fund the famous Tremaico bus tour of southern Chile. Jorge Cheuquian, a young participant who makes tape recordings in his village and sends them to Osorno by *micro* to be played on the air, said: 'Here the radio is at the disposition of the peasant.' In Chapter 16 we shall attempt a quantitative estimate of how much horizontal (i.e. peasant-to-peasant) communication there is on The Voice of the Coast.

Due to the mutual eagerness of the radio staff and the PPH members to achieve peasant participation in radio programs, we find a symbiotic synthesis of objectives (of the staff) and non-objectives (i.e. grassroots initiatives) that does not fit very well the concept of counting grassroots initiatives as evidence of attitude change. Here we note the facts, even though their relationship to our theory is a bit awkward.

Number of centres where non-objective has been achieved: 31   Dances.
Nature of non-objective: Jorge Zuleta says that the life of the peasants is so hard that one of their greatest needs is to create together more *espacios de alegria* (spaces of joy). The perspective of the enemies of PPH is less poetic and more choleric: one man, for example, complained to the police that he was beaten up at the home of a participant after a party, blaming the *centro* for creating a rowdy atmosphere.

(Here we count centres that hold dances mainly for fun, although there is overlap between *convivencias*, get-togethers, and *beneficios*, fund-raisers. We lump together dances with food (*onces-bailables*) and without food.)

Number of centres where non-objective has been achieved: 27   Auto-education.
Nature of non-objective: Although one would not distort the facts beyond recognition by calling all of PPH self-education, we are counting here centres where there is concrete evidence that the group has caught the spirit of PPH so much that it has organized at least one course. Here, 'course' means somewhat formal learning, in which the roles of teacher and student are somewhat differentiated. Those who wear Ivan Illich tinted-glasses may object that a group that differentiates teachers from students has not caught the true spirit of what PPH ought to be; they will see

evidence of the right kind of *auto-educacion* not here, but in the craft activities.

(a) In 9 centres, a member or neighbour assumed a leading role in teaching others. In Tacamo, the *centro* decided to learn something useful: pruning fruit trees. They persuaded an experienced pruner to teacher them, and since neither they nor the experienced pruner had pruning shears, they borrowed the necessary implement from Father Winfredo. In other centres, members taught sewing and sisal-weaving. We quote part of a member's account of her experience as a sewing instructor.

> There are *señoras* who have no idea how to cut. They don't know how to cut the clothes for their children. They are going to waste the material. So the second meeting of the month we have set aside for making clothes, to do the cutting, and the other times I always bring my sewing box because there will be some who will bring something to cut there. And afterwards, they may think that since I know how to cut, I don't want to explain to them. I imagine that they may think I am proud, that I don't want to explain to them, and I teach them without any profit motive, only to help them. They are all grateful to me for the explanations, and even the sector-coordinator is also grateful.

(b) Eight centres combine fund-raising with asking FREDER to send them an instructor. For example, they raise money to buy wool, and then they ask for a two-week FREDER course in weaving. During the course, they turn the wool into shawls and blankets, which they proudly exhibit at end-of-year festivities. Usually they keep their products for household use.

(c) Sixteen centres decided to ask FREDER to send them a course, without the kinds of preparation or follow-up just mentioned in (b). From the point of view of FREDER's promoters, PPH has accomplished nothing in these cases, because when the promoters go to the country to offer a course, they always get more applicants than there are places anyway. But it is significant that some course requests are the outcome of a deliberative process in which the peasants decide what they need – even when the request is only filed in the backlog of unfilled orders.

(d) In one case, a PPH coordinator learned how to make

artificial flowers of paper and cloth, and gave courses not only to her own *centro* but also to several others. One of her students commented: 'It was a new thing for our *centro* to learn that people like us could give courses. The members had always thought that professors had to come from Osorno and that you needed lots of papers.'

(The total number of cases in categories (a), (b), (c) and (d) above is greater than 27 because some centres fall into more than one category.)

Number of centres where non-objective has been achieved: 23　　Gifts for children at the end of the year.
Nature of non-objective:　　At the end of the year, every *centro* has a graduation ceremony for the children and the parents. We are not counting the ceremony itself as a non-objective, because it appears to be an unstated objective of the staff for the peasants to organize *actos*. These *actos* are the occasion of many grassroots initiatives, including using the funds raised to buy the children gifts. Here is Sra Juana Laucucheo's account of the 1979 *acto* at Huilma.

> We held a raffle to have a *fiesta* at the end of the year, for the children – this was to buy presents for all the children. For all the families, all together, we made an *once*. We gave them *café au lait* and all kinds of sweets. [The gifts were] T-shirts, balloons and packages of sweets. And we had them recite poetry too. And it was *bailable* too – afterwards we all danced. And for the adults we also had a barbecue.

Number of centres where non-objective has been achieved: 17　　Knitting (craft activity).
Nature of non-objective:　　Usually, the ladies teach each other how to knit better. At Huilma, they exchange knitting; the lady who receives has to continue the garment using the same kind of stitch; if she doesn't know how, the lady who gave it to her has to teach her.

15　Textile painting.
The sector-coordinators are under a great deal of pressure to keep their centres going by thinking of ways to motivate people to attend. My sense of the textile painting activity is that it is

slightly more accurate to describe it as a good idea that some sector-coordinators succeeded in promoting, than to describe it as the result of an attitude change. There are no doubt elements of the latter too, as is evidenced by the fact that every square centimetre of cloth and every cubic centimetre of paint was purchased with the proceeds of fund-raising events – which would have been impossible without a high degree of group solidarity.

14   Making a community first-aid kit.

At Cumilelfu, it is a veterinary kit to give first-aid to animals. At Chapuco, the PPH centre has ceased to exist, but the *botiquin* has been transferred to the school, where it continues to function. I examined the first-aid kit at El Monte, and found that it contained cotton, adhesive tape, aspirin for adults, aspirin for children, alcohol, cough syrup, hydrogen peroxide, and a local pain reliever that is stronger than aspirin. It is administered by a member who once worked as a maid in the infirmary of a boarding school.

12   Embroidery (craft activity).

At centres that consist mainly of mothers (about 60 per cent of the centres), they often stay on after the formal part of the meeting to do embroidering, knitting, flower-making, or textile-painting. The works are exhibited at the end of the year, together with the worksheets completed by the pre-school children.

11   Funerals.

When someone in the community dies, the *centro* helps organize food for the family, a wreath, and a *velorio*. The *velorio* consists of sitting near the body during the first 24 hours after death.

11   Singing and composing songs.

Much of the singing is oriented toward composing songs for the Festival of Country Music sponsored by FREDER in December every year. In 1979, a PPH group won first prize. In the 6 *centros* in the area known as San Juan de la Costa, the coordinators are encouraging singing in Mapuche and, in general, pride in the Mapuche culture.

10   Making clothes for children.

Usually, old clothes are taken apart and made into new clothes to fit the children. At Mashué, the material is exchanged so that the children will not know that their new clothes are made from their siblings' old clothes.

7   Aid for needy neighbours.

'In Las Quemas, at one of the last meetings of the year, it was agreed to help a lady with five young children, since her husband had been fired from his job and thrown onto the street, two months ago; they had nothing to eat. They were invited to participate in meetings, and they delivered to them food contributed by all the participants.' (From Miguel Oyarzun's 1979 sector report.)

7   Poetry.

Children recite at *actos*, and original compositions are sent to The Voice of the Coast to be broadcast. For a sample, see 'El Fervor Campesino', in Chapter 2.

5   Woodwork (craft activity).

This activity occurs in some of the centres where young men are prominent among the membership. (Young people predominate in about 30 per cent of the centres.) It consists of carving ornaments, such as seated monkeys, and toys, such as model boats. There is no teacher.

5   Planning a community building.

These are cases where the building is at the talking stage, although at Caracol the land has already been donated. At Huallinto, the group decided to repair the road and then make a building, but has not yet done either.

4   Artificial flowers (craft activity).

4   Library.

A member takes change of the few magazines the members contribute, plus a few FREDER contributions, and administers their circulation. This activity takes place in all and only the centres of one sector-coordinator, and is evidently an idea that he promotes.

4   Demanding a clinic.

The *centro* has complained to the authorities that they lack needed and deserved medical attention; see Chapter 15.

3   Sisal-weaving (craft activity).

3   Repair of building.

The men do the work and the women bring the lunch. The repairs are of a school, a chapel, and a previously existing community building.

2   Building a community building.

In two cases, Los Hualles and Dollinco, the building has been completed; see Chapter 2.

1   Wiring the school for electricity.

1   Asking for a new *micro* route.

In the Chahuilco area, the centres were successful in getting an improved bus service.

1   Supporting the grievances of woodcutters deprived of their livelihood by being forbidden to cut wood.

1   Building a ping-pong table.

1   Ceremony in tribute to the local schoolteacher on her retirement.

1   Aid to old people's home.

We have deviated from Part B of the verbal image, because we have a better list. We are happy to report that the complete and confirmed list did not contradict but rather augmented the verbal image. If we had followed Part B to the letter, the reader would have noticed a striking difference from Part A, because many of the answers look like:

(a) Agree: 2
(b) Disagree: 34

The preponderance of negative answers in Part B gives us reason to believe the following.

(i) The members of the centres did not nod their way through the sessions where the verbal image was reviewed. As one participant said of the examination of the verbal image in her *centro*: 'We realized that we couldn't tell lies.' (For the verbal image as a whole, the responses to the statements were: (a) agree 66 per cent, (b) disagree 31 per cent, (c) amended statement 1 per cent, no answer to item 1 per cent.)

(ii) Since many actions took place in one or a few places, we deduce that local people took the initiative in responding to local needs and opportunities.

We now terminate our detour from the verbal image, returning toward the end of Part B, at statement B32 to be exact, in order to cite, sentence by sentence, what the peasants say about certain achievements that are less tangible than the ones we have just considered.

32. The child enrolled in PPH, when he is in school the next year, already knows the letters and the numbers, and school is much easier for him.
    (a) Agree: 44
    (b) Disagree: 0
    (c) Amendments: none
    (d) Explanatory comments: none

33. The PPH plan of studies serves to improve the nutrition that the children need, particularly how to prepare the food for the baby.
    (a) Agree: 44
    (b) Disagree: 0
    (c) Amendments: none
    (d) Explanatory comments: none

34. One makes better use of the cereals we sow ourselves, and of the vegetables. The cereals that the peasant himself produces are not well utilized. According to the PPH plan of studies these things are made understood.
    (a) 42

(b) 1

(c) None

(d) The peasants tend to grow nutritious foods such as wheat, peas and oats, but to be so impressed by modernity and so lacking in self-confidence that they exchange the good things they have for junk from the city.

35. One learns in what form to give food to a child, and one learns to take advantage of legumes and fruits that perhaps the peasant has mistakenly disregarded.
    (a) 43
    (b) 1
    (c) None
    (d) None

36. Alcoholism is so attractive that one sees too much of it, and because of it the man arrives at perdition; it harms the marriage, that is, the family. One speaks a lot of this in the PPH centre, and you can see that people now do not drink so much. Among all those of the centre, you see changes. The people who do not attend continue the same.
    (a) 30
    (b) 11
    (c) Two *centros* modified the statement to say that older people do not change, but younger people do.
    (d) None

37. The peasant is very quiet, perhaps due to timidity. Also, it may be because his lack of studies causes him to lack words to continue conversing. In PPH one learns to speak, since there the material is prepared especially to start a conversation.
    (a) 44
    (b) 0
    (c) None
    (d) None

38. The games provide considerable benefit. One gets to thinking about how one should act when the wife (or the husband) starts an argument.
    (a) 37

(b) 7
(c) None
(d) None

39. Already many in the community have changed. The mothers themselves correct the behaviour of the children, and the marriages are better. Since we are all united there, the mothers themselves do the correcting.
    (a) 41
    (b) 2
    (c) The centres at Concos Macun and Huempeleo specified that the mothers not only correct their own children, but help correct those of neighbours.
    (d) None

40. You used to hear a lot of fights, and the mothers hitting the children, but now it is much better, because we are all united and we talk about everything.
    (a) 37
    (b) 4
    (c) One centre said the statement required modification, but it did not suggest a modified version.
    (d) None

We have now seen an image of how the project works, in the first instance an image constructed from the peasants' own words, and we have learned something about actions performed as a result of the project. The various lines of evidence converge and support each other. That there was attitude change and what kind there was is shown by what the peasants say and by what they do. The evidence concerning achievements is made more plausible by the evidence concerning the process that led to them, and we are more likely to believe that an attitude change process actually took place because we see evidence of concrete achievements.

NOTES AND REFERENCES

The plausibility of seeing PPH as a project likely to achieve the reform of alcoholics is enhanced by considering it as a way to build ego-strength – not, however, in terms of Cattell's notion of ego-strength as a measurable factor, but rather in reference to the concept (implicit in Cattell and explicit in later writers) of ego-strength as the power of what Freud (in the tradition of Plato; see *Republic*, bks 2–4) called the ego, i.e. the power of the rational self to integrate and to harmonize the divisive elements of the personality. The strengthening of the ego in this sense is, as the work of Jerome Frank shows, equivalent to integrating the ailing individual (in this case, the alcoholic) into a caring community. See Jerome Frank, *Persuasion and Healing* (Baltimore, Md: Johns Hopkins Press, 1961). For a discussion of Cattell and his relation to Freud, see Rom Harré and Paul Secord, *The Explanation of Social Behaviour* (Totowa, NJ: Littlefield, Adams, 1973) chap. 13.

10 Triangulation

> With the truth everything agrees, but a false statement
> soon comes into conflict with the facts.
>
> Aristotle

The Reasonable Social Scientist kindly consented to read the
drafts of this book, and she even agreed to come to Osorno on her
next trip to Chile to enable us to discuss the evaluation of PPH
personally. She called me on the telephone when she landed in
Santiago, and we arranged a breakfast meeting the following day
in Osorno. We met at the *Gran Hotel*, where we were the only
customers. In Osorno, only foreigners eat scrambled eggs in
public places at 8 o'clock in the morning. The Reasonable Social
Scientist began promisingly, by saying that she had found the
first nine chapters interesting. I asked her to summarize the
change her *problematique* underwent as she read from Chapter 1 to
Chapter 9.

'I would describe it as a shift from economics to social
psychology to anthropology,' she said. 'At first, the evaluation
seemed to be an exercise in social economics, an effort to
estimate the efficiency of a program. But it turned out that the
main variables, both on the cost-per-person side and on the
benefit side, needed to be studied from the point of view of social
psychology. It was then that you introduced some ideas from
Harré and Secord's critique of social psychology, *The Explanation
of Social Behaviour*, a book I must read some day when I can find
the time, and you drew the conclusion that attitudes must be
studied with methods that fall more or less into the category
"ethnographic".'

'Another leading theme in my conversion,' the Reasonable
Social Scientist continued, 'has been the acquisition of a different
focus on the search for cause–effect relationships in social
behaviour. I had been accustomed, following Hempel and

110

Oppenheim, May Brodbeck, Ernest Nagel and others, to suppose that in the social sciences as well as in the natural sciences
we are essentially concerned with finding laws. Indeed, I was
inclined to agree with Jean Piaget and others, who have written
that science has outgrown the category of cause and effect. They
say cause and effect should be relegated to the status of a popular
superstition and replaced by the concept of scientific law, the
latter being composed of two or more variables and the logico-
mathematical relationships among the variables. I was, of
course, aware that when a social scientist is hired to do research
on a social problem, and he comes up with a statistic showing
that a phenomenon is due to the impact of something and not
merely due to chance, then the practical use people want to make
of his results is to manipulate the cause (even though in strict
scientific rigour there are no causes) in order to produce an effect
(even though in strict scientific rigour there are no effects). I was
also aware that linguists had carved out for themselves a field
sometimes called synchronic linguistics, studying the meanings
of words, that is the significant relationships among words, in a
language at a given time. But although I was willing to admit
that the study of meanings was a legitimate activity for linguists,
perhaps even sufficiently legitimate to deserve the honour of
being called science, I still considered it alien to the main
business of science, that is to say, to dynamic explanation, to
explaining why things happen, to specifying the forces – also
known as factors and variables – that produce the observed
phenomena. That is, I thought science was mainly about what
we would call causes if we allowed ourselves to use the word
"cause".'

I pressed my inquiry further. 'And what was the new focus
you acquired as you read Chapters one to nine?'

'Now I allow myself to think of meanings as causes,' she
replied, 'I can think of speech as guiding and directing behaviour. Of course, I realize that some people want to say:
"Social inquiries that aim to achieve understanding of how a
group or an individual perceives its reality are one thing; causal
models are quite another." I think I know what they mean when
they say that. What is new is that now I also think I know what
you mean when you say that in explaining the achievements of
PPH, in stating their causes, it is correct to refer to the norms,
i.e. the *consejos* and the *conclusiones*, that the peasants set for

themselves when they meet together in their *centros*.'

'You said earlier that you found the study interesting, but you refrained from expressing unqualified approval.'

'I do think that if you calculate in your third chapter that the program has 660 stated objectives, and then when you later evaluate the program you deliberately ignore them all and consider only the achievement of non-objectives, then your methodology is ... er ... extreme.'

'The approximately 660 stated objectives are in two places, in the manuals the coordinators use to conduct the meetings, and in the worksheets the parents take home for the children. The objectives in the manuals deal mainly with group processes, for example, "that the participants express their opinions on alcoholism". The ones in the worksheets concern child development, for example "that the child learn to hold a pair of scissors".'

'It sounds to me as though what you need in order to find out whether the stated objectives are being achieved, in addition to the non-objectives you have already discussed, are some measures of group process and child development. If you knew what is going on in the groups, then you would be able to say whether the sort of thing called for in the objectives, i.e. participation and the posing of problems, is happening, or whether, on the contrary, it turns out that in practice the coordinators adopt the authoritarian styles that Paulo Freire calls "banking" or "extensionist" pedagogy, i.e. delivering knowledge from teachers who are presumed to know everything to students who are presumed to know nothing. You also need some data on process to finish your case for attitude change. If, as you say, attitude change consists of changes in group norms and personal identities brought about by changing beliefs and manifested in action, then the actions by themselves are not all the evidence you need. You need evidence that the process leading to the actions was one where self-respect was acquired and beliefs were changed through dialogue in a group.'

'The verbal image,' I said, 'as confirmed by the ratification of the relevant assertions by all or nearly all the *centros*, already tells that PPH children are better prepared for school than they would otherwise be, and that the style of interpersonal interaction in the meetings is participatory.'

'The trouble with your evidence,' said the Reasonable Social Scientist, putting down her toast, and speaking in an annoyingly deliberate tone, 'is that you are believing what people tell you. It is not uncommon for the participants in a program to be carried away by a great wave of subjective enthusiasm, so that they are all convinced they are getting results – when objective measures show that nothing is happening.'

'I'm not as stupid as I look,' I said testily. After all, I had, with the help of Horacio Walker and Manuel Bastias of the CIDE office in Santiago, checked the picture derived from the interviews and the verbal image by a variety of methods. In my briefcase, I was carrying reports on direct observations of meetings, systematic observation, Garfinkeling, tape-recordings of meetings, participant observation, teachers' opinions, examination of completed worksheets, content analysis of worksheets, a draw-a-man test, an IQ test, counter-suggestion, observations by independent observers, content analysis of the manuals, and a case study. I did not recite this list of methods to the Reasonable Social Scientist, because I felt that, by telling her I was not as stupid as I looked, I had already expressed the gist of the matter, and because I did not want her to think I was trying to overpower her by a long list of names of techniques (of which some, such as Garfinkeling, were little-known and exotic) since, after all, the important thing is the logical relation between the evidence and the belief it supports, and not the mere use of methods with technical names. In short, since I did not want the Reasonable Social Scientist to think I was unreasonable, I discussed the issues with her one at a time, step by step, in an orderly way.

'First let me tell you,' I said to the Reasonable Social Scientist, 'about the ways we checked our image of participation in PPH. One method we used was to observe the meetings themselves.'

Direct Observation of Meetings

'In the 12 *centros* I observed, watching one meeting each, the process was the participatory one the verbal image depicts, but I had the sense that the people were inhibited by my presence. What I gained from direct observation, that I would not have gained otherwise, was admiration for the skill of the sector-coordinators. They are adept at gently nudging the participants into autonomy, supporting them when they need support, breaking the ice in tense moments, eliciting and encouraging initiatives from the group. When the volunteer base-coordinator (who is, in the majority of cases, a woman) is able to work in the spirit of PPH and is not too timid, the sector-coordinator remains in the background. When the volunteer base-coordinator needs help, the sector-coordinator backs her up.

'The principle that the coordinator should *sacar las conclusiones del grupo* (draw the conclusions from the group) is a norm that is well-established among coordinators, but the methods used are often unimaginative and sometimes crude. Frequently, the volunteer base-coordinator simply asks questions until she is given the right answer. That is what I mean by unimaginative. What I mean by crude can be illustrated by an instance when a *centro* was discussing the folk belief that milk with fruit causes stomach aches. Four participants in a row said it was true that milk with fruit causes stomach aches. When a fifth said, 'I give my little boy fruit with milk all the time and it doesn't hurt him at all,' the coordinator exclaimed *¡un aplauso!* (applaud!).'

Theatre

'As you know from reading the previous chapters, some informants composed *teatros*. The *teatros* provided another window through which to view a PPH meeting.'

'Emotion and conflict were expressed more openly in *teatros* than in observed meetings or in direct interviews. The basic structure of the meetings depicted was the same as that shown by other methods.'

Systematic Observation

'We also observed meetings in a systematic way, using a fixed method for taking notes on the proceedings. If all we are saying about how the process works is true, then quantitative observation should show a high degree of participation. We used the Florida modification of the Flanders method for observing interpersonal interaction.' I showed the Reasonable Social Scientist this table.

Participation in two PPH meetings

Group participation	53%
A coordinator speaking (either base-volunteer or sector-coordinator)	36%

Time spent in silence or confusion	11%
	100%

'For comparison,' I went on, 'we analysed what an experienced judge deemed to be a typical adult education class in Osorno, by tape-recording it and applying the same system.'

Participation in Osorno Ministry of Education adult education class

Group participation	5%
Teacher speaking or writing on blackboard	76%
Time spent in silence or confusion	19%
	100%

The Reasonable Social Scientist looked at my tables and said: 'You have a rough measure of quantity of participation, but you don't know how many participate. Perhaps a few people do all the talking.'

'My impression is that the coordinators try to get everyone to talk, but succeed with only about half. The informants report somewhat higher participation, although their main concern is rather the opposite: the coordinators sometimes are too pushy in trying to make shy people and newcomers speak.'

The Reasonable Social Scientist expressed concern that my eggs were getting cold. Out of politeness, I pretended to appreciate her concern, but really the only thing I wanted to do was to tell her about Garfinkeling.

'Garfinkeling is a set of techniques,' I began, 'due to a man named Garfinkel who, if he were not a social scientist, would be considered an imp. Among the varieties of Garfinkeling, one technique consists of encountering the norms of a group by violating them. I did my Garfinkeling at Caracol, where the norm I expected to encounter was that PPH meetings are highly participatory. When I was introduced to the members of the *centro* in the way that all visitors are introduced, I proceeded to pretend that I was expected to give a speech; that is, I gave a speech. It was pretty good – not pompous, or dull, or over the heads of the audience. After a few minutes, Tito Barrientos, the driver, thought it necessary to interrupt me to ask if anyone else had an opinion on the subjects I was discussing. Whether they had opinions will never be known, because I continued before anyone could opine. After another few minutes, a coordinator interrupted me to suggest that the group discuss whether my views were correct. I felt unwanted, but I ignored his suggestion. I talked a while longer, and then gave it up. I was tired of being an idiot. The participants said nothing at all during or after my remarks. After my performance, the coordinator could not get them to say anything. When I left, they were still sitting in stony silence, and they did not say goodbye.'

Tape-recordings of Meetings

'Four meetings were tape-recorded by sector-coordinators. They were similar to the meetings observed, the ones told about by participants, and the ones dramatized.'

Participant Observation

'Participant observation,' I went on, 'consists of participating in the observed activity yourself. In a meeting at Somasur, I answered the questions posed by the coordinator, and took part in the conversation the same as any other participant. We talked about how we use powdered milk. The conclusion we drew was that we should make more puddings. Several days later, my four-year-old daughter and I bought a prepared pudding mix at a market, prepared it at Jorge Zuleta's house, and served it to the Zuleta family and our own. The sequence consisting of dialogue–*conclusiones*–action that I participated in was the same as the one Horacio, Manuel and I had observed by various methods.'

The Reasonable Social Scientist commented that although she was not, as a rule, greatly impressed by participant observation studies, of all the participant observation studies she had ever seen or heard of, this was the one by which she was least impressed. Recalling the first great participant observer, Malinowski among the South Sea Islanders, considering the years he spent living as if he were one of them, noting his ability to blend himself into their way of life so thoroughly that they forgot he was an outsider, the Reasonable Social Scientist suggested that Malinowski would turn in his grave were he to discover that someone fancied himself a participant observer because he exchanged ideas on powdered milk with several women at Somasur and made a pudding afterwards.

I was compelled to admit that in this study, participant observation was underutilized. However, just being in Osorno for three months (from mid-July until mid-October 1980), constantly alert for useful information or for tell-tale signs that cherished beliefs about PPH were not true, is, if not a form of participant observation, then at least a form of immersion in the context that shares with it some of its advantages.

'Furthermore,' I said to the Reasonable Social Scientist, 'we also examined the manuals used by the coordinators, and studied their in-service training. None of the evidence was inconsistent with the picture of group process portrayed in the verbal image.' I produced a rather bulky textbook from my briefcase, and read to the Reasonable Social Scientist from it. 'As John B. Williamson *et al.* say in *The Research Craft*:

> The logic behind the use of multiple measurement techniques is elegantly simple. It is referred to as the logic of triangulation. Just as in trigonometry one can indirectly but precisely measure the location of a point by appropriate sightings from two other points, so also can one apply this method of triangulation to social measurement. Specifically, all indirect measures have their own peculiar weaknesses. However, by concentrating on the point at which a series of independent, indirect, and perhaps weak indicators converge, we can effectively minimize their separate errors and maximize their overall validity. Simply put, there can be strength in converging weaknesses.

'I should say,' I added, 'that our use of triangulation differs from simply using multiple techniques, because we already possess a verbal image of the object of our study, and we are using triangulation to check it.'

The Reasonable Social Scientist paid the breakfast bill and excused herself. The driver was waiting to take her to the university at Valdivia, and besides, she had to deliver some spark plugs, which she was carrying in her purse. She was visiting the university in connection with some research her agency was supporting on Chilean peasants. 'Very little is known about Chilean peasants,' she said. 'There is practically nothing on them in the literature.' The spark plugs were for a used motorboat donated by the Icelandic government to a cooperative of poor fishermen who live on the coast near Valdivia. Although some spare parts had been provided when the gift was given, it had been overlooked that the motor required a Danish spark plug not available in South America. The Reasonable Social Scientist had promised the Danish Ambassador to the United Nations, who had kindly provided the required items, that she would deliver the plugs to the fishermen personally. However, she would return to the *Gran Hotel* late that night, and would be available for breakfast again the next morning.

For much of the rest of the day, I fretted. The Reasonable Social Scientist had remarked that little is known about Chilean peasants. But surely they know a great deal about themselves. From their point of view, little is known about social scientists. I asked myself what difference it would make if a lot were known about Chilean peasants – how it would affect the general state of human knowledge if the literature in the archives of the world's universities were filled with scholarly works on them, and, in particular, whether scientific advances in the field would enable me to find out what Manuelito's father had done when Manuelito was caught stealing a baby pig. The reader may think I had forgotten the incident, as a mild-mannered sort of person who accepts defeat easily would, but if that is what the reader thinks, then he mistakes my character. For in fact, when I am frustrated, I sulk for months. When Maria refused to tell me what happened, I took it as a professional insult, and contemplated reminding Maria of my credentials as an investigator, my quantitative and qualitative training in epistemology, methodology, phenomenology, statistics, heuristics and dialectics. I wanted to impress upon her that I could discover such large, superior and weighty truths that, out of respect for all my merit and rank, she should tell me what happened when Manuelito returned home, bruised and bleeding after being caught stealing the pig.

Not having dared to attempt to intimidate Maria, and having been unable to obtain the desired information then or since, I asked myself whether a suitable research program could efface the effrontery whereby the peasants contrive to keep their secrets to themselves. I concluded that it could not, that the expertise of a human group concerning the details of its own everyday reality is incorrigible.

NOTES AND REFERENCES

The quotation from Aristotle is from the *Nichomachean Ethics*, vol. i, bk viii.

Rom Harré and Paul Secord's *The Explanation of Social Behaviour* was published by Littlefield, Adams at Totowa, New Jersey, in 1973.

Concerning causes, see the Chapter 7 notes.

For methods of systematic observation of interaction, see the special issue of the *International Review of Education* edited by Ned Flanders and Graham Nuthall (with articles in English and French), 'The Classroom Behavior of Teachers' (Den Haag, Holland: Nijhoff, 1972); and Ned Flanders, *Interaction Analysis in the Classroom, a Manual for Observers* (Ann Arbor, Mich.: University Microfilms International, 1976). The Florida modification of the Flanders technique consists of setting up a parallel set of categories based on exactly the same criteria, for coding student behaviour; for example, in addition to 'teacher does x', there is a place for coding 'student does x', where x might be, for example, 'asks a question'.

On Harold Garfinkel, see his *Studies in Ethnomethodology* (Englewood Cliffs, NJ: Prentice-Hall, 1967); Harold Garfinkel, 'Studies of the Routine Grounds of Everyday Actions', *Social Problems*, vol. 11 (1964) p. 225.

The quotation on page 117 was from John B. Williamson *et al.*, *The Research Craft* (Boston: Little Brown, 1977) p. 84.

11 The Triangulation Continues

To lengthen our time to talk, the Reasonable Social Scientist had asked me to come at 7 am the next day, an hour when the breakfast area was still closed and no coffee was obtainable. As I sat in the reception area of the *Gran Hotel* and shared my notes on the triangulation of our image of PPH's success in promoting child development, I was drowsy. Nevertheless, I endeavoured to be as accurate as possible.

TEACHERS' OPINIONS

I asked three teachers to discuss each first-year child in their schools, and to classify their readiness for school at the beginning of the year as excellent, good, acceptable or poor. Independently, I ascertained which children had been enrolled in PPH. The results were tabulated as follows.

Teachers' opinions of school readiness of children – three schools

	With PPH	Without PPH	Sum
Excellent	5	2	7
Good	15	17	32
Acceptable	9	24	33
Poor	0	6	6
Totals	29	49	78

(Note: This table suggests that in any given village or locality, a little over a third, 29/78, of the children are in PPH. We have no reason to suppose that such an estimate is far off as a measure of the percentage that PPH reaches of the population of the villages served.)

'You say you ascertained independently which children were in PPH,' commented the Reasonable Social Scientist, 'but surely the teachers must have known who you were and what you represented, and therefore they must have known what to say to tell you what you wanted to hear.'

'My interest in PPH was not a secret, and their biases were not secrets either. One teacher was an ardent fan of PPH. She had sent the worksheets to her grandson who lives in Osorno, and she attributed to PPH her grandson's success in passing the entrance examination for *Colegio San Mateo*, an élite school for boys. The second teacher was a participant who had enrolled her own four-year-old, but her theme song was not one of praise for PPH, but rather the complaint that children do not benefit as they should because the parents do not properly supervise the use of the worksheets. The third teacher denied that she had ever heard of the program and was reluctant to attribute anything good to the children who had been in it. We know from other sources that her unawareness was feigned, and we know her motive: fear of being accused of cooperating with FREDER and PPH, because they had been accused by some powerful people of being subversive.'

'So it is your view that the biases of the respondents cancelled each other out.'

'Not really. If I had to depend on the three teachers' opinions alone, I would not draw any conclusions.'

'Perhaps,' said the Reasonable Social Scientist, 'you say that because you lack confidence in the quality of your data. Do you think your data are good enough to justify the use of statistical tests?' It was cold in the reception area of the hotel, and the Reasonable Social Scientist's chilly attitude did not improve the atmosphere.

'Your question perplexes me. I want to answer yes, and I want to answer no, but mainly I want to say that you could have asked a better question. I want to say yes, the data are good enough to justify the use of statistical tests, because they probably comply with the mathematical assumptions underlying statistical tests as well as a lot of the data that gets "processed" in that way – in fact, just for fun, we did run a non-parametric test and found significant results at the .05 level. And I want to say no, because I don't think carrying out a significance test is the best way to use this data. But mainly I want to say that you could have asked a better question, namely: "What logical conclusions follow from all the information you were able to gather?"'

'You did not gather very much. You interviewed only three teachers.'

'I tried to compensate for the small number of interviews (3) and the fairly small number of children (78) by discussing the case of each child in considerable detail.' I gave the Reasonable Social Scientist some sample descriptions of children by their teachers. (The numbers in parentheses are age in years and months at the beginning of the school year – in Andrea's case, at the beginning of kindergarten – in 1980.)

Agustin (6,5): did not participate in PPH. Evidently under-nourished, timid. He is sickly and frequently absent. He learns very little, but he has ability in physical education. There are five children from his home in the school; of the other four, two are in second grade and two in third. The others are good students. When Agustin arrived, he could not hold a pencil; he knew nothing of numbers and letters. If you tried to talk to him he would cry. I gave him sweets to persuade him to talk – I had to bribe him to make friends. He has to walk $4\frac{1}{2}$ kilometres to school.

Griselda (6,11): enrolled in PPH. It is obvious that her mother helped her with the worksheets. When she arrived at school, she knew practically nothing, her hand and eye movements were uncoordinated, she could not relate numbers to sets. She could name three letters, l, m and a. She could recognize three numbers, 7, 5 and 4, but she did not understand them. On the other hand, she is active in her group, and she brings materials to work from home, even more than is needed. She is very concerned that her row of desks be the most orderly, the cleanest, that there not be any dust on the tables. She is undernourished; her family is very poor. Her father was out of work for a long time, and now works in the miminum employment program. She walks 1 kilometre to school.

Claudina (6,7): (did not work with PPH). She lives with her grandparents in order to go to school. Her parents live deep in the mountains, where there are no schools. Her achievement is good, even though she is very timid. She is enthusiastic and learns. She even knew how to read a few words when she came. She is outstanding in cooperating in the activities of her group. Undernourished, walks $\frac{1}{2}$ kilometre.

Heliomar (6,2): (in PPH). He did all his worksheets. He is outstanding in art and in coordination of his movements. He can distinguish the letters. He is also outstanding in telling stories, and in discussing a theme. He has a lot of personality. He knew all his letters when he arrived at school. He could locate himself in space, he knew up, down, right, left. He could relate numbers to sets from 1 to 9, organize a story in the proper sequence, do puzzles and cutouts. Walks 4 kilometres.

Faviola (6,11) (in PPH). Learned to read in the first month of classes. Otherwise similar to Heliomar. Walks 8 kilometres to school.

Andrea (5,8) (in PPH). A difficult case. There are family problems at home. She acts very grown-up for her age. Rebellious. She always says she is going to kill somebody, that she is going to poison them. She walks around with a cologne jar with water in it, and she says she is going to poison people with it.

While the Reasonable Social Scientist read my notes I thought of Faviola, who was no doubt walking to school in the rain at this hour, while we were waiting for a breakfast area to open in a hotel reception area, where it was at least dry. 'What is your purpose in gathering this relatively in-depth data?' the Reasonable Social Scientist asked when she had finished reading.

'I start with a knowledge of the mechanism at work: the children presumably do work in their own homes that is similar to first-year school work; they learn how to handle a pencil and how to follow instructions. . . . When they get to school, they are better prepared than non-PPH children, because in school they continue to do the same things they have been doing at home. If, in a given case, it turns out that a PPH child does poorly, there must be some reason why the mechanism failed to work in his case. The case of a non-PPH child who does well similarly requires an explanation – for example, parents who provided similar experiences without using this particular program's pencils, scissors and worksheets. As it turned out, when teachers ranked non-PPH children higher than PPH children, it was usually because the children related well to the other children. That makes sense, because PPH did not organize play groups, and there is no reason to expect the social adjustment in peer relationships of the PPH child to be better than average.'

'After I have my morning cup of coffee,' said the Reasonable Social Scientist, 'I may be able to understand what you are saying. As it is, I am baffled. Let me tell you what I believe research is, and tell you why what you are saying makes no sense to me.

'When I was a student at Heidelberg' – 'actually,' she interpolated, 'it was not really Heidelberg. Germany had difficulty reorganizing its universities after the war, so the USA sent a team of experts from the University of Tennessee to run the University of Heidelberg temporarily, and help it get back on its feet. I was a graduate of the Tennessee–Heidelberg program' – 'I learned that research consists of framing a null hypothesis, choosing treatment and control groups of suitable sizes, and applying statistical tests to the scores on tests of the two groups. Now, you do have a sort of null hypothesis, that PPH and non-PPH children do not differ in school-readiness; you have some poorly chosen groups of not-very-suitable sizes, and some data that are hardly worth processing. I gather that what you had in mind when you had the teachers tell you stories about the children was that somehow their anecdotes would compensate for the methodological weakness of your research; so I asked you what your purpose was, politely referring to the stories the teachers told you as "in-depth data", and then you said something about mechanisms that lost me completely. I don't see what "mechanism", or, as you sometimes say, "process", has to do with anything. Ever since Galileo proved that you should look at the facts instead of looking in an ancient book to see what Aristotle said (we learned this in our History of Science class at Heidelberg), the purpose of science has been to describe data in terms of mathematical laws, not to describe processes with words or pictures.'

'The triangulation I am doing is similar to Galileo's method in the following way,' I said. 'Galileo's law for freely falling bodies, $s = \frac{1}{2} gt^2$, does not describe the flight of any freely falling body. At least it did not until several centuries later when a nearly perfect vacuum was produced, making it possible to drop small objects in vacuums. In the absence of a vacuum, the friction of the air causes deviations from the trajectory predicted by the formula. Italian wiseacres of the 16th century deduced that if $s = \frac{1}{2} gt^2$ is true, then a feather and a lead weight fall at the same speed – a conclusion that experiment did not confirm. Galileo was not impressed. He had identified the basic mechanism in a way that could be made consistent with all the evidence by taking into account the facts of each case.'

'What would the logic of triangulation have advised if it had turned out that the non-PPH children were better prepared for school than were the *chicos* from the *centros*?'

'Then we would have had a case where the various lines of evidence failed to converge; we would have had to conclude that something we thought was true is false, and to track down the source of the contradiction by questioning the picture of PPH we had previously formed. We would suspect that the parents were prevaricating when they said they taught the children at home, or that the many completed worksheets we saw were counterfeited, or that the authors of the instructional materials erroneously prescribed useless activities....'

'So far so good,' said the Reasonable Social Scientist. 'But your study would have been more convincing if you had selected teachers at random and interviewed more of them, sent a paper-and-pencil questionnaire to all the first-grade teachers in the schools PPH children attend, and checked the official records to see which children passed and which repeated.'

'One hesitates to state the reason why the course you very sensibly recommend was not followed, because one does not want to say that illuminative evaluation is a second-best method to be used only where tests and surveys are impossible. On the other hand, if a well-wisher were to maintain that it is an advantage of the approach we have adopted that it is suited to the conditions that prevail in most of the world – chaos, conflict, confusion, militarism, poor communication, the unreliability of almost everything and almost everybody – then we would not deny that the approach has that advantage.'

'From the difficulty you are having in expressing yourself, I can tell that you need a cup of coffee too,' said the Reasonable Social Scientist. 'What you are trying to say is that in most of the world, the extensive use of tests, surveys and random sampling is impractical.'

'Quite,' I replied. 'In our case, we could not do a survey of the teachers or interview a random sample, because our situation was delicate in ways that citizens of third-world dictatorships will comprehend more readily than citizens of industrial democracies. We considered ourselves fortunate that the authorities were unaware of our study and left us alone, and we did not want to rock the boat by doing something for which we would have had to ask permission. The teachers in the province had instructions not to cooperate with PPH in any way. It happened that there were two schools in the area that had not received these instructions because they were classified as "private" – an essentially meaningless classification stemming from long-forgotten history (having been founded by *hacienda* owners for the children of the *hacienda*). Nowadays, the state hires the teachers and prescribes the curriculum, but the slightly different legal status of the private schools was such that the teachers were not specifically instructed not to talk to us. We spoke to the directors of those two "private" schools. The third teacher interviewed runs a kindergarten, the only one in an area served by PPH. I went to see her because kindergartens also fall in a special administrative classification, but her fearful demeanour showed that she was providing us with information only against her better judgment and at considerable risk. We could have interviewed several other teachers whom we knew to be willing to violate the orders they had received, but we chose not to.'

PROGRESSIVE FOCUSING – LOOKING AT COMPLETED WORKSHEETS

The Reasonable Social Scientist drew my attention to a point I had raised a few moments ago, the question of whether the worksheets were properly completed. 'You mentioned earlier on,' she said, 'that one of the teachers interviewed thought that the children don't learn as much as they should because although they take the worksheets home, they don't use them properly.'

'Yes,' I said, 'in the process of checking the claim in the verbal image that the children do better in school because of PPH, we ran across a problem we had not anticipated. Constantly modifying one's research priorities as one learns more about the program under study is called "progressive focusing", a concept originally developed by Malcolm Parlett and David Hamilton.

When we started the study, we did not focus on whether the children completed the worksheets, but we did begin with the intention of progressively changing our focus as we learned more about PPH.

'When I followed up the question of whether worksheets are properly used in the homes, with the teacher who had raised the issue, it turned out that she had something else on her mind that we had not expected – she thought that teachers like herself should be counted as beneficiaries of PPH. The PPH children set the tone of the class and make her work easier. Also, she told us, the parents understand and appreciate the work of the teacher. They say, "How on earth do you manage to teach so many children when it taxes my patience to teach one?" But she also said that the great achievement of the program is in the community. "That is, we are beginning to live in community in the true sense of the word. For example, if someone is sick, the family asks the neighbour to help carry the sick person to the hospital."'

'The teacher's complaints about parental supervision of the use of the worksheets were: (i) some parents are so eager to make a good impression that they do the worksheets themselves and pretend the children did them, (ii) some parents let the children stop early, leaving the work half done.'

'Interviews with sector-coordinators,' I continued, 'confirmed the teacher's view of the use of worksheets. When they were three months into the first year of the program, the sector-coordinators reviewed all the completed worksheets, and made the following estimates concerning how well they were done.'

Approximately 50% worksheets well done.

Approximately 35% poorly done. The work was considered poorly done either when it was clear that the child had undue help from the parent, or when it was begun but not finished. The two criteria accounted for roughly equal portions of the poorly done category.

Approximately 15% very bad. These were cases when the work was not done at all, or where the child played with the material, doing whatever he wanted to do.

The Reasonable Social Scientist pointed out that it is not necessarily a bad thing for children to play with materials, doing whatever they want to do. Distinguished psychologists recommend that when children are introduced to new materials, they be given a period of free play before structured activities begin. I agreed with her, adding, however, that the problem is somewhat more complex than her remark suggests: realizing that free play at the right time is a good thing may require some dialogue with experts in child psychology, which would require an adjustment of the spirit of PPH to facilitate the assimilation of expert advice. It would also require an expert willing and able to relate to the spirit of PPH, perhaps the sort of person Gramsci would call 'an intellectual of the people'.

The Reasonable Social Scientist said she found my remarks tantalizing, and she hoped that in a future chapter, there would be more about how to find the right relationship between professional expertise and cultural action.

I went on to say that in interviews with nine sector-coordinators, we learned that all of them believe that parent supervision of the use of worksheets improved markedly in 1980 compared to 1979.

'How much improvement has there been?' the Reasonable Social Scientist asked.

'We don't know,' I said. 'In interviews with the sector-coordinators, the estimates of percentage of worksheets well done were over 80 per cent, but the program director, Jorge Zuleta, who takes a look at completed worksheets every now and then, does not think the percentage of well done worksheets has gone above 60 per cent.'

The Reasonable Social Scientist did not say anything for a while. When she did speak, she raised the conversation to a higher level, or else took advantage of a minor confession of ignorance to mount an attack on our whole methodology – depending on how you look at it. In the light of our rather miserable performance in determining how many worksheets are properly done, she raised the question of whether, in general, our reliance on interviews is altogether excessive.

'You will have to remind me,' she said, 'of the reasons for beginning the study with interviews, for I have forgotten what the reasons were, and if I remembered them I might not believe them. First you constructed a verbal image based on interviews, confirmed and corrected in group discussions, and you proceeded from there to use parallel investigations to triangulate the verbal image. But why didn't you do it the other way around? Everyone knows that interview data are unreliable, because people express their subjective impression and give free rein to their biases. Why not begin with something objective, like analysing the contents of instructional materials, or tests? Then you could use interviews as a secondary source in case your objective data had overlooked something.'

I replied by reminding the Reasonable Social Scientist of certain matters we had already discussed, and, I had thought, agreed on. 'Our cost-effectiveness study, and our consultations with experienced educators, led us to the conclusion that attitude change was the most important topic to study, and our analysis of the concept of "attitude" showed that beliefs and actions need to be examined in order to study attitudes. 'Furthermore,' I told her, 'what you call "subjective" relates closely to what PPH *is*. PPH is what peasants think, feel, say, and do.'

A maid was trying to tell us that breakfast was ready and we could enter the breakfast area and seat ourselves, but I was too excited to stop talking. 'I know what you are thinking,' I said to the Reasonable Social Scientist. 'You don't even have to tell me. You are thinking that I like peasants and I like PPH, and I am giving you an ideological speech about dignity. But I am really trying to underline a point of logic.'

'Perhaps if you would sit in one place,' said the Reasonable Social Scientist, 'instead of pacing the floor and gesturing like an angry Italian, I would be better able to grasp your logic.'

'The point is,' I said very calmly, 'that a social reality is constituted by the practices of the people who participate in that reality. The language they use to describe what it is has a certain priority over any descriptions given by outsiders. Even official documents, like the proposals made to funding agencies on file in the CIDE office at Santiago, do not say what it is, in the basic sense in which the people who live it every day are able to say what it is. Indeed, all the printed material is only *material de apoyo* (supporting material). A content analysis of the material comes second, because the primary reality is the peasants' perception and use of the material, not the material itself. Tests come second too, because we need an image of the programme formed in the field in order to know what to test – we would be flying blind if we defined a test beforehand in Santiago, in order to measure the achievement of an objective stated in a programme document.'

Fortunately for the pleasantness of our relationship, as soon as I finished speaking we moved immediately to the breakfast area, where we were again the only customers. After a Chilean breakfast of coffee with hot milk, fresh hot buns, butter, apricot jam, liverwurst and eggs, I went on to present the results of three more parallel (triangulating) studies.

CONTENT ANALYSIS OF THE WORKSHEETS

'We looked at the worksheets,' I said, 'to see what the children study. If alleged gains appear in areas they have not done work in, then we suspect the gains are illusory, or are not due to the program. If, on the other hand, the children in the hills west of Osorno perform the kinds of activities that produce cognitive growth and readiness for school in the rest of the world, then it is a reasonable inference that cognitive growth and readiness for school are likely to be produced in the hills west of Osorno.' I showed the Reasonable Social Scientist a list of the kinds of exercises found in the worksheets.

I.   Perception: visual discrimination, discriminating sounds, coordinating eye and hand, fine motor skills (e.g. holding a pencil), gross motor coordination.

II.   Thinking: language, social knowledge, physical knowledge (e.g. names of things), classifying, putting things in a series, numbers, spatial relationships, time.

III.   Levels of representation: this material is adapted from the work of the High/Scope Foundation of Ypsilanti, Michigan, which helps children to develop what Piaget calls 'the symbolic function' first by relating objects to objects, then by using a part of an object as an index to the whole object, then by using abstract symbols (such as words).

IV.   Emotional growth: the exercises seek to encourage curiosity, creativity, motivation to learn, and good parent–child relationships.

'The analysis of the contents of the worksheets,' I said, 'is consistent with our other evidence; children make progress in the areas covered by the worksheets when they carry out the activities the worksheets call for.'

A DRAW-A-MAN TEST

'In spite of circumstances that made systematic testing of children difficult, we were able to carry out a modified draw-a-man test. The main modification in comparison to usual draw-a-man tests is that because of

(a) the vast differences between peasant children and the children for whom test norms exist, and
(b) the small numbers of children of each age in the groups who drew pictures for us,

we did not compare the children with norms, but rather with children from the same villages who had not been in PPH; and instead of comparing drawings by children of the same age, we asked a university professor of child development, Mariana Chadwick, who teaches at the Catholic University of Chile at Santiago, to act as a rapid-automatic-calculating-machine comparing drawings by children of different ages – making a global judgment that one drawing is better or worse than another, making allowances for the fact that one may be older or younger than the other.

'A random sample of PPH children, and an intentional matched sample of non-PPH children from the same areas, drew human figures under standard conditions, i.e. with the same paper and pencils and on hard surfaces provided by the same clipboards. Professor Chadwick sorted the pictures, without knowing which were experimental and which were control, having before her only the picture itself and the age of the child in years and months. We, of course, had numbered the drawings so that we were in on the secret of which were by PPH children and which were not. The results were as follows.

1 best picture:	control
6 runners-up:	5 PPH
	1 control
15 good pictures:	10 PPH
	5 controls
19 acceptable pictures:	9 PPH
	10 controls
15 inferior pictures:	5 PPH
	10 controls
6 poor pictures:	1 PPH
	5 controls
1 worst picture:	control

'The lowest 7 drawings were children who did not draw at all, either because they could not or because they cried. (The one counted as 'worst' was the oldest child who did not draw at all.)'

'The control group,' I went on, 'was not significantly different from the experimental group in terms of family size, parents' educational level, size of dwelling, access to media, type of sanitary facilities, and distance from neighbours. But the experimental group had significantly more *minifundistas* (tillers of tiny farms) as compared to landless workers, and significantly more Indian surnames as compared to Spanish surnames. We asked Professor Chadwick to do another blind sort within the PPH group, to see whether in our sample, *minifundismo* v. landless worker, and type of surname, had a significant influences on drawing quality. They did not. Incidentally, these data confirmed a point about which we never had any doubt – that PPH is actually reaching the poor, and not enrolling middle-class children. When we looked at the ages of the children whose pictures Professor Chadwick had classified, we found that the advantage of the PPH children existed entirely at ages 5 and 6. The younger children who were just beginning PPH did not do better than controls. The older children, who had been in school for a year or more, did not do better than controls who had also been in school for a year or more. It appears likely that with respect to fine motor coordination and other skills used in drawing, PPH gives children a boost at the point when they enter school, but the children without **PPH** catch up with them later.'

'Is it your finding, then,' the Reasonable Social Scientist asked, 'that the child development advantages of PPH are temporary?'

'We are not really trying to answer the question of how long the effects last. We are using the draw-a-man test data to study a different question – the question of whether the interview data are believable. A man from Dollinco, for example, told us: "The worksheets are educational, not just for the children but also for adults. I at least had a son that I enrolled in PPH, and they gave him worksheets. For me the program was good in this respect, because this year he is in school, and since he already knows the letters and numbers, school is much easier for him. Not just for him, because I have a cousin and an uncle, they also have their children in the program, and for all of them it is the same."'

'Apparently,' the Reasonable Social Scientist said, 'you have a certain amount of confidence in what your interviewees tell you, and when what they say is confirmed by independent tests, your confidence increases.'

'We can't check everything they say, but we can triangulate the image that emerges from their testimony by checking the few things for which we can obtain other kinds of data. Since so far the things we *can* check agree on the whole with the verbal image, we have confidence in the parts of the verbal image we cannot check. But let me tell you about a study using an IQ test, which was by itself inconclusive, but which harmonizes with our other evidence.'

RESULTS OF ANOTHER STUDY – AN IQ TEST

'All our evidence is consistent,' I said, 'with the results of study using the same PPH worksheets done in Trapiche, near Curicó, Chile, in 1977. A rural kindergarten class and a comparable group of children using PPH worksheets were given the WISP intelligence test (a Chilean version of the Wechsler scale) before the two treatments and again 4 months later. The PPH children improved an average of 6.2 points from pre-test to post-test, while the rural kindergarten children improved 3.4 points from pre-test to post-test.'

The Reasonable Social Scientist appeared to enjoy her breakfast, and to have no objections strong enough to voice concerning
the general thrust of the evidence I was presenting. She said, 'At
this point, I think it would be unreasonable to doubt that the
verbal image is basically correct with respect to child development, except for the peasants' claim that they do the worksheets
properly – on that point, Jorge Zuleta is probably right to
estimate that over a third of the worksheets are poorly done.
What worries me more is a certain matter that concerns adults
more than children – the possibility that the rather vague claims
toward the end of the verbal image are divorced from reality. In
the middle part, where peasants were asked whether they had
performed concrete actions, many answered "no", but as the
statements became more vague, the number of "yes" answers
rose. I am referring to the claims that people have adopted more
nutritional eating habits; stopped excessive drinking; achieved
self-confidence for public speaking; and have established better
human relationships with their children, their spouses and their
neighbours. I am worried that when those statements by informants were brought up for discussion in the *centros*, the people
just nodded their heads in agreement out of a desire to be
cooperative, since the statements are so unclear that it is hard to
produce definite evidence either that they are true or that they
are false.'

COUNTER-SUGGESTION

'We took some steps,' I said, 'to check to vague claims to which
you refer. The possibility that the *centros* simply passively
acquiesced with vague claims in the verbal image was checked
by the method of counter-suggestion with four participants: two
were informants elected by their *centros*, who had participated in
the elaboration of the image, and two were others selected by
chance.'

To be more precise, I went to the *feria* one Saturday morning
hoping to find, among the peasants who had come to town to sell
produce and buy provisions, some PPH-members on whom to
try counter-suggestion. I managed to round up four women, two
informants I already knew and two others, and to engage them

in conversation in a sleezy restaurant next to the fairgrounds. They enjoyed a free lunch as they talked to me, keeping one eye on the window to be sure their *micros* did not leave without them. (It turned out, incidentally, that one of the ladies had been sold a sack of flour marked '25 kilos' that actually contained only 20, and I spent part of the rest of the day helping her to obtain the additional 5 kilos of flour she had paid for but had not received.)

'At the time of our conversation, the *centros* had not yet reviewed the verbal image. The technique consisted of reading a text that said the opposite of what the verbal image said, to see whether the four of them would go along with the opposite. It became evident that with a little forcefulness, I could intimidate them and get them to agree to anything. However, if the information was simply presented as a question to them, seeking their opinion as to whether it was true, they resisted the counter-suggestion, and told the same story the informants had told in the first place.'

'The only exception was item B36, which claims that the people in PPH have given up excessive drinking. My way of saying the opposite was to say:

> Alcoholism is so attractive that there is too much of it, and because of it men are lost, marriages are damaged, that is to say, the family is damaged. This topic is discussed a great deal in the PPH centres, but the people who are heavy drinkers do not change. They do not take the lessons seriously, and they go on drinking the same as before.

'All four of the women I talked to agreed that this statement was true. Three of them went on to claim that in some way the discussions of alcoholism do some good – because the young people whose habits are not yet formed refrain from becoming heavy drinkers; or because although lessons alone do not change husbands, the combination of the meetings plus persuasion by the wife in the home does produce results.'

OBSERVATIONS BY INDEPENDENT OBSERVERS

Now I presented the Reasonable Social Scientist with another kind of evidence. 'More light on the somewhat vague claims you

mention is shed by the reports of some independent observers.'
Three foreign visitors had already spent rather long periods of
time getting to know PPH-Osorno when our study began.
Although they had left behind them written records of their
observations, I did not read them until my own field work was
completed. Lisa Sullivan is a Spanish-speaking US citizen who
recently graduated as a human relations major from Earlham
College; Bernardo Salazar is a young social worker from Colombia. Together they visited 15 *centros* in May 1980; they
presented their findings at a meeting of the sector-coordinators
in the by-now-famous pink house. Here are some excepts from
the minutes of the meeting, taken by Jorge Zuleta.

> The participants themselves told us that the program enabled
> them to overcome timidity and personal insecurity. Now
> everyone participates, expresses opinions and ideas, etc. Also,
> their family life is better; the children have learned a lot, for
> example school is easier for them now; according to what the
> teachers say, they are much more advanced than those
> children who have not participated in PPH (Lisa).
>
> The greatest value we have seen is the organization that
> PPH has generated among the peasants. This type of orga-
> nization is better than those already existing, because it is
> more open, more dynamic ... I believe that what is important
> is not in the units of the program, but the dynamics that are
> created in the meetings; in other words, the most important
> thing is the methodology that stimulates the creativity of the
> group and the search for solutions (Bernardo).

'Sister Thelma Arrogabe is an Argentine nun,' I went on, 'the
director of a large radio school named INCUPO (*Instituto de
Cultura Popular*). She spent the month of April 1980 with
PPH-Osorno – one week tramping from house to house with
Teresa Catalán, the sector-coordinator in Entre Lagos; one week
as the constant companion of Nora Schwaeger, the sector-
coordinator in Riachuelo; and two weeks in various other places.
Sister Thelma said,

> The change that most impressed me was the respect the
> peasants had developed for their children. One noticed that
> after a year of the programme, there was a great respect for the

children; they had discovered an affectionate way of relating. Also, the demand on the part of the women that the husbands respect them and the children. Another beautiful thing was the relation among the members of the *centros* – cordial, warm (*cariñoso*), they felt they shared something in common.

'The independent observers saw PPH prior to the time when the *centros* took up the topics of alcohol and nutrition. Although they confirmed the claims in the verbal image concerning interpersonal relationships, they did not mention decreased alcoholism or improved nutrition.' I drew a chart on a napkin.

Earlier:	Treatment X present	Benefit X present
	Treatments Y and Z absent	Benefits Y and Z absent
Later:	Treatments X, Y and Z present	Benefits X, Y and Z present

I explained to the Reasonable Social Scientist that the Xs refer to interpersonal relations, the Ys to alcoholism, and the Zs to nutrition. The pattern shown in the schema helps to answer the objection (which is perhaps a rather far-fetched objection anyway) that the benefits observed might not be due to PPH, but simply be virtues of the peasants that were there before, during and after PPH. In other words, the fact that the independent observers saw all and only the benefits PPH was working on, strengthens our belief that PPH is working.

CONTENT ANALYSIS OF THE MANUALS

'Of all your evidence,' the Reasonable Social Scientist said, 'the most persuasive has been the content analysis of the worksheets. I'd like to see a similar analysis of the manuals used to facilitate discussions among adults.'

'Do you mean to say,' I asked, 'that your confidence in the existence of the claimed benefits would be increased by evidence that topics extensively discussed are of kinds that plausibly lead to the benefits claimed?'

'Exactly so,' said the Reasonable Social Scientist. 'Benjamin

Bloom has argued recently that the most important variable in explaining learning is time-on-task, which is another way of saying that people tend to learn what they study, and to learn it more the more they study it.'

'The contents of the units for adults in the manuals,' I said, 'are (as the verbal image in Chapter 8 says) especially designed to start conversations. There are more questions than statements. No money has been spent on hiring specialists who might improve the accuracy of the information transmitted, and in some cases it is inaccurate (it is claimed, for instance, that onions are rich in vitamins); the whole point is conceived to be to draw the peasants into conversation, not to deliver information to the peasants. The CIDE staff members who prepare the units draw on their own and the institution's experience in working with the desparately poor and the marginal, not on subject matter expertise. Indeed, the contents of the units are so sparse that we shall not waste time if instead of summarizing, we reproduce in full the substantive points it takes the *centros* two years to discuss.' Perhaps I should have given the Reasonable Social Scientist a list of topics to read, but, thinking that since I find all this material fascinating she would too, I read the whole thing out loud to her.

First Unit: Child Development. What are the problems that slow child development? An image to be discussed shows a well-nourished and a poorly-nourished child. Other images show poor hygiene, lack of affection, and problems with homework. The question is raised of how the family can help the child learn. The group is asked to propose other problems in addition to those posed by the images, to think of the community organizations that might help solve the problems, and to suggest what they might do themselves. (The last part is repeated in all the units.)

Second Unit: To Learn to Write. The following questions are raised: Why do people need to learn to write? What difficulties are there in learning? Is learning to write similar to learning to knit? What activities help children learn to write? (There is a picture of a child shelling peas.) Of the things that parents and siblings do in the house, which would serve to help a child learn to write? (The idea is to integrate helping children learn into the daily routine of the peasant household, avoiding having to set special time aside for lessons. Cost-effectiveness analysts should note this point.)

Third Unit: To Learn to Speak. Is it important to call things by their correct names? How do children learn to speak? How can the family help the child learn to speak? The child learns to read and write better when he has previously heard the words and become acquainted with the things they refer to. If he has a better vocabulary, he will have more confidence in speaking in groups. (The manual tells the coordinator what the main objective is: 'Your work is to lead the group to discover the importance of conversation among adults and children in the home and in the community.')

Fourth Unit: Parent–Child Relationships. This unit follows the typical four-meeting sequence, which it might be well to repeat here, using this unit as an example, for the sake of clarity. (i) In the first meeting, there are conversations motivated by pictures. (ii) In the second meeting, there is a workship; in this case, making toys for children out of scraps and waste material. (iii) In the third unit, the work is with a problem sheet; in this case the problem sheet is a drawing of a father whipping with a belt a boy who just sawed the leg off a chair. (iv) The fourth meeting is dedicated to reviewing what the group has done and how it was done. The contents of this unit are as follows. How do people treat adults and how do they treat children? How does a person feel if no one ever expresses affection or shows interest in which he is doing? How can one express affection for a child? Do children play just to entertain themselves? How should parents respond when children ask questions?

Fifth Unit: Children Ask Questions (Sex Education). The images to be used to start conversations include a baby sucking its mother's milk, a rooster on a hen, dog on dog, child with finger on tummy of pregnant woman, older sibling sees new baby for first time, child takes bath, child touches herself, adolescents necking in the street while children and neighbours make fun of them. (Some peasants objected that the last-mentioned image shows an urban problem.)

Sixth Unit: Children Learn from Us. Children identify with their parents. It they see that their parents love each other and talk over their problems together, they will learn the value of affection (*cariño*) and communication.

Seventh Unit: To Learn to Count. Mathematics is useful in daily life. Before learning to count, add and subtract, the child learns from games that include classifying objects and ordering objects from smallest to largest; and from learning words such as more, less, all, few, some, etc.

Eighth Unit: Children and Alcohol. Images are used to provoke discussion of folk beliefs concerning alcohol, that it cures colds, quenches thirst, brings joy, keeps one warm when it is cold and cool when it is hot, makes one a real man, shows that you are a boon companion and true friend. The coordinator is told what conclusions the group is supposed to draw: whether one should take another drink or not depends on health, age, whether one takes drink with meals or on an empty stomach, and the quantity one has already drunk.

Ninth Unit: Us and Alcohol. What effects does alcohol produce? What is the significance of a person being an alcoholic? Is alcoholism a disease? What can the family do the prevent alcoholism a disease? What can the family do to prevent system, and liver, which is especially grave if the drinker is a young child.

Tenth Unit: The Family and Food. Ideas on the causes and effects of poor nutrition are drawn from the group with the aid of pictures of malnourished children and adults. In the workshop (second) meeting, measurements of height and weight are discussed. The third meeting features reflection on folk-themes concerning milk: milk should be given only to small children, powdered milk is less nutritious than real milk, milk gives children diarrhoea, milk with fruit produces stomach aches, milk is to be consumed mainly as something added to tea or coffee. Powdered milk should be made with warm boiled water. Use half a cup of water, add 3 tablespoons of powder, beat well, then add another half-cup of water. The unit also gives recipes for milk pudding, rice with milk, and apples with milk. The people are encouraged to exchange recipes among themselves. (Note: The Voice of the Coast supports all the units with appropriate *teatros* and other programs. The manager of the station, Celedino Fierro, predicted that when the *centros* started the tenth unit, The Voice of the Coast would start receiving milk recipes in the mail to be read on the air – a prediction which proved to be correct.)

Eleventh Unit: Food and Growth. The images feature a healthy and a sick ear of corn, the idea being that people, like crops, need proper nutrition and care. Good nutrition includes foods from group 1 (proteins), group 2, fruits and vegetables (vitamins), and group 3 (calories).

Twelfth Unit: Let's Use What We Have. People are invited to discuss home gardens, raising animals, and preserving their own food. Pictures feature chickens, geese, rabbits, bees, pigs, dry preservation of vegetables, slaughtering a pig, canning, children helping with the tasks, the family working together.

Since the Reasonable Social Scientist became a little bored as I read the contents of all the units to her, she looked at the accompanying pictures while she listened to me with one ear. The peasants, too, like the pictures best. It is hard to think how they could be improved, except for doing a little more adapting of the pictures called 'problem sheets' (i.e. pictures that pose a problem for discussion) to local conditions. Occasionally the peasants have a picture to decode that poses an urban problem they do not have, such as the problem of two young lovers trying to find a place to be alone.

Having finished looking at the pictures, the Reasonable Social Scientist asked if we had done anything to check the claim that married couples in PPH understand each other better and get along better. 'If that claim is true,' she said, 'I shall consider starting a PPH *centro* in New York City.'

A CASE STUDY

I had also taken an interest in the question raised by the Reasonable Social Scientist, and had investigated it by means of a modest case study. 'My wife and I,' I said, 'made friends with a couple who, according to the sector-coordinator, had been on the point of breaking up, but had now become more united than ever.' I told the Reasonable Social Scientist about our experience.

'The objective problems of Raul and Ana are enough to drive any couple to divorce, if not to suicide. They live in a wooden shack with no light, no heat and little food, in a semi-rural village next to a town where, until recently, there was a sawmill. Raul has been out of work for several years, and since the sawmill closed, unemployment in the area has been even higher than it was before and even higher than it is in the rest of Chile. (It is impossible to obtain accurate unemployment figures; the government admits to 16 per cent.) Our informants say "everyone" in the village is unemployed, which is perhaps true if one considers only one's own social class, only men (some women work as maids), and counts as unemployed those with irregular employment (e.g. in road-building) and those in *el mínimo*. Raul counts as out of work in the last category mentioned, since he ekes out less-than-a-living ($33 a month) in *el mínimo*, the government employment program. Ana also worked in the *mínimo* for a time; now she stays at home and makes a little money knitting, between household tasks. Some of the men in the area turned to stealing cattle, and got caught. Raul himself took up selling vegetables illegally from door to door at night, when he got home from the *mínimo*. It was illegal, because he could not afford to buy a licence. He was caught by the police, and although he was under arrest only briefly, his stock of produce was confiscated. Jessica, age 7, Ana's child by an earlier marriage, did poorly in school; the teacher said she was mentally deficient, which Ana denied. In any case, Jessica was diagnosed as physically ill, requiring a hernia operation, and she was told she could not attend school until after the operation. The public health service gave Jessica an appointment for the operation six months away, at 7 in the morning, in Osorno, leaving it to the parents to find a way to get to Osorno at an hour when there is no public transportation, or else a place to stay if they came the previous day. After the operation, Jessica had to leave the hospital at noon, even though her recovery had just begun and the parents had no way to transport her home. Rodrigo, 3, is sickly; the times we saw him he was red with fever, and we wondered whether he would live. Even though they live in a cold, rainy climate, among the four of them they had no umbrella and no coat.

'Although we visited their village, the three occasions when we saw the family together were all in Osorno: a morning followed by a lunch, a supper, and a search for a place to stay on the evening preceding Jessica's operation. Raul was intent on following up leads on possible jobs in Osorno, all of which proved to be fruitless. Jessica, who had been studying at home with PPH worksheets while she was not allowed in school, drew some pictures for me with great eagerness and a great capacity to concentrate her attention. Since Ana had been elected president of the Board of Directors of her *centro*, and was an informant for the PPH evaluation, she was something of a celebrity at FREDER; Raul appeared to take his wife's prominence in his stride.

'Ana confirmed the sector-coordinator's report that a year previously, she and Raul had been on the brink of separating. She also provided, on various occasions, insight into the process by which PPH had helped their marriage. She goes alone to the meetings – indeed, all the people who attend her *centro* are women – but they review the main points of each meeting at home. (Raul wants to go, but cannot because he is in the *mínimo* during the day. The meeting cannot be shifted to a night hour to accommodate the *mínimo* people who want to attend because, among other reasons, it is not safe to go out after dark.) Raul and Ana have learned to talk about their problems, and she has learned to appreciate the difficulties he faces. One of the PPH activities was a *teatro* the members of the *centro* created and acted out among themselves. Ana later recreated it for me, and I transcribed it.' I asked the Reasonable Social Scientist if she would be so kind as to read the female parts while I read the male parts.

Teatro

Scene: a home.

Sra Graciela: We have nothing to eat, nothing at all, and you wander around all day. I stay here in the house, and I don't know what you are doing out there, whether you are trying to find work or spend your time standing on the corner staring into space, and our children have nothing to eat. They have to go to school, they don't have pencils and paper for school, and you probably don't make the effort to work.

Sr José José: What can I do if I don't find work, woman? I have looked and looked. The bosses are angry and don't want to give work to the poor, and on top of that I come back home and you fight with me and you don't understand me. At this point I don't know what to do. I think I am going to leave you and the children.

Sra Graciela: Go! I will stay with my children, and you will have to send me money. You will see that you will find work.

Sr José José: Come here, Rosita, let's see if you as my daughter can help me.

Rosita: What, *papá*? Here I am.

Sr José José: Look, daughter, what advice do you give me? I have no work. Your mother says that because I am lazy, I don't look for work, she says I pass my time standing there on the corner.

Rosita: Well, *papá*, what can I do? I am studying, and I don't think of anything but my studies. Those are your problems. Those are your problems, *papa*. And now I don't have any shoes.

Sr José José: ¡ *Chita*! I don't know what to do. Even my children hate me. Come here, son. Come here, Manuelito. You, since you are a little man, you can help me, now that everybody is against me.

Manuelito: And how can I help? I am a little boy. I am studying. If I were a big man I would work, because I see that in the house there is not even bread, and I am hungry, and you without work, *papá*.

Sr José José: Well, I am going to go out again.

End.

I explained to the Reasonable Social Scientist that the *teatro* illumines the mechanism or process by which the benefit was achieved. 'From this *teatro*, and from discussions and games where they analysed their family problems,' I said, 'the women drew the conclusion that they should be understanding and forgiving toward their husbands.'

'The way you go about triangulating,' said the Reasonable Social Scientist, 'reminds me of the point W. W. Charters, Jr, makes in his article, 'On the Risk of Appraising Non-Events in Program Evaluation'. Charters says evaluators too often look at results without ascertaining that the processes supposedly leading to the results were actually in place and functioning. You go a bit farther, holding that the existence of a mechanism or process known to be likely to produce a result forms part of the evidence that the result really happened.'

I am always grateful when I am understood, and I thanked the Reasonable Social Scientist profusely for her kind attention. 'You are the best listener I have ever had,' I said. 'Why can't everyone be reasonable like you?'

She may have been embarrassed by my hyperbolic praise. Perhaps she thought my sentiments were immature or insincere. She did not say anything to me as she paid the bill and thanked the waitress, leaving her a generous tip. However, as she departed to visit five day-care centres in Cautín, she agreed to meet me for breakfast again the next morning at 7.30am. I was impressed by her stamina.

When the Reasonable Social Scientist left, I felt abandoned. I needed to talk to someone because I thought that in my effusive gratitude, probably I had said the wrong thing to the Reasonable Social Scientist, and I wanted to say the right thing to somebody in order to reassure myself that I was socially acceptable, and also because reading Señora Ema's *teatro* had given me a stronger dose of reality than I was able to endure. Sometimes, when reality gets to you, you can use talk as an anaesthetic, to numb your mind. So I said to the waitress, 'It's a nice day, isn't it?'

'Yes sir,' she said.

'It's raining, of course,' I went on. 'But I like the rain. It's like God's tears.'

'Yes sir,' she said again.

Since my conversation with the waitress did not seem to be off to a good start, I gave it up. I sat by myself for a while and then went to The Voice of the Coast office to work on organizing my notes.

NOTES AND REFERENCES

The reference on p. 138 is to Benjamin Bloom, 'Time and Learning', *American Psychologist*, vol. 29 (1974) p. 682ff.

Extensive data on PPH families, which show that PPH actually reaches the poor, were collected by Manuel Bastias (Manuel Bastias, 'Caracteristicas de las Familias Estudiadas', mimeo. (Santiago: CIDE 1980)).

The Trapiche study using an IQ test is discussed by Robert Halpern, in 'Early Childhood Programs in Latin America', *Harvard Educational Review*, vol. 50 (1980) p. 481, 490.

The article mentioned on page 144 is W. W. Charters, Jr, and J. E. Jones, 'On the Risk of Appraising Non-events in Program Evaluation', *Educational Researcher*, vol. 2 (1973) p. 57ff.

12   How Teresa was *Capacitada*

What appears in the manual is just a list of suggestions. The methodology itself is the style we learned when we were initiated into the program in the beginning. There we grasped the form in which we were going to work.
Sergio Ramos (sector-coordinator, San Pablo)

The methodology draws out the inner richness and value of each person.
Jorge Zuleta

The substance of the Reasonable Social Scientist's first remarks at our next meeting was, if I may paraphrase her words, that on the whole she was convinced that PPH is well worth its price, and that a similar program elsewhere would very likely be well worth its price also, unless of course one's scale of values were such that participation and community organization are undesirable, in which case one would be well advised to spend one's money on modes of instruction that focus on the achievement of specific child development objectives to the exclusion of PPH's adult education and community solidarity benefits (not because it is clear that such alternative programs would achieve the child development objectives cheaper or better, but because they would at least not produce grassroots participation, which, in the hypothetical case, the Reasonable Social Scientist was assuming, the funding agency in question does not want).

'I would like to be more convinced than I am,' she said, 'that the apparent results are real. However, there comes a time when one needs to stop reviewing and checking one's image of the benefits of a program, and to start examining *how* the results were achieved rather than *whether* they were. This is especially the case,' she went on, 'if the person contemplating a program similar to PPH is in a position to correct some of the mistakes made in PPH-Osorno.'

She asked to be allowed to explain what she meant. 'In deciding how much of one's time and effort to spend triangulating one's image of the benefits, one has to ask what one would do with the additional information the additional triangulation would bring. If the new information confirmed what we already believe, we would proceed as before. If it showed that one or more of the benefits we attribute to the program is partly or wholly imaginary, then there are two possibilities: either the PPH approach does not yield that kind of benefit, or an error in PPH-Osorno prevented the benefit from accruing in that particular case. So the planner planning a program like PPH needs to know *how* the results were achieved, even for the purpose of predicting benefits, since the benefits the planner is interested in are not, strictly speaking, the ones PPH-Osorno produced, but the ones PPH-Osorno showed to be possible, plus the others one can get from standing on PPH-Osorno's shoulders and learning from its mistakes.'

I noticed that she did not say 'minus the benefits possible only in the especially favourable conditions of Osorno in 1979–80'. I did not ask her the reason for the omission, because I did not want to complicate our conversation at that time, and in any case the topic was low on my list of priorities, since most of the arguments for attributing the success of PPH in Osorno to peculiarly favourable conditions are either quite weak (such as the claim that peasants enjoyed the meetings because their appetite for meetings had been starved by six years of martial law – which is untrue, since the typical PPH village also supports a mothers' club, a sports club, a youth club, and two or three other meeting-holding organizations), or else too obvious to belabour, such as the point that the soil in which PPH grew was prepared by the history of Chile.

Having given me that foregoing sound advice, which took somewhat longer than the account I have written here takes because I have taken the liberty of briefly paraphrasing her lengthiest comments, the Reasonable Social Scientist retired to her room to get some rest, rest she richly deserved after her hectic travel on the previous days. Her plan was to spend the day resting, and then to begin to visit the countryside in order to acquaint herself first-hand with the people and with the Parents

and Children Program; to that end, she had postponed her
return to New York considerably beyond the date originally
scheduled.

I was thus left with the task of assembling my notes in order to
show how the PPH methodology works. As I mentioned previously, I had interviewed representative participants from each
of the ten sectors, as well as each of the sector-coordinators.
From the latter interviews, I obtained accounts of their training
(*capacitacion*). I was not personally present at the training
sessions. In addition, I talked with Cecilia Yañez and Manuel
Bastias, who conducted the training of the sector-coordinators;
with nine volunteer base-coordinators; with Father Winfredo;
with Jorge Zuleta; and with the Director, two announcers and
one script-writer of The Voice of the Coast. I visited the place
where the coordinators were trained, and generally took advantage of opportunities to chat with passengers on *micros*, customers
at markets and fairs, solid citizens of Osorno in cafés and
sometimes in their private residences, peasants working in fields,
priests in churches, nuns in schools, and passersby anywhere. I
had even paid a call on the Provincial Director of Education, a
government official, to solicit his opinion of PPH, only to be told
that he knew nothing whatever about it and had no opinion.

I wanted to write a draft as soon as possible, in order to
circulate it among sector-coordinators, staff-members, and
others in a position to criticize and correct it. It is a tenet of the
illuminative approach that one should test one's picture by
checking it with other people's perceptions – to find out, for
example, whether what I perceive as typical is also what others
perceive as typical.

I decided to begin by describing the training (*capacitacion*) of
sector-coordinators, relying primarily on the account given to me
by one of them, Teresa Catalán, and telling the story from her
point of view. Next, following a suggestion of Horacio Walker, I
would tell the history of a typical *centro* – how it began, the
problems it encountered, and its present status – relying primarily on notes from conversations with volunteer base-coordinators,
but beginning with Teresa's role in getting a particular *centro*
started. The following is an account of how Teresa learned the
methodology, or perhaps I should say 'became attuned to the
spirit of the methodology', when she was trained.

Teresa's *capacitacion* began early in the morning on 8 January

1979, with a *micro* ride from her home in the locality known as Riachuelo, to Osorno. Her feelings while she was on the bus were mixed. It was midsummer, and her father needed her to help with the sheep, goats and pigs, with the potatoes and other vegetables – all produced for their own use with a little left over for sale. Besides, she did not think she would get the job. Twenty people were to be trained, and only ten selected to be PPH sector-coordinators. She thought her lack of schooling would exclude her – she had only 2 years of school, while the average candidate had 8. On the other hand, her father had wanted her to go, in spite of his need for help. He had been an active Christian Democrat in the years before the dictatorship, one of the first members of the cooperative and the small farmers' committee, a minor official in the technical aid service associated with the agrarian reform. After the *coup* of 1973, he was fired from his government job and he withdrew involuntarily from politics, but he encouraged his daughter to participate in FREDER. Teresa, for her part, had always wanted to go back to school; she had been unable to study while working, because she had worked nearly all her life as a live-in maid or on her father's farm. At 24, she was much too old for a regular school, but she was an avid consumer of FREDER courses. Her fellow students had elected her to be a monitor of a FREDER course of special interest to us, the one in 1977 that was a one-month pilot PPH program. Her experience as a monitor had earned her an invitation to the PPH *capacitacion* – another short course that might or might not lead to a job.

The trainees met at the studios of The Voice of the Coast on Cochrane Street in Osorno. It took all morning for the group to assemble, because the *micros* from different points in the country-side arrived in Osorno at different hours. The fare was reimbursed. Teresa knew some of the people: Sergio Ramos, a neighbour from Riachuelo who was active in Christian organizations; Nora Schwaeger, who, like Teresa, had been a monitor in the 1977 pilot program; Cecilia Yañez, who had helped lead the *capacitation* for the 1977 program

When enough people had gathered to justify a trip, they were taken by jeep to Rahué Mission, one of a string of missions run by the Capuchin Fathers. Italian capuchins came to the south of Chile in the 19th century. Later, Spanish capuchins took up the work, and now Dutch capuchins, among them Winfredo van den

Berg. Rahué mission consists of four buildings and a small semi-subsistence farm: beans, chard, artichokes, beets, lettuce, leeks, peas, potatoes, onions, strawberries, a few rabbits, a dozen chickens, a half dozen fruit trees. Of the four structures, one is a house for priests, one a house for nuns, one a dormitory and conference centre. The fourth is a new A-frame chapel. The old chapel was burned down shortly after the *coup*; someone poured kerosene inside and outside and set fire to it. The tower of smoke could be seen in Osorno, 8 kilometres away. Although no one ever knew who did it, the local peasants say it was a foreign priest; he also burned several other churches in the area, before the bishop ordered him to return to his own country.

Only 16 people came to the *capacitacion*, not the 20 Teresa had feared. Only 13 were candidates; FREDER had been unable to produce the 20 candidates that CIDE had wanted for sector-coordinator jobs. The 13 were peasants with experience as monitors in FREDER courses; 3 had been in the pilot PPH program; several had miscellaneous organizing experience in Christian youth groups, the peasant league, small farmers' committees. There were, in addition, the two trainers, Cecilia Yañez and Manuel Bastias; and Celedino Fiero, the administrator of PPH who later became the manager of The Voice of the Coast, after the revolution at the radio station which you will read about in Chapter 17.

The first activity was putting one's belongings in one's room, and making one's bed. The men stayed downstairs, and the seven women upstairs.Teresa's roommates were Nora Schwaeger and Maria Catriyao. After that there was lunch, and after lunch there was nothing to do but drift from place to place and talk to people. Teresa wandered through the vegetable garden to the cemetery behind it. It was overgrown with weeds and brambles except for a few paths. The majority of the graves had no names; the simple wooden crosses had borne names at one time, but over the years the rain washed away the paint until the names could no longer be read. Small irregular rectangles made of the same unpainted wood and tiny crosses marked the graves of unknown children. Teresa walked back from the cemetery through the garden, and struck up a conversation with the gardener, whose name was José. José said a person could survive on a plot of 50 square metres, properly cultivated. He told Teresa about the time he had worked on a cattle ranch in the far south, in Aysen. 'We had so much meat there was more than we could eat,' he said. 'I have nothing to complain about in life. I have never gone hungry anywhere I have been.'

Classes did not begin until six in the evening. The group met in the main hall, a rather large (7 metres by 10) room made of knotty pine walls and flooring, and a low plywood ceiling. One end of the hall served as a dining room, and at the other end the chairs were arranged in a circle beside a large stone fireplace. The side of the room opposite the fireplace was mainly glass windows; if you looked out the windows, you saw the garden and the cemetery. The windowsills were adorned with indoor plants in old coffee tins, and the walls were adorned with slogans: 'Every radio course is a new dawn for the peasant in the south of Chile.' 'Friendship requires two duties: love your friends and do not forget them ever.' 'Violence enslaves, peace liberates.' 'Peasant training: food, nutrition, health, rabbits, geese, fruit trees, vegetable gardens, beekeeping.' 'No one is literate who cannot read his heart.' 'Seek Jesus; find a personal faith that orients all your life.' 'Cleanliness is culture.' 'Kitchen – keep out.' The last sign mentioned was on the door leading to the kitchen, and its precept was constantly violated.

Cecilia explained that the purposes of the *capacitation* were to get to know ourselves, each other and the PPH program. The first thing that had to be done was to introduce everybody. The group divided into pairs: you and your partner talk for twenty minutes, then you introduce her to the group and she introduces you. Teresa's partner was Sonia Curran, a quiet girl who was reluctant to talk about her private life – but then, so was Teresa. Sonia comes from a locality where there are no other young women – all the others have gone to Osorno to be maids. She has two brothers and a sister. She works at home doing knitting and sewing; sometimes she goes to other people's houses to watch the children while the housewife goes to town. What she dislikes most is drunken men and boys. The leaders in her community disappeared after the *coup*; now there are no leaders and no organizations.

After everybody was introduced, Cecilia and Manuel (Manuel Bastias, the other trainer) put 60 photographs on the floor. They were $8\frac{1}{2}$ by 11 blow-ups of black and white photographs. There was a man working, a young girl with flowers, a woman in jail, a sheaf of wheat ready to harvest, children, landscapes, families, crowds, conversations, sadness, joy. Each person was to select the picture she most identified with, the one that best reflected herself in her role in the community. Everybody spent 15 minutes in silence, studying the pictures.

Then each person presented the picture he or she had chosen, and explained the reasons for the choice. Cecilia chose the woman in jail. She gave as her reason that she felt imprisoned because she did not know how to face life.

Teresa chose a picture showing a team of two oxen hitched to a plough, with one person guiding the plough and another walking behind, sowing seeds. She chose it because it really reflected her labour at her father's farm, where she and her father work the soil almost every day. (Actually, at their farm it is only half a hectare that they plough with oxen and plant; they rent the oxen for the ploughing from a neighbour. Most of their land is too steep to cultivate; their farm is mostly a hilly pasture where 6 sheep, 11 goats, and 1 cow graze.)

After everyone had presented the picture he or she identified with, Cecilia pointed out some common themes in what people had said when they explained what picture they had chosen and why. Everyone's self-description had shown a desire to serve others.

That night, as she went to sleep, Teresa realized that she felt confused. She did not know what secret purpose might lie beyond the activities they were being asked to perform. She kept her doubts to herself, because she supposed that everyone else understood, and she was afraid the others would laugh at her if she confessed her confusion.

On the second day, Tuesday 9 January, classes began at 9 am with a game. You whisper the name of a gift in the ear of the person in the circle who is seated on your right, for example, 'I give you a pencil'. To the person on your left you whisper what the gift is for, for example, 'it is good for writing letters'. Then each person tells what she was given and what she was told it was good for, which leads to comical combinations like: 'They gave me a flower and told me it was good for writing letters.'

Then Manuel and Cecilia explained the next activity. They were to divide into groups of three, and draw pictures of the main problems in their communities, with magic markers on poster paper.

Teresa found herself with Nora again, and with a young man as handsome as a fabulous Arabian prince, Ponciano Rumian from Cumilelfu. The young man whose presence electrified the young women was not, in reality, Arab, but rather Mapuche; people who do not know the Mapuche tribe may be surprised to learn that a Mapuche man can be as handsome as a mythical sheikh from the *Thousand and One Nights*. Ponciano Rumian was already famous as a singer. His group, the *Huetchemapu* (a Mapuche word meaning 'young people of the land') has revived interest in indigenous music.

Ponciano, Nora and Teresa decided that the main problems of their communities are: (i) alcoholism, (ii) lack of organization, (iii) lack of electricity, and (iv) lack of schools.

To show alcoholism, Teresa's group drew drunken men, and houses representing clandestine stills. They talked about the way clandestine vendors proselytize among the youth, making propaganda for the pleasure of drink. Men are drinking more. Drunken women are beginning to appear in considerable numbers – something you did not see 10 years ago. Crime is rising too, often associated with alcohol.

To show lack of organization, they drew a meeting hall crossed out with an X to show that no one was there.

To show lack of electricity, they drew a dark house and the poles of a transmission line, marking the poles with an X to show that the line did not exist.

The groups worked on the drawings until 11.15 am, and then paused for a coffee break. At the coffee break, four visitors were introduced. They were Alicia, Miguel, Florencio and Miriam. Each gave a short talk. Alicia is a widow, a peasant-woman from a village near Curicó, a city about 650 kilometres north of Osorno. She organized PPH in her community, but she did not want to be a leader. She wants everyone to make progress together, not for some to stand out above the others. Miguel and Florencio are *campesinos* from near Curicó. The purpose of their visit was to tell of their experience with PPH, and to bear witness that through the program it is possible to do something. They expressed gratitude for the affectionate welcome they were given everywhere they went in the Osorno region. Miriam participates in PPH in a semi-urban slum near Curicó. She said it was harder to promote the program in the city than in the country, because the city people are more *egoísta*.

Except for the meal hours, the rest of the day was spent working with the material generated in the drawing exercise.

(i)   A representative of each group presented and explained the group's drawings. The *rapporteur* for Teresa's group was Ponciano.
(ii) The trainers led a discussion in which the themes of the groups were summarized, and listed on poster paper with magic markers.
(iii) They split into groups of three again, to analyse the causes of the problems. Their assignment was to reach consensus in the small group on the main causes of each of the problems on the big list developed in (ii), and to report the small group's conclusions to the assembly.

The problems on the big summary list, and the opinions of Teresa's group regarding their causes, were as follows.

ALCOHOLISM – family quarrels, unemployment, need to escape to forget problems, had habits formed in youth, 'to be a man you have to drink'.
MALNUTRITION OF CHILDREN – mother undernourished, peasants sell so much they don't keep enough for themselves to eat, lack of money.
LACK OF HYGIENE – lack of concern, lack of awareness of the problem.
LACK OF COMMUNICATION – lack of interest in organizing groups so that people can express their ideas and feel that they are human beings, traditional rivalries among families, families centred on their own concerns.
LACK OF ORGANIZATION – fear, lack of places to meet, lack of trained leaders.
LACK OF PUBLIC SERVICES – absence of coordination among the people to ask for services, little unity to make contributions (such as voluntary labour, or money to pay for the fuel for government machines that come to repair roads).
OUT-MIGRATION – no creation of employment in the area, exhausted soils, attractions of the city, large families that can't live on the land they have, tiny farms.
EROSION OF THE SOIL – Teresa's group spent so much time

analysing the causes of other problems, that they did not have time to discuss erosion.

(iv) The next step was for the groups to make lists of the persons or institutions to whom they might turn for help in solving their problems. Teresa's group listed government agencies – the agricultural technology service, the police, the health service, the ministries. They also listed the church and the Red Cross.

Tuesday was a long day. Everybody was tired. They had a good supper, pottered around the house and chatted, and went to bed.

Teresa awoke the next morning feeling more confused than ever. She could not comprehend the objectives of the work they were doing. In talking with some of the other trainees during breaks the previous day, she had found that they were sceptical. They felt that they were analysing the obvious. Apart from reaching agreement on what everybody already knew, they did not expect to learn anything of any use for solving the problems of the peasantry.

Wednesday's work began with a game that consisted of distorting old sayings by adding the words 'in front' and 'behind'. For example, from the old Spanish saying, 'the shrimp that goes to sleep is carried away by the current', you make, 'the shrimp that goes to sleep in front is carried away by the current behind'. Silly games were not an important part of the training, but they were a part Teresa remembered. They helped people to relax and to overcome timidity.

Manuel presented some national statistics that confirmed what they already knew from experience: 38 per cent of the population with less than 2000 calories per day, unemployment, 19.9 per cent (March 1976), alcoholism in the working class, 40 per cent, mental deficiency in working class children at age 6, 40 per cent, etc.

Next, they were supposed to work with some slides, but there was a power cut. They filled in time with a giggly game called 'electricity'. The one who is 'it' goes out of the room while the group chooses the one who has the 'electricity'. Then 'it' comes back and stands in the centre of the circle, while the others tantalizingly offer their hands to be touched. 'It' carefully makes up its mind whom to touch. When the 'it' touches the person who has 'electricity', everybody gives a great shout, as if the 'it' had been shocked. 'It' cooperates in the illusion by jumping into the air.

The 'electricity' illusion did not work like a charm. The power still did not come back on. The assembly discussed the problem, and it was unanimously agreed to work with slides by taking turns holding them up to the light.

The photographic images depicted the familiar problems: malnutrition, alcoholism, retarded children, etc. About each image, Cecilia asked the same questions:

(i)   What do we see?
(ii)   Is this situation one commonly seen? Does the slide remind you of some of your personal experiences?
(iii) Why does this happen?

The answers went as before: the listing of causes, the listing of institutions from which one might expect help. It was then that Manuel asked: 'Why don't you list the family among the institutions that might help?'

A great light dawned. Perhaps the family . . . a set of interests everybody has . . . the most basic of all the institutions . . . a point of entry, a source of leverage. Teresa began to understand PPH.

After lunch, Teresa went for another walk, this time with Maria Catriyao. Maria is one of ten siblings, unlike Teresa who lives with only her father and step-mother. Maria had always lived back in the hills, several hours walk away from the muddy course of the daily *micro*, unlike Teresa who had been a maid in Osorno. They walked past the garden and the cemetary to a field inhabited by six bulls and the transmitting tower of The Voice of the Coast. The tower was dynamited in 1976 – another unsolved crime – and then rebuilt with help from Holland. They parted a barbed-wire fence, and crossed to another field, where they found wild edible plants: *cardo*, a weed the peasants use for salad; watercress; trees bearing white *maqui* and black *maqui* – like grapes, but small and bitter. 'I'm not at all worried,' said Teresa. 'In fact, it doesn't matter to me at all whether I am selected or not.' Maria thought it likely that they would both be chosen, since only 3 of 13 were to be rejected, and the two of them had been monitors in the pilot program. As they talked, they came to a straight line of redwood trees marking the boundary of *Fundo Chile*; on the other side of the boundary, everything was orderly and well cultivated, in contrast to the motley disarray on this side. José, the gardener, had warned them that the *Fundo* does not welcome trespassers, and the dogs on the other side of the redwoods repeated the message. They dared not enter and steal a peek at the wonders reputed to be on the other side: prize cattle, formal gardens, a deer park surrounded by an iron railing where live the descendants of deer that were a gift from General Goering. The *Fundo* was, until recently, the property of a man who died mysteriously when his private plane crashed into the deep waters of Lake Rupanco – a death much lamented by the peasantry because he was a good *patrón*; he always slaughtered several animals on holidays, in order to provide meat for his employees, and he ordered extra land sown with vegetables and grains so that none of his people would go hungry.

When Teresa and Maria got back to the mission, they were given a sort of test, although they were told it was a survey. Here is part of it (there are 23 questions in all).

1. The coordinator should pay special attention to:
   (a) the contributions of each person;
   (b) the most important things that are said;
   (c) the contributions of the most timid.
2. With respect to the theme of the meeting, the coordinator:
   (a) should never say what he thinks;
   (b) should not impose his opinion on the group;
   (c) knows that his opinion is best and tries to bring the group to think the same.
3. The coordinator:
   (a) makes sure everyone feels free to speak, without obliging anyone to speak;
   (b) makes sure everyone always gives his opinion, including the most timid;
   (c) asks the persons who understand the topic best to speak.

Then something happened that made Teresa think Maria would certainly be chosen. A pedagogical issue was posed concerning how to work with two contrasting slides, one showing a well-nourished child and the other a malnourished child. There were two transcripts of classes using the slides: a class led by Professor A and a class led by Professor B. Professor A was obviously the best: she asked the people what they saw in the pictures, encouraged them to share their experiences, and asked for opinions on the causes of malnutrition. Professor A was in fact Maria – the transcript was taken from a tape-recording of a discussion she had led in the pilot program.

The whole group acted out the two classes, by reading the transcripts. Teresa was able to show that even though she had only 2 years of school, she read better than people with 4 or 6 years. Afterwards, they broke into small groups, to answer written questions on the exercise. Teresa's group gave the following answers.

1. How did the participants in the two classes feel?
   A's class felt good. They were motivated to seek solutions to the problems.
2. What did the coordinator do?
   A accepted people's opinions. She made the participants find the causes. B gave the answers himself.
3. What did the groups do?
   In A's group everybody talked. B's group listened.
4. Who got the benefit from the images shown on the slides?
   A's group analysed the differences between the well-nourished child and the malnourished child.
5. Who is the better coordinator?
   A.

After tea, Cecilia and Manuel discussed the methodology, and passed out the manual for Unit 1 of PPH. They emphasized the five basic points of the methodology.

1. Look at the image and discover what it shows.
2. Ask the participants to tell their experiences.
3. Encourage discussion of the experiences.
4. *Sacar conclusiones.* (Look for possible conclusions.)
5. Remind the group of what they have said, and summarize.

In the evening they stopped early to go for walks; and, later, to dance, play guitars and sing. One of the singers was José

Hueyelef, a trainee who had recently won first prize at FRED-ER's *Festival Campesino* with his composition '*Mundo Pequeño*'.

Mundo Pequeño	*Little World*
Yo canto a la vida	I sing to life
porque vine a este mundo	because I came to this world
no comprendo ni me explico	I do not understand
porque vine a esta vida	why I came to this life
llena de pecado	full of sin
y hermanos desposeídos.	And dispossessed brothers.

Estribillo: Chorus:

> Yo quise un mundo pequeño   I wanted a little world
> de paz armonia y cariño   of peace, harmony and love
> que el niño sea como grande   where the children would be
> y el grande sea como   like grown-ups
> sea como un niño.   and the grown-ups would be
> Quiero cantar   would be like children.
> a la humanidad   I want to sing
> guitarras sonarán   to humanity
> oiré mi propio canto.   guitars will sound
>   I shall hear my own song.

Admiro al poeta	I admire the poet
que vive soñando	who lives dreaming
hablando de cosas	speaking of things
que llegan al alma.	that reach the soul.

Hermanos queridos	Dear brothers
oidme de mi canto	listen to my song
Cristo vino al mundo	Christ came to the world
para liberarnos.	to free us.

Miguel Oyarzun played a folk song from Chiloé.

La Naranja	*The Orange*
Deja correr la naranja	Let the orange roll
Que ella buscara su centro	It will find its centre
No la partes con cuchillo	Don't cut it with a knife
Que mi corazón va adentro.	My heart is inside.

Then Ponciano sang a song in the Mapuche language.

Thursday began with 'Simon says', a game well-known to the English-speaking reader. They practised with the manual for Unit 1, going through the four-meeting sequence taking turns playing the parts of coordinators and participants: (i) work with images, (ii) workshop and worksheets for children, (iii) problem sheet with worksheets, (iv) review and summary with worksheets.

Friday was a great success, because of the feather game. The teams tried to keep a feather in the air by blowing it upward, while trying to sink the other team's feather by blowing it downward. The rest of Friday morning was more practice with Unit 1.

On Friday afternoon, Teresa and her partners failed an exercise. Each group was given a problem and asked to perform a skit showing a solution. Teresa, Nora and Ponciano had this problem: a sector-coordinator arrives in a community and finds that the volunteer base-coordinators are feuding with each other. What can he do? In the skit composed by Teresa's group, the sector-coordinator told the base-coordinators to engage in dialogue with each other to resolve their differences. However, the spirit of PPH prescribes a different solution: the sector-coordinator should return the problem to the base-coordinators: 'What do you think should be done about your feud?' Of course, they were not told they had failed the exercise; but in their hearts, they knew they had erred. On Friday evening before the sun set, they walked to a nearby orchard and picked cherries.

On Saturday morning, Teresa was given the good news: she was accepted; she was *capacitada*.

13   Building Trust in
Ex-Estacion

> The task of the coordinator is to create conditions of
> affection and trust in the meeting.
>
> *Jorge Zuleta*

From Osorno, a paved road runs east towards Argentina,
passing through flat, fertile pastures where prosperous farmers of
German descent raise prize cattle by modern methods. In the
period 1970–3, much of this land was seized by peasants led by
militants of the Movement of the Revolutionary Left, an irregular private army that opposed the socialist government of
Salvador Allende on the ground that Allende was too moderate.
Some historians and political scientists confess that they cannot
explain why Allende's legally-elected government permitted
armed activist groups to exist, while those who say they can
explain it – the most plausible explanation being that Allende
expected the irregulars to defend him against the regular army –
disagree with others who also say they can explain it. Whatever
the explanation may be, the fact is that these green pastures were
once inhabited by tattered peasants living in makeshift shelters
decorated with Chilean flags and the red banners of the MRL.
The landowners recovered their lands after the *coup d'état* of 11
September 1973.

As Lake Puyehue comes into view, the green land in front of us
turns to blue water; the colour of the sky does not change – a
cloudy grey. Across the lake, in the hazy distance, rise the blue
mountains that separate Chile from Argentina; I open the car
window and feel the cold, wet wind, and I remember that the
landowners have not forgotten anything. For several kilometres,
the road runs east and west along the south shore of the lake.
Here there is a semi-urban area which does a tourist business

three months a year when Argentine holiday-makers come to enjoy Chile's natural beauty and comparatively low prices. We turn right off the paved road, onto a muddy path that stretches south away from the tourist district, into a shoestring community of unpainted shacks; each house has a garden plot, some have a few animals. They do not have electricity. The people here are ranch-hands or lumber-workers when jobs are available; since in recent years few jobs have been available, most of them work in the *mínimo*. This is Ex-Estacion, a locality named after a no-longer-existing station of a no-longer-existing railway.

After the *coup d'état*, the police went from house to house in Ex-Estacion to arrest supporters of the former government. They took them away in a truck; some never came back, others came back so changed by prolonged torture that their friends and relatives scarcely recognized them. One of those arrested was the mayor, a socialist woman who ran a small grocery business from the front of her home, a few doors away from the house where the PPH *centro* now meets. By coincidence, I had an opportunity to interview her in Santiago in July 1980; the contact was made through a church-related legal-aid organization which was then trying without much success to press a suit for damages on the woman's behalf. Let us let her tell her story in her own words:

When the armed forces seized the government on 11 September 1973, I wasn't surprised. What will happen to me, I wondered? I soon found out. At 5 o'clock in the afternoon of 16 September, the *carabineros* from _____ came to arrest me and four other people, including my husband, who had never been active in politics. The police had an order from the Commander of the Regiment in Osorno.

We were taken to a jail, where we were imprisoned until 1 am, when we were released to a band of civilians wearing black masks and gloves. They pushed us into a black van and drove us over back roads to a hanging bridge over the Rio Bueno. There we were forced to get out and line up. The men were tied with rope, for some reason my arms were left free.

We stood about three metres apart, and to the left and right of each of us were stationed masked men with machine-guns. My husband was at one end of the line, and I at the other. I heard the shots and screams and the splashes the bodies of my *companeros* made when they tumbled into the deep, cold water about fifteen or twenty metres below. The man who was supposed to murder me, however – standing at my left – couldn't get the job done. He was so nervous he was trembling from head to foot. Two times he tried and failed to pull the trigger. The man on my right was furious. 'If you can't shoot, push!' he yelled, and either he or the other one gave me a whack in the kidneys with the butt of the gun. As I fell, I heard them shooting at me.

Fortunately, I know how to swim, and the fast-moving current quickly carried me down the river. My lungs almost burst as I kept my head under water as long as I could. I finally emerged, crying out as I gasped for breath, about 200 metres downstream, pulling myself up by the thick blackberry bushes which grew profusely there. I scratched myself terribly, of course; one does what is necessary to save one's life.

At first, I was disoriented, and unintentionally walked in the direction I had come, toward the bridge. Finally I realized, however, that I was on the *fundo* of Senor ＿＿＿. I went to the peasants' huts. Certain that they would be terrified to house me if they knew my situation, I made up a name and a story that my husband had tried to kill me. Then I knocked on the *lechero*'s (dairyman's) door. He and his wife took pity on me, allowing me to sit by the fire until dawn, when the *lechero* went to milk the cows. Then his wife loaned me some dry clothes and brewed a pot of tea; I was able to sleep in the bed the couple had just vacated.

When the *lechero* returned at noon, however, he knew about the killings of the night before. The *fundo* owner had gathered all the *inquilinos* together and had told them with great satisfaction that I and other Leftists had been pushed from the hanging bridge. Since the *fundo* owner was happy at the news, the *inquilinos* tried to appear pleased too, but the *lechero* – not knowing my identity – confessed to his wife and me that the notice filled him with sorrow. 'Señora did a lot for us,' he objected; 'she didn't deserve to be murdered.'

I broke down then, and revealed my identity. As I had suspected, the couple was afraid to shelter me; it was a terrible risk for them. But they agreed to keep me one more day.

During the night, we were awakened by the sounds of screams and shots coming from the bridge. Last night's scene was being repeated.

The next afternoon, the *lechero*'s wife took a bus to Osorno to deliver a message to my mother. I begged my mother to reveal to no one – not even to my children – that I was alive. I asked her to provide a disguise for me so that I could get out of the south. The *lechero's* wife returned with the clothes, and I cut my hair and applied make-up liberally to my face – something I'd never done before. Then I got on a bus and headed north.

THE FIRST CONTACTS

Teresa Catalán brought **PPH** to Ex-Estacion in 1979 in the month of March, that is to say, in late summer. You are acquainted with Teresa because in the previous chapter you read about her *capacitacion*. The records of **FREDER** showed that Ex-Estacion was a place where people had once signed up for radio school courses, although not recently. Teresa took the bus to the point where the paved road intersects the muddy path, and from there she walked south, knocking on doors. We shall let Teresa, too, tell her story in her own words.

They did not invite me into the houses because they did not know me and they were ashamed. When we started to work there, the people were very badly dressed and they did not keep up their houses; their self-confidence was so low that they paid no attention to their personal appearance and the appearance of the house. The people there had suffered a great deal; they ended up fighting among themselves. The fights among children would lead to fights among adults. The people there were very rebellious, because the things that had happened had left them very rebellious – they did not forgive and they did not want to forgive. They would fight about chickens and pigs, about animals that were stolen or that wandered away and wrecked somebody's garden. They had no organization at all. The mayor ignored them completely; he is also the Judge, and he got tired of hearing their complaints. They brought him too many cases. "I don't want to hear anything more of those people," he said.

I knocked on the door, sometimes for a long time, and finally someone would come, stand there and say nothing. The lady or a child would come, not the man. I would say: "*Buenas tardes*. I am making visits (*yo ando visitando*), and I am Teresa Catalán, a staff-member of The Voice of the Coast [they all know the radio station], and I am looking for a place to hold a meeting for a program called Parents and Children. We provide some gifts of pencils and worksheets, and we help the parents to work with the children at home, provided that we can find a place to meet, and provided that the community accepts the program."

They asked me for explanations, but I said we would have to hold a meeting and then it would be explained. They lose interest if you tell them everything at first.

Sometimes I went to a house and they threw me out, and I never knew why. It is hard to understand people.

At one house, I could hear the man in the back room ranting and raving as if he were drunk. He was shouting. "There is no bread! There is no bread!" I was afraid. The lady asked me to go away. When I was part of the way down the road, they shouted to me to come back. I returned and they apologized. The man was not really drunk. He was pretending to be drunk in order to play a friendly trick on the neighbour, who is usually the only one who comes to visit. He had not expected a stranger to pay a call. We talked, and they offered me their house for the first meeting.

THE MOTIVATION MEETING

In the technical vocabulary which the PPH staff has devised to describe its operations, *la capacitacion* is followed by *la motivacion*. *La motivacion* is, in turn, followed by another *capacitacion*, since one of the products of the *motivacion*, as we shall see, is a group of volunteer base-coordinators (in Osorno approximately 100 of them) who need to be *capacitados* in essentially the same way that the sector-coordinators were *capacitados*, i.e. as described in Chapter 12. There is a first *capacitacion* (of sector-coordinators); a *motivacion*; and a second *capacitacion* (the second is of volunteer base-coordinators – in Osorno they were split into three separate groups, for three separate, successive, week-long intensive mini-courses).

From then on, the calendar is marked according to which *unidad* the *centros* are doing. Each of the 12 *unidades* cooresponds to a manual, and it is important that all *centros* do the same *unidad* at approximately the same time, so that the radio broadcasts will be relevant to the meetings. *Unidades* one to six were done in the first year, 1979; after the summer holiday, the new year began with a *remotivacion* followed by *unidades* seven to twelve. Parallel to the *unidades* are the *auto-capacitaciones* (group-teaches-itelf meetings), held by sector-coordinators once a week and by volunteer base-coordinators once a month. What the reader lacks, to be fully initiated into the essences of the mysteries of PPH, are accounts of the *motivacion* and the *auto-capacitacion*, since the reader is already knowledgeable on the subjects of *capacitacion*, *centros* and *unidades*; and since once he masters the concept of *motivacion*, he will have no difficulty with *remotivacion*. We shall complete the reader's initiation into the mysteries by continuing the history of the centre at Ex-Estacion in the form of a tale told by a volunteer base-coordinator. We think it best to select as the reader's informant for this purpose, a composite base-coordinator named Señorita Isabel, aged 19, whose history of Ex-Estacion is a *pastiche* derived, in fact, from interviews with several base-coordinators from several centres. Incidental remarks not taken from transcripts of interviews with base-coordinators are enclosed in brackets [ ].

'Señorita Teresa was the one who brought PPH to us. She came to our house and asked us to come to a meeting. My mother said: "She behaved correctly. She came to visit us and invited us to attend a meeting. You should go to return the courtesy for us. I am too old." The meeting was also announced on the radio. It was at Sra Juana's house. It was hard for Srta Teresa to get a house for the meeting, because we do not own the land here, and people don't know what might happen. God willing, some day we may own the land our houses are on.

'Señorita Teresa greeted me warmly (*me recibio con cariño*). My cousin Rosario was there, and my aunt Irene; there were about 18 people in all, mostly people I hardly knew, people I recognized by the colour of their clothes. Over half the houses did not send anybody.

'The speakers at the motivation meeting were Florentino and Alicia from Curicó. They are country people like us; they have the same problems we have. They showed us "films" [i.e. slides, colloquially called "*películas*"] of a malnourished child, a discouraged man, a child unable to learn ... About each picture they asked us:

1. What do we see?
2. Is this situation one that is commonly seen? Can you tell some personal experiences?
3. Why does this happen?

They said that in Curicó, they had been able to do something by working together, with the support of the Parents and Children Program (*Programa Padres e Hijos*, PPH). When the parents teach their children at home, the children do much better in school. They were offering the PPH course to Ex-Estacion at no cost; it did not cost anything because PPH had help from the church. Before the program could begin, we had to decide that we accepted it, and we had to elect two representatives who would be responsible for the coordination in our community. Then they left the house, so that we would be alone to make our decision and elect our coordinators.

'At first, no one said anything. Then my aunt Irene raised the question of whether the course might lead to trouble of some kind. She did not say what kind. At this, Don Mario, who had been a political prisoner for two years, became emotional. "How long," he asked, "are we going to be afraid to do the least little thing?" After another silence, one of the ladies said: "This is not a political program. It is an educational program. It is for our children." From that moment on, it was settled that we would accept the program; the discussion turned to who would be the coordinators. The first people nominated were Mario and Ruth. Don Mario declined because he could not get time off from the *mínimo*. Sra Ruth accepted at first, and then later said she did not believe her husband would let her. Her husband could not be consulted because he was not at the meeting. In the end, the group selected two unmarried young women: Rosa, a girl I didn't know, and myself. Since the group placed its confidence in me, I did not want to say no.

'When the visitors came back, Don Mario told them what we had decided. The visitors told Rosa and me that the time and place of our *capacitacion* would be announced on the radio, and that our expenses would be reimbursed.'

THE MEMBERS OF A *CENTRO* VIEWED BY A VOLUNTEER BASE-COORDINATOR

'Now I shall tell you about the members of our *centro*; then about the *auto-capacitacion*; and last about some problems our centre has faced.

'My cousin Rosario comes regularly, but she sometimes misses a meeting when her baby is sick. Although she is married, she is still a young girl; she likes to listen to the older mothers because they give her ideas on how to bring up her children. She does not speak, but she follows the conversation; you can tell she is paying attention, because when you ask her a question, she answers.

'Don Mario's attendance is irregular. In general, the men do not come often to our *centro*; they send their wives and sometimes the children, or else they do not come and do not allow anyone else to come either. When Mario comes, he has a lot to say. He cannot read or write, but he has a lot to say. Often he says: "We should all be equal because we all have the same needs." He takes offence easily; sometimes he stays away for a month because he is quarrelling with me or with one of the families that participate.'

[In roughly 60 per cent of the *centros*, the mothers dominate, as they do at Ex-Estacion. In 30 per cent the *juventud*, the unmarried young men and women, set the tone. Married men dominate only in about 10 per cent of the *centros*, i.e. in the heavily indigenous sector known as San Juan de la Costa, but it is common to find a man or two playing a prominent part in a centre where the majority is formed by *las mamas* or by *la juventud*. Membership in the centres is by families, and a family is counted as present if it sends one or more representatives.]

'Sra Silvia began to come because her children were coming. I went to her house and told her that since her children were learning, she could learn too; she could learn another system for teaching them, how to guide them. She was convinced because her children liked the program; they came home with the worksheets and asked her questions she could not answer; so she decided she would go to the meetings to learn the worksheets herself. Nevertheless, even though she had made up her mind to go, she did not actually go until I visited her personally and invited her. Her children began to come because I met them on the road one day on my way to the meeting and said to them:

"Let's go. We are going to sing, we are going to play." They asked permission of their mother, and came with me. I have visited all the houses in Ex-Estacion several times; even if it is a short visit, I go to see everybody, including the people who do not participate. I don't go so that the people will feel an obligation to come to meetings, but from a natural interest in talking with them about their children, or about anything at all. I find out the problems that exist in the community, the economic situation and the problems of each family. I am Catholic, I go to mass whenever I can, but the fact of being a member of a community is a natural quality that everybody has; one must have a humanitarian vocation to serve others and understand the needs of the people. Before the PPH program came, people knew me very little – they didn't know me the way I really am. They thought I was proud. Now they have told me I am entirely the contrary of what they used to think. Their problems are the same as mine, so I cannot pretend the problems don't exist.

'Sra Lidia is the sister of Silvia. In her case, also, the children came first and finally brought their mother.

'Sra Norma could not go at first, because she had a tiny baby and could not leave the house. Now the baby is about 9 months old, and she comes about once a month, bringing the baby with her. Twice, her husband came with her.

'Sra Elba was persuaded to come by Sra Lidia. Lidia told her: "It is an educational programme where people discuss things that are important. Why don't you come to see for yourself how we run the *centro*?"

'In July of this year, Elba was absent for three meetings in a row because they knifed her brother. It was fight over land; he claims to own some land back in the hills, as the heir of his grandfather. When he went to plough it, some other people who claim to own the same land attacked him and knifed him. Elba had to take charge of his hospitalization in Osorno, and of making a criminal complaint against the attackers. Everybody in the *centro* understood the reasons for her absence, and helped her as much as they could.

'Sra Inez dropped out of the *centro* from envy. She attended the first year; then in the second year she began to change, because she found out that *Caritas* was giving food to us base-co-ordinators. They gave us 50 kilos of flour, 15 kilos of powdered milk, and $7\frac{1}{2}$ kilos of lard – five times in two years. We did not expect it; it was not payment; it was a gesture *Caritas* made in recognition of the sacrifices we make. Anyway, Ines complained that we were not helping the people from goodwill, but so that we would have something to eat in the house; it was a kind of envy. She went from house to house complaining that because we are coordinators, we have something to eat, but she did not convince anybody. These people who create problems ought to be ignored; it is enough that the others understand one's intentions in serving them.

'Sra Ana was one of the original members. Her assistance has been regular except for a period when she worked in the *mínimo*. At one time, she and her husband both joined the *mínimo*, but they had to give it up because there was no way to take care of the children and house when both of them worked; now she makes a little money knitting at home.

'Sra Teresa is another regular member. She says she has learned many things, especially the words to reply to her children when they ask her questions about sex.

'Sra Jovita is motivated because her child is learning from the worksheets. She listens to The Voice of the Coast from morning to night, never missing a PPH Radio Theatre. She loves the third and fourth meetings of the month, when we play dramatic games and compose "radio-theatres". We do not broadcast the *teatros* we make up at the meetings, but maybe some day we will.

'Jaime is the only man who comes regularly. He is about 25, and unmarried. He has a steady job as a carpenter and handyman on a ranch. When he first came, he did not speak at all; now he has learned to speak so well that his boss complains that he talks back. Some people say he comes *por interés*, because he is interested in me. Some people say he is *egoísta* because he is looking for opportunities to speak on the radio. People give him a hard time, but he comes anyway. Jaime is one of the people who are *firmes*, *comprometidos* (solid, committed).

'The ones I have named are from the families that participate now. There were some others who left, one because the lady had a problem with Sra Jovita. The two could not be together, so if one stayed the other had to go. Srta Teresa tried to reconcile them. She said: "We have to have *union* (union) and *comprension* (forgiveness, understanding), and not pay any attention to the fights of the children, because children fight and then the next moment they are playing again." Senorita Teresa was only guessing when she supposed that Jovita and the other women were *peleadas* because their children fought; she did not know the real reason. My aunt Ruth left when her child started school. She said that the programme was not for her any longer because she no longer had any pre-school children, but the real reason she left was lack of interest. Sra Carmen moved to another town, and Sra Ursulina left after a few meetings – she had expected something else; when she found out that we were not distributing free food and clothing to the people, she left.'

LA AUTO-CAPACITACION

'The first time it was my turn to lead a discussion in the *autó-capacitacion*, I felt no fear. I did not feel anything. I felt, as we say, as if I were using family words. The other base-coordinators told me afterwards that I was not nervous, I did not make any mistakes. It was in the winter of 1979, at the house of Melinda, a base-coordinator of the *centro* at El Colorado; coordinators from five centres were there, all the ones from the area between Lake Puyehue and Lake Rupanco. There were 13 of us altogether: 6 coordinators (one centre sent two), Srta Teresa Catalán, Jorge Zuleta, Melinda's mother, and Melinda's four sisters, aged 12, 14, 17 and 19. The mother and the sisters had to join the meeting because there was only one wood stove – anyone who got too far away from the stove would freeze.

'I left my home at 7 in the morning and took the *micro* to El Colorado. A heavy frost had fallen during the night. Everyone arrived at Melinda's house at about 8.45 am, some with Jorge in the jeep and the others on the *micro*. We all brought donations for the breakfast and the lunch, and ingredients to make a cake since it happened that the *auto-capacitacion* fell on Melinda's birthday. For breakfast, I brought bread my mother had baked the night before; we had the bread with butter, and tea, and then we did the general panorama.

'In the general panorama, each *centro* gives an overview of how the program is going in its community. The reports were mainly bad: the people want something concrete, something that will bring them money. They say: "Why should we talk about nutrition when we don't have any money to buy food?" Jorge's advice was to return the question to the group: "What can we do that is concrete, that will bring us money?" He gave the example of the *centro* at Tacamo where people asked the same question, and went on from there to organize for themselves a course on how to prune fruit trees. Another problem was that a coordinator had been forced to resign. The ex-coordinator works for CEMA-Chile (a government-sponsored organization for married women), and the mayor's wife found out that she was in PPH.

'After the general panorama, we did the questions. They were the five questions of the fifth *unidad*: What questions does a child ask? Why does the child ask questions about sex? How should one answer this type of question? Who are the persons who should answer? Why do we feel ashamed about sex? Srta Teresa copied each question from the manual onto a piece of paper, leaving one piece blank, because there were six coordinators and only five questions. Then she folded the papers and put them on the table; each of us picked one and unfolded it; you had to lead a discussion of the question you picked, unless you drew the blank.

'Not only did I have to lead a discussion, I had to lead the first question! I asked the question, and the others answered as if they were participants. It was hard to get someone to talk until someone shared an experience: a coordinator said her father never let her go out of the house alone, even when she was 20 years old. Everyone there had similar experiences to share.

'We spent all morning on the questions, while Melinda's mother prepared the lunch with the ingredients we all had brought. I brought hard-boiled eggs and boiled beets for salad for everybody. PPH program money paid for the meat. Before lunch, Jorge summarized the discussion: "It is a problem that exists because of the lack of sufficient communication between parents and children, and the low level of consciousness among them. Since the people who really are country folk are accustomed to the man working all day, they expect him to arrive home at night tired and hungry. He expects his wife to work all day too, to work all day in the house, and he forbids her to leave." Jorge told a story about a pair of sweethearts who embraced and kissed as they passed a schoolyard; the children stared at them and followed them down the street – the children's bad behaviour was the fault of the parents, because the parents had not prepared them to take such things in their stride.

'After lunch we did the rest of the manual for Unit five: the images; the workshop with worksheets; the problem sheet with worksheets; the summary with worksheets. We role-played the meetings, taking turns being coordinators and participants.

'The last part of an *auto-capacitacion* is the *crítica constructiva*, the constructive criticism. We all make suggestions to each other to improve our methodology.

'This year, we usually do the *auto-capacitacion* all together in Osorno instead of in our sectors. I like it better in Osorno, because when there are people there from all the centres, we can learn more from each other.'

THE PROBLEM WITH ROSA

'We almost lost the centre because of the problem with Rosa. Srta Rosa, the other base-coordinator, stopped coming; Sra Monica stopped coming; other *señoras* dropped out, until there were only five adults at the meetings.

'Every time someone is absent, I go to their house to find out why. That is the work of the base-coordinator – to make people feel that because they are important, their absence is noticed.

'When I visited the houses, the ladies said they would come to the next meeting, but then they did not come. Sra Monica did not even say she would come. She said her husband would not let her go. When I asked to speak to her husband, she said I would have to come during the lunch hour because he was working. The next day I went during the lunch hour to talk to Sra Monica's husband. I told him his family should participate because we needed *union* among the people to go forward (*para salir adelante*). He said he did not want his wife leaving the house because she had a lot of work to do, many children to care for. He finally agreed that she could come, but not every week.

'After that, attendance stayed low. Sra Monica came irregularly, and the other coordinator did not come at all. Then one day Sra Monica came to my house to say that her husband had told her that she definitely could not go to PPH, ever. She broke down and told me that the basic problem (*problema de fondo*) was *la coordinadora, la coordinadora* and her husband. Rosa had gone to her house drunk, one day when Monica was not at home.

'I told Señorita Teresa, and Señorita Teresa went to see Rosa. She had trouble finding her. When she found her, she said that we always have to expect coordinators to be careful of certain things, because they have to be examples. Rosa agreed that it was best for her to resign her position as a base-coordinator.

'After that, attendance rose, averaging 11 adults [family representatives] per meeting.'

THE PROBLEM OF LACK OF INTEREST

'Attendance went down during the worst weather of the winter; then it went up again as the weather improved in the spring. In spite of the improvement in the spring, PPH lost several centres during 1979. Before the summer holiday, we held a meeting of the base-coordinators in Osorno, to analyse the *centros decaídos*. [A *centro* is called *decaído* when so few people show up for a meeting that the lesson has to be postponed until the next week; if postponements continue, the *centro* falls behind the others until its *unidades* are out of phase with the radio and the *auto-capacitacion*; the original motives for poor attendance are compounded by discouragement at being behind the others, and the centre is likely to cease to exist. Of 54 centres that started in March 1979, 44 lasted until the end of the two-year program.]

'I said at the meeting that 100 per cent of the *centros decaidos* would have been saved if we had used slides. In *la motivacion*, slides were used, and the people expected a programme with "films". Instead, they sent us pictures. The work of the coordinator is easier with slides, because you don't have to keep telling people to pay attention. Jorge and Celadino said no one had ever promised to send slides; if some of the sector-coordinators had said there would be slides, then they were speaking without authorization.

'When all was said and done, the meeting drew two conclusions about how to revive interest in PPH.

(i)   Invite well-known radio personalities to visit the centres. For example, Uncle José Luis (see Chapter 2) taped his

program, "Children's World" with city children. If he
would come to the country to visit the *centros*, the parents
would bring their children to be taped for broadcast.

(ii) Do handicraft work in the meetings. This was the idea of
Ermimia Alvarez, a base-coordinator from Pilmaiquen. It
happened that a base-coordinator from San Pablo knew
how to make artificial flowers out of paper and cloth.'

THE PROBLEM OF THE BENEFIT

'We needed to raise money to buy materials for flower-making.
Our idea was to raise enough money to buy material for
embroidery too, and then to ask FREDER to send us an
embroidery instructor. When it became clear that the money we
were able to raise by holding raffles among ourselves was not
going to be enough, Sra Jovita suggested that we hold a *beneficio*
(a fund-raising dance), and sell refreshments. When she went to
the police to obtain a permit to hold a *beneficio*, they told her to
come back another day, and when she went back they told her
the mayor said no, because PPH is political.

'We don't do anything that is political. Several times we asked
the mayor to come to our meetings, in order to see for himself
what we do, but he has not come. The participants do not know
what to do. For any kind of public fund-raising event we need a
permit.'

THE PROBLEM OF THE POLICE

'The day before the election [a plebescite called by the military
government on 11 September 1980], the police came to Ex-
Estacion to look for the Communists they said were holding
meetings there. They looked everywhere but they did not find
any meetings.

'In spite of everything, seven families are *firmes*. [All together,
there are about 25 families in the locality. In addition to the
seven, five to eight more could be counted as participating by
loosening the definition of what counts as participation. Eleven

are enrolled.] We have grown accustomed to working together so much that we do not think it is right (*lícito*) that the program end after two years. The community has changed since PPH began; the mayor has started paying attention to us. CEMA-Chile has organized a mothers' club; the municipality is putting in sewers; the government sent us a course on home gardening (*huertas*). People have more pride and treat each other with more respect. We have elected a Board of Directors, and we intend to go forward with our *centro* as best we can.'

14 Why They Come, Why They Don't Come

An attempt to explain why *las personas* attend PPH meetings must be careful not to attribute to the program more charm than it has. Attendance has not been high – it has averaged about half that of vocational training (*capacitacion laboral*) courses given by the same institution (FREDER) with the support of the same radio station in the same communities. (The average attendance is approximately 12 for PPH, 24 for *capacitacion laboral*.) An account of motivation to participate should not encourage anyone to think that a programme like PPH is likely to be easy – on the contrary, persuading participants to attend is likely to be a fight every step of the way. Although child development at the pre-school level and *union* appear to many analysts to be keys to coping with poverty, they are not ordinarily high priorities in the everyday lives of the poor.

The daily struggle to maintain attendance is waged by the sector-coordinators and the volunteer base-coordinators. Their persistence and ingenuity contribute at least as much to attendance as the program itself. (Here, 'the program itself' means PPH's guiding ideas and values, plus the support materials – worksheets, pictures, manuals.) Hence the problem of attendance merges with the problem of maintaining the morale of the coordinators, especially the volunteers, those whom Jorge calls *el voluntariado*. Maintaining morale has its seamy side; if a sector-coordinator fails to keep at least five centres going, she will be fired. If a volunteer's centre decays to the point where it ceases to exist, then she has nothing to coordinate and no flour from *Caritas*.

The poor need much encouragement if they are going to take time for a program like PPH. As one volunteer base-coordinator said: 'The people have a great deal of difficulty in attending, but they attend in spite of the difficulty.' After transcribing some *teatros* that reinforce the premise, we shall summarize a series of structured interviews in which coordinators were asked to say what brings people to PPH and what keeps them away. It will then be argued that it would be worthwhile to budget a little more money for some extra attractions that would bring in more bodies and souls.

WHY THEY COME, WHY THEY DON'T COME, IN THE PEASANTS' OWN WORDS (*TEATROS*)

Sra Fresia: 'I can't go because I was washing clothes. I have so many children, I have a lot of laundry to do.'

Srta Inez: 'I have problems sometimes with dad (*el papá*). Dad says: "Why do you have to go out so much? You have a home (*casa*). You have a lot to do at your home, Besides, you get together with bad company." I say: "I'm not going to pay attention to you anymore. I'm just going. Because there I can talk over my problems with my friends." '

Srta Alicia: 'I have no problems about going to the meeting. My parents don't dare stop me. They just let me go.'

Juan tries to come on time. Sometimes he is late; then he apologizes, explaining that he walks a long distance on foot. *Las personas* understand him (*lo comprende*), because we all know the roads are bad.

Sra Silvia misses sometimes because her husband forbids her to go when she has not finished all her housework. She has to work in the garden, take care of the chickens, and she says to him: 'It doesn't matter to me if the housework gets done.' She she goes anyway, because she is illiterate, and in PPH they are teaching her the letters and the numbers.

Srta Raquel comes to all the meetings. She has no problems in her home, she has no children. She comes to participate (*por participar*), and gives enthusiasm to the centre.

Sra Araucaria many times she does not come, since her children are in school. She has her weaving to do, and work in the garden, but she makes the sacrifice of coming, because she wants to become a coordinator. She wants to have good attendance, so that next year the group (*la asamblea*) will elect her coordinator.

Ivan comes voluntarily because he likes the program; he gives people enthusiasm. His father never forbids him to partici-pate. The father says to the son: 'There you will receive better *consejos* than I can give you.' The father does not receive (i.e. accept) the *consejos* of the conversations we have in PPH. But the son appreciates them, and so afterwards he will be a good son. He says: 'I don't thank my father for his *consejos*; I thank the PPH program.'

Sra Luisa: 'I almost was not going to come to the meeting, because my husband (said): "So don't go, because who is going to make the lunch? You (*Ud.*) are always wandering, wandering (*andando, andando*), and I stay here alone."'

Sra Clara: 'I almost didn't come to the meeting because I was working in the garden, making starter beds for seedlings.'

Sra Rosa: 'I was doing the laundry, and I left my laundry to come to the meeting, because the meeting interests me more, because I am illiterate and here I am learning with the worksheets.'

WHY THEY COME, WHY THEY DON'T COME, AS ANALYSED BY COORDINATORS

Nine sector-coordinators were asked, one by one, to express their views on the motives for attendance. On the whole, they found the units more motivating than the worksheets, which suggests that there would have been less progress in child development if the parents had not been enticed into the program by discussions of adult topics. We know from the verbal image (Chapter 11) that participants frequently perceive the worksheets in less than enthusiastic terms, as 'a task they give us', that 'we comply with'. Some units motivated more than others, in the following rank order.

Parent–Child Relationships (Unit 4) – most motivating
Children Ask Questions (Sex Education) (Unit 5) – tied for second
Children Learn from Us (Unit 6) – tied for second

Children and Alcohol (Unit 8) – fourth most motivating
Child Development (Unit 1) – fifth
The Family and Food (Unit 10) – sixth
Us and Alcohol (Unit 9) – tied for seventh
To Learn to Write (Unit 2) – tied for seventh
Food and Growth (Unit 11) – ninth
To Learn to Speak (Unit 3) – tenth
To Learn to Count (Unit 7) – least motivating

(For brief descriptions of each unit, see Chapter 11.)

In a different series of interviews (with seven sector-coordinators and two volunteer base-coordinators), the motives of the peasants who do not attend PPH were analysed. Five respondents mentioned fear of being associated with FREDER and the clergy (*las curitas*), because they were accused of being 'political'. This topic was always approached via circumlocutions such as, 'they don't come because of distorted ideas some people have about the program'. We suspect that the other four respondents who did not mention this point had it in mind, but did not say it.

Five mentioned inability to attend because of work. The men cannot attend if the session is scheduled during their working hours; women may be unable to leave the garden or the house.

Five mentioned lack of interest. The people 'don't take education seriously'.

Four mentioned long distance – members must walk up to 10 kilometres to attend.

Three mentioned disappointment because the people expect the programme to deliver food, clothing, or knowledge that will lead to paid work. One coordinator said that the people say: 'Why are we attending this meeting here, that doesn't deliver anything concrete that can provide money?

Three said some people do not go because one or more people they dislike do go.

Two mentioned *egoísmo*.

Two said people do not like to meet in private homes. It is a mark of the suspect status of PPH that it is not allowed to meet in public places.

Two mentioned people who came to a meeting once and did not like it – they did not like being asked to participate when they preferred to listen.

The following motives for non-attendance were given one mention each: some parents without pre-school children think the program is not for them, and so do some unmarried young people; men think the program is for women; the old people do not join anything; some people think they learn more staying at home and listening to the radio; if you go to the meeting, they are sure to ask you for a donation.

We also possess the results of a door-to-door survey in Mata de Caña, one of the places where a *centro* decayed and died. The moral is clear, and it is supported by other reports: attendance dropped because people stopped coming, because attendance dropped, because people stopped coming. When a person walks five kilometres to a meeting, only to find that it has to be cancelled because only one or two others showed up, the walker is likely to stay at home next time. If he comes and finds no meeting at all, because he was the only one not informed that this week's meeting was cancelled, next time he is sure to stay at home. Interruptions figure prominently in the histories of lost centres: the *centro* was expelled from the school and missed some meetings while looking for a new meeting place; the coordinator became ill or moved away, and meetings were suspended until a new one could be found; a meeting failed because of fear of the police; the office at Osorno did not deliver the materials on time. An interruption is a loss of momentum that may prove fatal. Conversely, bringing in a few new members strengthens the commitment of the old members.

PROPOSALS FOR INCREASING ATTENDANCE AT PPH MEETINGS

Staff-members are quick to tell you that increasing attendance is not an end. The achievements of a small group may be great – it may set a new tone for a community or renew a person's life – while a large group may be merely a crowd of observers (*mirones*) hypnotized by a spectacle. Increasing attendance is a means to incorporate people into a process (*para incorporar a las personas al proceso*).

In comparing PPH attendance to vocational training courses

(at the beginning of this chapter), we omitted the fact that cost per person per meeting is lower for PPH. This is true because even though attendance is lower, costs are so much lower that PPH ends up being cheaper per person. (Here, we count only those who attend meetings, not considering as beneficiaries the children, the other family members, the communities, and the listeners who hear PPH Radio Theatre.) PPH is an inexpensive model because not only do the people teach their own children, they also teach themselves how to teach their children.

If additional expenses are incurred in ways that attract more members, cost per person will remain low. It may even be lower. We calculated above (Chapter 5) that if slides and projectors increase attendance by 20 per cent, then cost per person per month will fall from \$1.62 to \$1.38. It is tempting to make similar calculations for other proposals, showing how increased attendance would offset increased expenses, thus lowering cost per person. We would calculate break-even points, showing how much increased attendance would be needed to maintain cost per person per month at a stationary level, while reaching more people through investment in added attractions.

We refrain from making such calculations, partly because the data, the estimates and the projections are eminently 'iffy'; and mainly because they would probably draw attention away from the crucial questions. For example, there is no doubt that PPH could increase attendance by delivering flour to participants. Here costs are not the main issue; the crucial question is how to deliver flour without changing the social meanings of the scenes and the actors, without making PPH into a system for the delivery of goods and services. If PPH ceases to be a means for helping people to overcome apathy and to affirm their dignity, then it will be a failure even if attendance doubles or triples. We do not want to be accomplices to burying that crucial question under cost and attendance figures. The reader who feels overprotected – who feels quite capable of resisting the magnetism of cost per person ratios expressed in crisp numerical form, who will focus, in spite of them, on social meaning – can easily calculate break-even points for himself; and they will be more useful calculations anyway, because they will be based on the cost of slides, flour, tape-recorders, and so on (and on the less obvious costs soon to be discussed), pertinent to the reader's time and place rather than on costs in Osorno in 1980.

Slides (Herein of Folk Art and Music)

The coordinators interviewed believe that attendance would have been better with slides. Nevertheless, nobody wants to re-open the debate on slides in Osorno – the staff agonized so long over the pros and cons of the magic lantern that only a sado-masochist would move to reconsider the decision not to use slides. The rest of the world, however, is, for the most part, not yet committed on slide issues, and it may find the following synopsis of the argument instructive.

An evaluation of the 1977 pilot PPH program, where slides were used, attributed the increase in attendance from the first to the third meetings to slides, and to the word getting around that there was a program with slides. The same communities had lower average attendance in 1979 when slides were not used. We present some attendance figures below, not because they constitute a knock-down argument, but because they are typical of the data we have, and consistent with the opinions of the people interviewed.

PPH attendance in January 1977 pilot program and PPH attendance (average of four meetings) in April 1979 in all communities in both programs

| Community | 1977 (slides) | | 1979 (no slides) |
	1st Meeting	3rd Meeting	Average for April
Chapaco	18	17	13.75
Cumilelfu	7	17	9.25
Lomo de la Piedra	19	19	6.75
Cantiamo	7	6	8.25
Los Hualles	14	27	10.25
Huali	14	14	14.25
Rio Blanco	23	20	13.75
Total for 7 communites	102	120	76.25

Note: Children are not counted in the attendance figures. Attendance counting children would be, in the mean case, approximately a quarter greater.

A volunteer coordinator reported from Bahia Mansa that

Protestant missionaries regularly draw crowds of 100 people there, while PPH draws 20, primarily (in her opinion) because the people are fascinated by the missionaries' *películas*.

The weightiest objection to slides is that they do not generate confidence in what the peasants can do with their own resources. They fascinate, but do not empower. A drawing, on the other hand, is a plain thing, of the sort a peasant might make himself.

A low level of audio-visual technology is consistent with the message that the program is mainly created by the peasants themselves, albeit with the aid of some materials of a sort they could also create if they wanted to. PPH is not a gift sent down from above by those who have access to superior resources.

The replies to the foregoing objection are of two kinds.

(i)   With access to cameras, the peasants could participate in making slides. Even those who did not push the flash buttons, who merely posed, would find the new technology closer to them and more subject to their influence.

(ii) The moral to be drawn from the attractiveness of slides is perhaps not precisely that slides are needed, but rather that some kind of attractive display is needed. Therefore, resources should be invested in folk art and music with the aim of producing the same degree of attraction in a way that *las personas* feel as an extension of their individual and group identities.

Another set of objections to slides concerns hidden costs and dangers – the administrative headaches and conflicts they lead to. The hidden costs and dangers are:

(i)   the cost of the time and energy of the sector-coordinators who carry the projectors;

(ii) the labour and material for darkening rooms – the labour can become a benefit if it becomes a community sewing project;

(iii) the danger of losing momentum when a meeting is cancelled because of equipment failure;

(iv) the danger of hurt feelings when the equipment is considered so valuable that most people cannot be trusted with it; and

(v)   the cost of administrative time spent dealing with items (i) to (iv).

These objections could be answered by advocating that the budget be increased to pay for more audio-visual equipment so people will not fight over it, and more personnel so people will have time to cope with the headaches. Hence the conclusion of the argument may be that a generous audio-visual budget is best, a bare-bones budget worst, and none at all second-best. It is better to have no projectors than to have so few that the crystal of good human relations is shattered (*se triza el cristal de las buenas relaciones humanas*), fighting over who can and who cannot use the projector, and when.

Tape-recorders

The tape-recorder debate is *mutatis mutandis*, the same as the slide debate, but the case for tape-recorders is stronger. Father Winfredo's greatest frustration with PPH is that PPH Radio Theatre is produced by sector-coordinators when they meet in Osorno, rather than by peasants in the country. A supply of recorders would facilitate making recordings in remote places, creating more horizontal (peasant to peasant) communication via radio, as well as permitting other entertaining and instructive activities in the *centros*.

Handicrafts and Vocational Skills

The objection to handicrafts – a proposal to boost attendance frequently proposed and already partly implemented – is that the PPH staff has no expertise in handicraft instruction. On the one hand, requests for handicraft and vocational courses are outcomes of PPH, because they are grassroots initiatives resulting from the application of the methodology. On the other hand, when PPH offers vocational and avocational skills instruction, it begins to look as though the program is an end in itself, an exemplar of Murphy's Law (any bureaucracy will invent tasks to keep itself occupied), an improvization. A way to meet this objection is to:

(i) channel grassroots requests for instruction to existing agencies able to provide it, the obvious one to turn to being the *capacitacion laboral* department of FREDER;

(ii)   continue to promote the idea that the peasants themselves can organize courses;

(iii) promote the application of PPH values and methodology
in handicraft instruction, by organizing *auto-capacitacion*
workshops for vocational skills instructors.

The key to making the above solution work is an institutional
commitment by FREDER to use its instructional resources to
support PPH. If, God forbid, inter-office rivalry and jealousy
should divide the PPH office and the *capacitacion laboral* office,
then PPH, instead of having another carrot with which to attract
members, an inside track for getting a vocational course, will
have a half dozen FREDER course promoters running around
the countryside insulting PPH *por inutil* (on the grounds that it is
useless).

Gifts of Instructional Materials for Children

It is impossible to make a general recommendation about how
much to give, when and to whom. Everything depends on how
the gift is taken, the meaning the receivers give to the gift. For
example, Jorge Zuleta counts it as a wise decision, in its context,
to deliver pencils only in the first year of the program, because
during the second year, many communities, having appreciated
the utility of pencils, organized to provide pencils for their
children themselves.

Nevertheless, it seems likely that more deliveries of material
would increase attendance, provided that they can be made in a
way that does not undermine the program's *ethos*. One might
even go so far as to say that it is impolite not to deliver materials
when the worksheets themselves require them, since otherwise
the peasants are embarrassed by their proverty. For example,
worksheet number one asks the children to glue cut-outs, but
most peasant families have no glue. Worksheet 17 asks the child
to draw a dog, a rooster, a cat and a pig, but provides only a
small piece of paper.

In order to keep PPH reasonably consistent with its own
ideology, deliveries should be incidental to PPH activities, and
complementary to time and materials donated by *las personas*,
avoiding gifts that cast the peasant in a passive role. One might,
of course, argue that there ought to be a different program with a

different ideology, one that teaches the fairness of transfers of goods from the haves to the have-nots. Be that as it may, gifts cannot simply be added to PPH, because a program that consistently violates its own meaning will transmit contradictory signals to its participants and consequently will not work at all.

Delivery of Food and Possibly Other Items, such as Clothing

In Unit 10, a gift of powdered milk was successfully integrated into a lesson on how to prepare powdered milk. In the workshop session (lesson 3 of Unit 10), each *centro* prepared a dish that called for several ingredients – for example, a cake. The gift of milk was combined with the work, the planning, the ideas, and the complementary ingredients furnished by *las personas*. The coordinator also distributed milk powder to take home. The combination of a lesson and a practical activity with nutritional support provides a model for making gifts of food compatible with the spirit of PPH.

There is no doubt that periodic food gifts from *Caritas* encouraged the coordinators, and that the gift of powdered milk in Unit 10 encouraged all the participants. The relationship between a program like PPH and an agency like *Caritas* is, in principle, a symbiotic one. The agency is going to deliver powdered milk anyway as part of its mission to relieve hunger. By distributing it via a program the agency gets more for its money by using its powdered milk to catalyse child development, adult education and community organization benefits. The program for its part, works a little better with a little nutritional support.

In addition to the problems mentioned above, in connection with gifts of instructional materials for children, food and other possible deliveries (such as used clothing) require a great deal of careful, conscientious, judicious, sensitive, tactful and intelligent management in order to prevent jealousy. On the whole, providing flour, powdered milk and lard for coordinators produced little jealousy in Osorno, but as the alert reader will have noted (see the previous chapter), it did produce some.

Legitimating the Program

Visitors to Ex-Estacion (to cite as an example the case of a *centro* with which the reader has some acquaintance) are surprised to find how eagerly they are welcomed. We interpret the warmth of such welcomes, in part at least, to the gratefulness of embattled peasants who find that someone from elsewhere is aware of them, and recognizes the right of their organization to exist, and, indeed, is so interested in them that he or she makes a trip back into the hills to pay them a visit. Expelled from the schoolhouse, watched by the landowners, suspected by the police, these peasants need a Christmas greeting from the bishop, a public display of their handicraft work, a *saludo* (greeting) from a friendly police officer, a visit from an observer from Santiago, a foreign country, or an international agency. Constant encouragement from The Voice of the Coast helps only up to a point, because the radio station operates in the face of the same threats that threaten PPH.

To some extent, the peasants create their own legitimacy, by organizing ceremonies at which they applaud, for example, the 'graduation' of their five-year-olds who have done the worksheets. FREDER has recognized the importance of the presence of Father Winfredo, or some other dignitary from Osorno, at such *actas*.

Miscellaneous Suggestions for Increasing Attendance

Other promising ideas from our informants are: (i) schedule more meetings during hours when working men can come; (ii) bring radio personalities such as Uncle José Luis to the *centros* more often; (iii) modify the support material to make it more rural: as was mentioned previously the problem sheets (*hojas problemas*) sometimes show city problems, such as that of a couple embracing in the street for lack of thickets to hide in – the localizing of the material could be part of *auto-capacitaciones*; (iv) add a sheet or two of blank paper to the worksheets; (v) let newcomers listen without participating; (vi) when the unit proves to be dull, play games: a favourite game starts by tying a chicken's feet and blindfolding the players, and the winner is the one who first catches the chicken, locating it by hearing it cluck – 'Some chickens peck hard!'; (vii) add more work on human relations skills to the *capacitaciones*, without neglecting the present focus on analyzing the causes of problems; (viii) organize playgroups so that the children can play with other children their own age; (ix) introduce more substantive information (*contenidos*) in the later units.

We should not, however, lose sight of the forest while examining the trees. The people's sense that in PPH they affirm a self they want to be, their enjoyment of the role of being a participant or coordinator, is basic to motivation, whatever may be the ups and downs associated with simpler and less elusive considerations. It is true that parents want their pre-school children to be prepared for first grade; it is true that if a community makes a first-aid kit, it is because the members know they need better medical service than they have; it is true that people come to embroidery classes because they enjoy learning the skill, because they enjoy having embroidered items, and because they may sell some. And, although the volunteers do not think of themselves as working for 50 kilos of flour, their morale goes up when they are given it. But the extra 'oomph', the mystique, that enables PPH to achieve more than the delivery of goods and services, is in the set of attitudes and values which the participants gain through participating. 'The secret is in the methodology,' says Winfredo.

NOTES AND REFERENCES

Conflicts between young women who wish to attend PPH meetings and their fathers who want them to stay home, may relate to the broader question of whether the young women will stay on the farm under the control of the *jefe del hogar* (head of the household) or migrate to the city to work as domestic servants. 'The role of the woman has a clear function in the family unit, and it is important economically. This traditional role is maintained principally in the adult women; the younger women have developed other kinds of expectations and want to migrate' (Sergio Martinic, 'Caracteristicas Basicas de la Familia en una Comunidad Campesino-Indigena', mimeo. (Santiago: CIDE, 1977) p. 12).

There is a vast literature on the pros and cons of slides, the uses of tape-recorders, and so on, sometimes known as 'development communications literature'. For some sources see the notes to Chapter 5.

15   Jorge Zuleta: the Poet as Activist

> The first time I saw Jorge, he gave us *confianza* (trust, confidence). We were not afraid because we felt we were all of the same family. Since he trusted us, we trusted him. When a person has to speak in front of a group, it gives the person confidence to know that Jorge will be there.
>
> *Ermimia Alvarez*
> *(Volunteer base-coordinator, Pilmaiquen)*

Now that we have seen a good deal of how **PPH** works, we need to consider the person who makes it work, and how the person in question does it. I believe that a correct name for the way Jorge Zuleta makes **PPH** work is cultural action, and that you (the reader) could do cultural action too, if only you had a frame of reference for appreciating its significance and its nature, and a graphic image of Jorge Zuleta.

Throughout the world, people are feeling that they are living in an epoch when society is disintegrating. Although people differ on whether they blame capitalist rapacity or creeping socialism; the narrow-minded logic of the scientific method or the rising tide of unreason; patriarchy or permissiveness; too much television or too little communication; too much industrialization or too little; too much individualism or too little individuation; overeating or hunger; militarism or the insolent temerity of the criminal element; the rape of mother nature by modern agriculture, or the backwardness of the peasants who have not yet learned how to rape mother nature; the left side of the brain or the new translations of the Bible; the dehumanization of art or the high price of wine – everyone agrees that one of the results is loneliness.

190

I have provided a list of diverse sentiments, each representative of the feelings of contemporary people of one sort or another, in one social circle or another, in one or another of the places I have been, who sense in one way or another that they live in a world that is falling apart, because I think there is a danger that in focusing on the details of how PPH works in Osorno, one may overlook ways in which PPH represents a generalizable type of response to the need of our times. The generalizable type of response, of which PPH and especially Jorge Zuleta's work in Osorno is an example, can be called cultural action. The need of our times, the theme that runs like a red thread through many diagnoses of contemporary social maladies, can be called loneliness; or isolation; or alienation; or, following the Frankfort school, the impossibility of discourse; or, following Antonio Gramsci, the fragmented consciousness of the exploited classes; or, following Raimundo Panikkar, the absence of God; or, following Richard Sennett, the decline and fall of humanity conceived as persons who exist for each other in a community; or *abandono* (abandonment). The last word has a special significance for me, because at a meeting I attended, a Peruvian woman gave an inspiring report on a successful cultural action project among Indians in the *sierra* (mountains) of Peru, which she concluded by saying: *No se abandona a nadie* (Nobody is abandoned).

Let me try to describe how cultural action works.

Cultural action is humanizing. The participants increase their appreciation of each other as persons. Facts of nature and facts of culture are distinguished; a peasant may understand for the first time that, as a person, he is not a thing, and that the degradation to which he is subjected is not a fact of nature. The educational process demonstrates, by doing more than by saying, that the dignity of a person is a gift of greater value than the worth of a natural object.

In the account of Jorge Zuleta's work given below, the humanizing aspect of cultural action is made manifest in the descriptions of Jorge's interpersonal relations.

Cultural action is also constructive. In places where one can use the word 'revolutionary' without being arrested, one can call it revolutionary. In it, people transform the themes (i.e. meanings) of their culture, by talking with each other about them in the light of their most urgent problems, and by working together to implement the conclusions they draw. If culture can be considered (following Clifford Geertz) to be a guidance mechanism complementary to biologically innate behavioural tendencies, then cultural action can be considered the repair and reconstruction of a guidance mechanism. There is growth in the capacity to cooperate, and in the adjustment of cultural meanings to physical realities.

The constructive aspect of Jorge's work is visible in the way he facilitates the use of thematic material already existing in the culture, to build a better culture. Jorge's work is an example of a general sort of work, cultural action, and cultural action is a response to a general sort of need, the need to communicate and to work together for shared ends – in other words, the need to organize solidarity.

The reader who has followed the twists and turns of our effort to evaluate PPH-Osorno is ready to appreciate that an understanding of Jorge, and an understanding of the sort of thing Jorge does, are essential. The evaluation of the results of the program turns out to require a description of the process through which the results were produced. The process is cultural action. The leading facilitator of cultural action in Osorno is Jorge Zuleta.

Jorge's physical appearance is socially ambiguous. He is tall enough to be a member of the well-nourished classes, but round enough to be a member of the class that lives on bread and noodles. His face is a combination of little boy and warrior: large soft brown eyes (in actual fact, near-sighted) and a large straight nose like a chiselled statue of an Inca or an ancient Egyptian. He dresses in work clothes, studiously avoiding anything that might mark him as upper-class, making it easy for peasants to believe that he is one of them – an illusion that is not all illusion, because he grew up as a semi-poor child in a semi-rural area. But it is hard to concentrate on Jorge's physical appearance; he looks at you so hard that your awareness of him looking at you dominates your awareness of you looking at him; he establishes a relationship of observer to observed such that he is the observer and you the observed – what he is observing, and encouraging, is not your body but your soul, your values, and you feel that you must not disappoint him. Even more – he is a whole crowd of observers, the personification of the generalized other. When he laughs, it is as though he had been suppressing laughter for a long time, with the friendly intention of saving you from mockery of the crowd, and finally, unable to control himself, he bubbles over – only to make amends quickly, in a way that assures you that he is on your side, whatever the crowd may think.

To appreciate Jorge's importance for the program, it is enough to appreciate the importance of the volunteer coordinator. The Parents and Children Program is run by the peasants themselves, with the support of people they have chosen from among themselves, the coordinators.

In this connection, the previous two chapters illustrated an important fact: the program is able to function only because volunteer coordinators are so committed to fulfilling the duties of their roles that they give energy and time to the program. The key to motivation must be that the coordinators like their roles, they like being the persons they feel they are when they are acting as coordinators of PPH. What this means in practice is: what Jorge expects them to do, they do.

What Jorge expects you to do is what you ought to expect from yourself as a person and as a member of a community. He does not give orders to his staff; he expects them to commit themselves. He does not express personal opinions; he formulates the consensus, a consensus anchored in certain basic values that determine *lo que no puede ser* (what cannot possibly be allowed) and *lo que tiene que ser* (what must be done).

Among the things that *tiene que ser* is showing respect for the peasant as a person. Jorge is assiduously polite and correct with everybody, especially with the poor. For him, correctness includes warmth and concern; people ought to be concerned with the psychological and physical welfare of other people – if we are not concerned we have failed ... our parents failed ... our society failed. He greets peasants warmly, not because he is trying to please them, but because it is *lo que corresponde* (what ought to be done). Promotion of their dignity is not a job or a tactic; it is living a value passionately felt. Jorge identifies with their humiliation as individuals and as a class; he is in revolt against it.

SOME OF JORGE'S PHRASES

To understand Jorge, it helps to listen to what he says. Here are some quotations that provide a sample of the sort of thing Jorge is likely to say.

'El coordinador de base es una persona que tiene que crear condiciones de mucho cariño en la reunion.' (The volunteer base-coordinator is a person who must create conditions of much affection in the meeting.)

'Yo creo que es bueno que tu lo sepas.' (I believe it will be good that you know.)

    – a frequent introduction to telling somebody something. Jorge rarely uses the formal *Ud.*, second person pronoun, preferring the familiar *tu*.

'Tu estás disfrazado, pero adentro estas más firme que nunca.' (You are disguised, but inside you are more committed than ever.)

    – to a friend who took to wearing suits and ties to reduce the chances of being arrested.

'Un honesto servidor.' (An honest servant.)

    – in *capacitaciones*, to mark the contrast between the coordinator and the professor who acts like a petty tyrant and pretends to know everything, the former being *un honesto servidor* and the latter not.

'Me gustan los vasos.' (I like glasses.) (He means the kind you drink from, not the kind you wear in front of your eyes – the latter are not *vasos* in Spanish, but *anteojos*.)

    – an echo of the *Odas Elementales* of Pablo Neruda, Jorge's favourite poet. In the *Odas*, Neruda celebrates simple things.

'Valorizacion de la persona.' (Valuing of the person.)

    – frequently stated as an objective of meetings, of *capacitaciones*, of PPH.

'No le cuadra en la cabeza.' (It doesn't fit in his head.)

    – said of a person unable to grasp, or to face, a reality.

'Las corbatas son muy pencas.' (Ties are very *pencas*.)

    – comparing a status symbol of the dominant class with *penca*, a tasteless weed the peasants eat sometimes when they have nothing else.

Jorge claims that the style of the Parents and Children Programme requires a new pedagogical vocabulary, one that reflects horizontal (i.e. equal) personal relationships.

'Instructional material' is replaced by 'support material'. The point of this change is that the contents of the programme are not considered to be in the materials, but to a large extent in the experiences contributed by the peasants.

'Instruction' becomes 'participation'.

'Instructor' or 'monitor' is replaced by 'coordinator'. (The English word 'facilitator' has no Spanish equivalent; if it had one, Jorge would probably use it.)

'Promoter' becomes 'generator'. This change is meant to distinguish between the promoter sent out from headquarters to sign up peasants for a course, and the participant who generates enthusiasm for a grassroots initiative – as was the case with Ruth Cofré generating the activity of sewing clothes for children (Chapter 8) or Ermimia Alvarez with artifical flowers (Chapter 13).

WHAT PEOPLE SAY ABOUT JORGE

Let us look now at some typical comments other people make about Jorge.

From a sector-coordinator: 'He does not oblige (*obligar*) people to do things. Rather, one makes a commitment (*se obliga*) oneself. He does not speak brusquely. He has a special way of asking that things be done – one commits oneself (*se obliga*) to do what needs to be done.

'In any circumstances – personal, family, or work – he is understanding (*comprensivo*). He always supports you in every way. Jorge values each person, so you feel good and continue working.

'If he sees that the work is not as it should be, he does not say it is bad. He gives suggestions for improving it. He is not like the people who say things in a way that depresses your spirits to nothing (*echar el ánimo al suelo*).'

'The time when Jorge went to Santiago was a difficult time, because when he is not here things do not go (*no marchan las cosas*). To find another person like Jorge, we would have to search in the night with a magic candle (*vela bendita*).'

From a visitor: 'For Jorge, people come before everything:

before the program, before the meetings, before everything. That is what he says and what he does.

'After being absent from Osorno, on his return he spent many hours with each of the sector-coordinators. He was getting his house and family together, but nevertheless he spent time with each one personally before giving them instructions or holding a meeting.

'He made the group take responsibility for decisions. For example, when the sector-coordinators were unhappy with the weekly *auto-capacitaciones*, he led them to propose a change, to make the decision, and to implement it. They decided to split into two groups of five. Each group met every fifteen days for the *auto-capacitacion* and for making the radio theatre programs for that week.'

MUSIC ON A TWO-TONE SCALE

While certain musicians have increased the number of tones on the scale in order to give more scope to their creative talents, Jorge has moved in an opposite direction, deliberately restricting the scope of his creative talents by dedicating himself to composing speeches with limited vocabularies. The following is a talk he gave at the inauguration of a PPH community building.

The truth is that I don't know if I'm cold, because I am tremendously touched (*emocionado*). Every day when, because of our work, we have to go to the country, we find so many beautiful things. It is impressive how the country family (*familia campesina*) every day gives us a series of examples of union, *cariño*, solidarity, of effort and sacrifice to go forward in everything. Then I don't know what to say, it's unbelievable. And today is a very beautiful day for the Los Hualles community and for us, because when we go back to Osorno we are not going to be able to tell, not able to tell everything we feel at this time here, seeing you, seeing the mothers, and the fathers, and the children of Los Hualles. First of all, we have the visit of Uncle José Luis, don't we [applause], who is going to speak to us. I am very, very touched (*emocionado*), and I think that Los Hualles is an example for us. It is an example for many people, and I also think that many people, many communities, are going to find out what is happening in Los Hualles and they also are going to think of something they can do.

I just want to ask of you one thing. This little house will do a lot of good if you are here. This little house will have warmth when you are in it, sharing feelings, giving opinions, telling about your lives, telling your problems, seeking solutions. The house is not going to have value if the house is not with people (*personas*). This little house needs your presence; it needs your speech (*necesita la palabra de Uds*).

I wish that every day you would ask more of us, because we [from the office at Osorno] are at your service. Really, we want to share (*compartir*) with you the good things and the bad things – the bad things in order to make them better. Really what we want is to serve, and happily (*felizmente*) we count on your support and *cariño* and *confianza*. So this little house needs your warmth and your presence as we also need them. You know how to get to the office and how to get to the radio, and you know they belong to you. Happily, through this tape-recorder, we have brought with us the microphone of the radio, and this belongs to you.

To end, I ask that as a symbol we take each other's hands strongly (*fuertemente*), because in this way we are going to demonstrate with warmth and with desire (*ganas*) to be united, that united we are going to go forward in the things that concern us (*que nos interesa*). Please let's all take each other's hands. In silence let's ask to be united, united we can go forward in everything.

IS JORGE UNIQUE?

Although in some sense everyone is unique, some people have raised the question of whether Jorge Zuleta is unique in the special sense that PPH-Osorno could not exist without him. If he is unique in this special sense, then it might also be argued that it is impossible to do the sort of thing PPH does anywhere else, since there is only one Jorge Zuleta, and he is not available because he is busy in Osorno.

On the contrary, I wish to argue that it is possible to analyse Jorge's language and the language of PPH in a way that shows a reproducible pattern. That is, Jorge practises a kind of cultural action that in principle could be repeated, with the necessary variations, in Indiana, Bombay, Mozambique or Penang.

Since Jorge is the only CIDE staff-member who works in Osorno, the language of PPH and the language of Jorge are indistinguishable there. If we count both transcriptions of Jorge talking with peasants and the words directed to peasants in the support material prepared by him and other CIDE staff members, we have fairly extensive records of Jorge-PPH discourse. One can abstract from them a thematic analysis that sheds light on the process through which PPH works.

The analysis to be given below complements the description of Jorge already given. Jorge's respect for people, his use of simple language, his gentle modes of persuasion, his tendency to speak as spokesman for values rather than for himself, and the way he encourages people to take responsibility, make him an effective cultural activist. Conversely, to combine the transformation of schemes as described below with an authoritarian style of interpersonal relationships would be impossible.

The analysis consists of distinguishing three kinds of themes: losables, usables and invaders.

(i) Losable themes are folk beliefs that the peasants will talk themselves out of if they take them up as topics for conversation. Examples are: 'you have to drink to be a man'; 'fruit with milk produces stomach aches'; 'women should not leave the house'. These are themes that are prominent in the culture; they are excellent for starting conversations because they are on people's minds. Cultural action changes the existing culture by raising the themes to the level of conscious reflection, helping people to scrutinize them in the light of their own experience.

(ii) Usable themes are growth-points, beautiful and functional values that exist in the culture, foundations for constructive change. Examples are as follows.

>   *entrega* – giving of oneself (literally, 'delivery').
>   *amistad* – friendship.
>   *cariño* – affection, warmth. It can also mean enthusiasm, as
>   when a peasant says his child does the worksheets 'with
>   much *cariño*'.

firme – solid, committed. Jorge distinguishes:
  firme en lo personal to describe a person who has brought order
  into his personal life, who tends to work on solving problems
  (rather than evading them);
  firme en la comunidad to describe a person who can be counted
  on to do his part in the community.
egoísmo – selfishness. This is a usable anti-value. Sector-
  coordinators sometimes describe themselves as struggling
  against the *egoísmo* present in the communities where they
  work. *Egoísmo* is the unlovely image of the self one fervently
  insists one is not.
union – unity. A popular saying is, '*La union hace la fuerza*'.
  (Unity makes strength.)
comprension – forgiveness, understanding.

The reader will appreciate the link between usable themes and
motivation. The usable themes, or growth-points, are the meanings within the culture that permit the creation of new meanings
and new roles. The new roles, such as that of volunteer
base-coordinator, are attractive because they serve values that
are already honoured. What is honoured in a country will be
done there.

(iii) Invader themes are not part of popular speech at all. They
invade from the dominant culture. Because they are often words
addressed by the powerful to the powerless they tend to remind
the poor of their humiliation. Because they claim to be true and
right, they cannot help suggesting that the peasants' words are
false and wrong. It is hard to introduce friendly invaders. It is
hard to make any invader theme compatible with the affirmation
of the dignity of the peasant as a person. Examples of friendly
invaders are:

  protein – not a word in the peasants' vocabulary, but a
    concept that would be useful to people who sometimes sell
    high-protein grains and legumes to obtain money to buy
    low-protein flour.
  play – is an invader when it is thought of as the natural and
    desirable activity of the child, the basis of its growth and
    learning.

In the technical vocabulary of PPH, the problem here called

'invader themes' is called 'the problem of *contenidos* (contents)'. In the inner circles of PPH, at Osorno and Santiago, it is now agreed that they have gone too far in making the *contenidos* minimal, and that they need to find the right way to introduce more friendly invaders, to generate a synthesis of popular culture with the cultural and scientific patrimony of humanity.

Which of the theories of cultural action, intellectual and moral reform, and the like, best interprets and describes what Jorge Zuleta does, is probably an unanswerable question. It seems reasonably clear, however, that his *praxis* among the peasants of Chile is the general sort of thing that many theorists, as well many activists, in various parts of the world have been declaring the need for. It is a general sort of thing that other people can do in other places.

POSTSCRIPT

A year later, I asked some students at Earlham College to try to think of suitable themes for cultural action in Indiana. They decided that television commercials provide many losable themes. If you just think about them, they lose their plausibility. Another losable theme would be the folk belief that anybody can succeed in business who is optimistic and works hard.

They thought an example of a growth-point or usable theme would be 'family'. 'People in Indiana are family-oriented,' said one student. 'They can get into a photographic essay like *The Family of Man.*' The same student suggested 'inadequacy'. 'Everybody feels inadequate. If you admit that you feel inadequate too, it establishes a basis for communication.'

Another student proposed 'American imperialism' as an invader theme. 'When people from the third world say America is imperialist, the people in Indiana don't understand it. They have no frame of reference for it.'

NOTES AND REFERENCES

Paulo Freire, *Cultural Action for Freedom*, is available as a monograph reprint from *Harvard Education Review*.

Harré's theory of social psychology suggests a plausible explanation of why cultural action and its opposite, which might be termed cultural destruction, work. 'By negotiating an agreement to adopt an interpretation, for most social purposes and for most social cases, we thereby enlarge the social world, since to adopt a novel interpretation is to create a new social fact. To persuade women to interpret marriage as exploitation rather than as a source of security, is to alter the social reality of the institution. This can be shown in the different emotional and attitudinal consequences of the adoption of the different interpretations. Changing the causal powers of something is to change its very essence' (Rom Harré, *Social Being* (Totowa, NJ: Littlefield, Adams, 1979) p. 237).

16   The Battle of El Monte

The bright October sun came at last to the green hills west of
Osorno. While its warmth beat down on the dense vegetation,
drying it out a little, after seven months of constant rain, a blue
Suzuki minibus, the latest acquisition of the PPH office,
threaded its way towards the village of El Monte, along roads no
longer mud but not yet dust, up and down cutbacks, beside the
banks of twisting streams, across fields of stumps where *leñadores*
had harvested firewood for the stoves of the city. With me in the
minibus were two short detectives wearing dark glasses, and also
the Reasonable Social Scientist. The Reasonable Social Scientist,
who was also wearing dark glasses, seemed perfectly at home.
One could not help but reflect how remarkable is the human
being's capacity for adjustment to a new environment, with all of
its new expectations and new, unspoken assumptions. She who a
few months ago had worked on the thirty-second floor, processing data and drinking black coffee, now found it perfectly
natural to drink tea with unbuttered bread, and to accompany
two detectives in a blue Suzuki minibus along dirt roads in the
green hills west of Osorno.

My thoughts soon turned from meditations on the malleability
of human nature to meditations on the Greek origins of some of
our fundamental concepts. Admirers of the Greeks sometimes
say that they were the only people in our Western tradition who
were able to name things for the first time. Everyone else has
been either carrying on a tradition or reacting against a tradition, or, in some cases, unconsciously using Greek concepts
without knowing their histories and without reflecting on their
metaphores de base. The Greeks had no tradition earlier than their
own; they started our tradition. Their words had no histories;
they started histories, coined metaphors.

The Greeks had three words with three different meanings,
where we have three words with the same meaning: *dynamis*,

kratos, energeia: force, factor, variable. When data are processed for use in inferential statistics, it does not matter whether 'educational level of parents', for example, is called a force, a factor, or a variable. Its 'impact' on something else, say, for example, 'scores of children on reading readiness tests', will be the same whichever of the three terms is used. If, on the other hand, we wish to translate a sentence including the English word 'force' into ancient Greek, it matters very much whether we are talking about *dynamis, kratos*, or *energeia*.

Energeia can be dismissed as not germane to the present purpose, but some people will protest that *energeia*, of all concepts, should always be foremost in the mind of the evaluator. They will point out that Aristotle defined human good as *psuches energeia ginetai kat areten* (force/activity/energy of the soul, acting according to excellence/virtue). PPH, the topic of the present evaluation, should be studied as a civilizing program, one that brings *energeia* under the control of *areten*.

Whatever may be the merits of the claim that *energeia* should on no account be dismissed, the present meditation is about *dynamis* and *kratos*.

Dynamis has several meanings. Its importance for a commentary on the set of events of which the errand of the blue Suzuki forms a part, as a thread forms a part of a net, is that it is the ancestor of the trio 'force, factor, variable', a trio which, in spite or perhaps because of its immense versatility, impedes our efforts to understand where the blue Suzuki is going and why it is going there. It was *dynamis*, in one of its senses, that was rendered as *vis* in Latin, when Greek science was absorbed by the Roman West. And *vis* ('force') became the central category of Sir Isaac Newton's *Principia*, a tale of *vis* from beginning to end. Newton shows the forces moving machines here on Earth (terrestrial mechanics) to be the same as the forces moving the heavens (celestial mechanics). Universal predictability, universal harmony. The great economists, such as Newton's admirer Adam Smith, thought of themselves and were thought of by others as discovering the analogous laws of social life.

When Emile Durkheim and others founded sociology, they needed no better argument to show the possibility of social science than the existence of economics: there is a social science, economics; therefore, social science is possible. In the history of the social sciences, economics was the original model for the others. When educational evaluators borrow the kits of tools of the social scientists, they sometimes do no more than adopt the techniques for measuring the impact of the force (factor or variable) on the phenomenon in question provided by the intellectual descendants of Durkheim's *Rules of Sociological Method* and John Stuart Mill's *Logic*, both conscious emulators of the economists and the physicists, children of the Latin *vis*, and grandchildren of the Greek *dynamis*.

Meanwhile, what has become of *kratos*? *Kratos* is the kind of force that people use against other people; it is the power of some over others. Thus the centurion says to Jesus: 'I say unto one Go, and he goeth; and to another Come, and he cometh, and to my servant Do this, and he doeth it.' We have traces of the Greek work *kratos* in demo*cracy* (the *kratos* of the *demos*) and in auto*cracy* (the *kratos* of *auto*, of one). If we bear in mind that *kratos* is a feature of reality no less basic than *dynamis* or *vis*, we shall use research methods suitable for understanding conflict, i.e. dialectic methods; we shall think of conflict as pervasive, and of harmony as exceptional.

The systems approach faces a dilemma: either (i) it ignores conflict, or (ii) it considers conflict.

Let us consider the first horn of the dilemma. Some examples will show that ignoring conflict is unacceptable, because one cannot get accurate information if one is unaware of conflict.

First example   When I ask peasants why they like PPH, they say: '*porque es educativo*' (because it is educational). They are likely to go on to prove their point by citing certain things they have learned, or to say generally that they have learned 'many things'. Why do they say this? They say it because they are engaged in conflict with some powerful officials, and with certain neighbours who do not participate. Their enemies say: 'PPH is political.' Their answer, their defence, is: 'No, it is not political; it is educational.' If I do not understand who is in conflict with whom, and with what rhetoric (i.e. with what meanings present in the culture) the conflict is waged, then I shall not know how to interpret the peasants' testimony.

Second example   It cannot escape the notice of an observer that Chile was the scene of a violent social struggle, and that the right wing won. In such an environment, a program which is affiliated with the only institution capable of above-ground opposition, the church, and which organizes the poor, is viewed with suspicion –

particularly by those persons within the government who are especially zealous right-wingers, and by those private individuals whose interests and values were especially threatened by the previous left-wing government. Some things are obvious, as Thoreau said, 'like a trout in the milk'. We are faced, then, with the problem of what to make of evidence that appears to contradict the obvious: the peasants say they get along just fine with the authorities; if they run into trouble, they often attribute it to a misunderstanding that could be corrected if the mayor would come to a meeting to see what they do; the sector-coordinators avoid reference to conflict when they talk, and Jorge Zuleta not only does not talk of conflict, but also *no acepta* (does not accept) complaints that the sector-coordinators sometimes make to him that they cannot do their work properly because of official opposition. The provincial education director, a government official, claims to have no animosity toward PPH, indeed to have no opinion at all about it, because he has no information whatever on the subject. (He is, of course, the same man who issued instructions that teachers are not to cooperate with PPH in any way.)

The reasonable conclusion to draw is that there are raw nerves that the people interviewed prefer not to touch. As Jorge Zuleta said in a candid moment: 'I cannot say that our work is dangerous, because if I do, my fear will be communicated to the sector-coordinators; through them, it will affect the volunteer coordinators, and the program will fall apart.'

Awareness of conflict is needed to interpret the data.

Third example If one asks volunteer base-coordinators to estimate how much attendance would increase over the long haul (not just at the first showing) if slides were used instead of pictures at the first meeting of each *unidad*, one gets large figures, of the order of 100 per cent, going as high as 400 per cent. If one asks sector-coordinators the same question, the estimates are moderate, around 30 per cent. If one asks CIDE staff-members the same question, one is given no quantitative estimates, but instead a series of reasons why pictures are preferable to slides. Although it would be foolhardy to attempt a definitive study of variations in estimated attendance projections among interviewees, the following must be relevant.

(i) When slides are used, battery-powered portable projectors are needed to go with them. The *ensemble* must arrive in working order, at the right place at the right time. The headaches – keeping track of where the projectors and slides are, tired batteries, lugging the projector from the *micro* stop to the meeting place, covering it with plastic to keep the rain off it, worrying about theft or loss, etc. – fall most heavily on the CIDE staff, heavily on sector-coordinators, and not at all on volunteer base-coordinators

(ii) There is a history of conflict over the issue (see Chapters 12 and 13). The history contains an element of injured pride: some volunteer coordinators felt they were not considered responsible enough to be trusted with expensive equipment.

Perhaps we can move on now to the second horn of the dilemma, considering it to be sufficiently shown that lack of awareness of conflict leads to inaccurate information, and proceeding to consider the consequences of awareness of conflict. It will be helpful to begin by outlining a conflict present in southern Chile in 1980.

A number of the peasants interviewed drew attention to their persistent struggle with cattle thieves. Walterio Huichapay, a sector-coordinator, for example, lost an ox; he and two friends spent several days tracking it, unarmed, aware that at any minute they might be attacked by an armed band or a larger unarmed band. The police were no help at all: they told Walterio to come back when he could prove who stole the ox and who had it. After three days, Walterio gave up the search. Even if he had found the missing animal, he would have had to sell it to pay the expenses of the search.

In general, the countryside can be described as a lawless frontier dotted by forts. The forts are the *haciendas* of the *huasos*, the prosperous landowners. The *huasos* possess barns, pickup trucks, guns, ammunition, dogs, influential friends, and enough personnel to mount a round-the-clock guard if necessary. Trying to protect a few animals outside the 'fortified' *haciendas* is not easy; some peasants have reached the point where they are selling their animals because they cannot defend them.

With the foregoing background, let us consider some examples of functions of culture in conflict. To be more precise, let us consider the functions of two words in the context of this particular conflict. The words *union* and *amistad*, so prominent in the speech of PPH participants, take on, when interpreted in context, the significance of responses to *desamparo* (unprotected-ness). They are traditional values; they are the suggestion of a strategy for survival, namely, binding together for mutual aid. However, they are only a suggestion, and a very tentative one because the strategy they foster is risky. The recent history of peasant organization has been disastrous. The more prudent course for any given peasant may well be to seek the protection of a *patrón* (boss) or to ally himself with a powerful *huaso* (if there is one in his locality), or at least to avoid acts (such as joining PPH) that may aggravate the *huasos*. *Union* is therefore a word that promises more than it can at present deliver; it is a project for the future; a hope. It will take many small successes (a dance, a first-aid kit, etc.), much growth of *confianza*, much testing of how much organizing the police and army will allow, before mutual aid can be an effective defence against heavy blows such as the theft of an animal. Meanwhile, *union* is delivering less tangible benefits: worksheets for the children, enjoyable meetings, *cariño*, some household hints and skills, someone to mourn at your funeral, etc.

Let me assert now something the reader was perhaps on the point of agreeing with anyway, even before reading my example of *amistad* and *union* in a context of *desamparo*. In general, cultures function in a context of conflict; consequently, the systems approach, like any other *problematique*, can be criticized from the point of view of what it does in a context of conflict.

The least that can be said in criticism of the systems *problematique* is that it is blind. By describing reality in its own terms, it fails to focus on other terms, such as *union*, *amistad*, *confianza*, that are *idées forces* that work, that do things, in the hills of southern Chile on a bright October day in 1980. One might make a second, somewhat stronger, charge: since the *problematique* defines itself as 'rational', 'scientific', and 'modern', by implication it denies the legitimacy, i.e. the 'rationality', of other terminologies – contributing in this way to the disintegration of the cultures that use the other terms. If you say to someone, 'Speak up and say what you mean clearly', and what you mean is, 'Speak in a terminology that is intelligible to me', then you are especially likely to succeed if you are armed and powerful, and your interlocuter is unarmed and powerless. Your success in making it a general practice to describe your terminology as 'rational' will be enhanced by your arms and your power.

A third, still stronger, charge is that the systems approach is an instrument of domination. In American educational literature, this harsh judgment is expressed by referring to 'management by objectives', and, indeed, it is the concept of 'objective', or rather the place of objectives in the systems frame of reference, that makes the accusation credible. Since the logic of the systems approach defines objective-setting as a phase of the decisionmaking cycle separate from research, implementation and evaluation, it lends itself to – although it would be too strong to say that it requires – thinking of objective-setting as a specialized function performed by an élite. The dominant group is the one that sets the objectives, even in the case where the goal is not the welfare of the élite, but the welfare of those whom the élite is trying to help. When the logic and the language of systems make it easy to rationalize domination, they can be classified among its instruments.

Focusing on conflict accomplishes a transformation of the systems approach. The approach cannot get off the ground without data, and, in most social research, it cannot get accurate data without considering conflict. When conflict is considered, the role of language in conflict shifts into focus and becomes visible. The world is turned inside out; it shows its seamy side. The systems approach steps down from its pedestal and joins the crowd, becoming one of many *problematiques* that act in the world as *idées forces*, losing its privileged status as impartial observer and analyser. The systems approach must be held responsible for what it does.

Thinking in terms of conflict also illuminates the language of PPH. Instructors vanish; coordinators appear. Instructional materials fade out; support materials fade in. Promoters are unheard of; everyone is talking about generators. The people who participate in PPH are not called the target population, nor subjects, nor Ss, nor beneficiaries, not even students or clients, but simply *las personas*, the people. All this happens because PPH is a deliberate effort to empower the poor. Therefore the PPH staff tries to use words that help the poor to think of themselves as active subjects.

When I shared my thoughts on these matters with the Reasonable Social Scientist, she took the view that my way of putting things was too circuitous and low-key. 'I am convinced by your premises,' she said, 'but you do not draw your conclusions in a consistent and straightforward way. The first time you quoted Aristotle, back in Chapter 7, you did it to show the ancient lineage of the view, which you consider correct and to be the view of contemporary informed opinion, that human action is largely under the guidance of *logoi* (i.e. of language). You should have cited Pavlov, who held that language is a second signalling system, one decisive for human action, superimposed on the conditioned response system. Later, in Chapter 15, where you described the work of Jorge Zuleta as cultural action, it became quite clear, although it was reasonably clear earlier, that the *logoi* in question are not the inventions of individuals, but languages of human groups. A word that is a theme in the life of a group, such as *cariño* or *unidad*, is an *idée force*; it is something that is at work in the world doing things. The struggle of a people to survive, to communicate in order to cooperate, to organize its life, is the struggle to strengthen its *logoi*, its culture. The systems approach is itself a set of *idées forces*; as such, it is a weapon used to strengthen a certain culture. By and large, it is a weapon used by the managerial élite to serve its own interests.

'When I think back on all those disgusting things I used to believe,' she went on, 'I see the systems approach as a form of genocide. When we planned and programmed *for* the poor instead of *with* the poor, setting objectives in our language instead of in theirs, we deprived them of the one thing they need in order to survive in a world of conflict – power, *kratos*. We described our work as "efficient" (a word notoriously associated with keeping costs down by keeping wages low), but we were not at all efficient in helping poor people attain what they need the most – the capacity to solve their own problems. We even talked about "educational services delivery systems", "health care delivery systems" and "target populations", as if the aim were to keep the poor as passive as possible while we took care of them. It makes me sick to think about it. The United Nations, in its own way,' she went on, 'through an elaborate ideology composed of welfare economics and management science, kept the poor powerless as effectively as the *huasos* who have no ideology at all, but simply a common fear that the socialists will take their land again, and a common interest in cheap, submissive labour. We said we did not believe in class struggle, but we participated in class struggle – on the side of the dominant class.'

The blue Suzuki stopped. The road was occupied by a herd of cattle, slowly moving toward us. As the herd reached us, and the cattle milled around the stationary vehicle on their way to some new pasture, I said to the Reasonable Social Scientist that although I sympathized with her sentiments, I thought she had overstated the case. 'In some respects, the systems approach really is efficient in the best sense of the word,' I said, 'and we do the poor a favour by initiating them into its use, just as, sometimes, we do them a favour by providing modern medicines. Furthermore, there is no exact correspondence between the adoption of a particular research or planning methodology, and doing what is in the best interests of the poor at a given time and place. "God is on the side of the poor', as the Baptist scholar Ron Sider (among others) has convincingly shown on the basis of biblical texts. But who else is? It is not necessarily true that those who say they are, are; nor that those who try to be, are; nor that those who profess to follow Freire, or Marx, or Jesus are doing what really helps, even if the people in question are sincere and conscientious. Presumably the poor are on the side of the poor, but only presumably – one poor person can betray another, intentionally or unintentionally. In short,' I said, as the cattle moved on down the road, leaving the atmosphere charged with unpleasant odours, 'the world is quite complex.'

It would be nice to report that the wicked wolf died and PPH lived happily ever after. Unfortunately, or perhaps fortunately from the point of view of the friends and relatives of the wolf who are not reconciled to his death and defamation, those who empower the peasantry do not live happily ever after. PPH faces another set of problems, as the following example will show, the problems of those who encourage the downtrodden to stand up for their rights, and then find it difficult to decide how to respond when they become embroiled in conflicts they did not anticipate.

In the PPH *centro* at the village of El Monte, an objective had been generated at the grassroots level: to get a *posta*, a clinic. *Las personas* put two premises together: (i) they were frequently ill and injured; (ii) there was a community building in the vicinity that their volunteer labour had built to serve as a clinic, but it was not being used as a clinic. The community clinic building had been absorbed by the local school, and I was told (but did not verify) that the schoolteacher used it as a pen for his pigs.

The members of the *centro* agitated for the return of the clinic to the community.

The schoolteacher fought back. He entered the clinic on the school's inventory so that it would be listed officially as government property. He called a meeting of the PTA, and obtained from it a resolution approving the transfer of the clinic building to the school – according to the *centro* members, he had cancelled an earlier PTA meeting he had called when he learned that the PPH members were coming, and later held a rump session with a group he could intimidate. (In all of this, I do not know the schoolteacher's side of the story.)

When the members of the *centro* met with the schoolteacher to protest his actions, he told them they were a clandestine group, subject to arrest for holding illegal meetings. He succeeded in intimidating them, for they sent a representative scurrying to FREDER headquarters to obtain a document that would attest their organization's right to exist and hold meetings. The representative was also worried that when the two-year PPH programme ended, the brethren at El Monte would be left to battle the schoolteacher with no outside support. Father Winfredo promised that El Monte would not be abandoned, and he promised a piece of paper authorizing the PPH centre to call itself an affiliate of FREDER.

A few days later, the teenage daughter of the president of the *centro* accused the schoolteacher of raping her. The *centro* composed a declaration, to be read on The Voice of the Coast, calling for the teacher's dismissal, and affirming that several parents had protested the sexual abuse of their daughters by the teacher. The parents of the victim threatened to kill the teacher. Jorge Zuleta persuaded them to complain to the police instead.

The police refused to investigate the charge until they had a medical certificate showing that the girl was in fact raped by somebody. Since the parents could not afford a private doctor, obtaining a certificate meant standing in line for an appointment at the public hospital, and then another *micro* ride to Osorno on the day of the appointment. When they at last had the certificate in hand, and delivered it to the police, the police asked for fuel money. The police would bring the accused in for questioning if the parents would pay for the petrol. The parents had no money . . . they passed the hat at the PPH office. When they returned to the police station with the petrol money, the police told them they could not make the arrest because there was no vehicle available – all their vehicles were tied up on other missions.

And so it came to pass that the blue Suzuki minibus threaded its way through the green hills carrying two short detectives wearing dark glasses. The detectives arrested the schoolteacher and took him to jail. There was joy in El Monte – *la union hace la fuerza*.

A complicated investigation followed: the schoolteacher accused someone else of having done it, several suspects were interrogated, one confessed, the confession appeared to be false, the victim's account appeared to be false, more extra-legal self-help was threatened ... but enough of the story has been told to make the moral clear: when the initiatives come from the grassroots, the organization may find itself embroiled in conflicts for which it is not prepared.

Jorge Zuleta tried to minimize the involvement of the PPH office in the *centro*'s battle with the schoolteacher. The *centro*'s resolution was not read on The Voice of the Coast. One of Jorge's reasons for caution was that he did not know whether the people who were asking him for help were telling the truth – at the time of writing, it appears that the charge that the schoolteacher raped the girl is false.

The problem posed by the battle of El Monte is as follows. Given: human beings as they are. Given: a programme that deliberately encourages its members to shake off apathy and intimidation, to act and to help one another to act. To determine: under what circumstances and to what extent should the program support its members?

NOTES AND REFERENCES

For a discussion of *dynamis* and *vis*, and the role of the latter in physics, see Max Jammer, *Concepts of Force* (Cambridge: Harvard University Press, 1957). For a discussion of the consequences for human self-understanding of the extension of the metaphor of *vis* used by Galileo and Newton, see the first part of Edmund Husserl, *Die Krisis der Europaischen Wissenschaften* (Hamburg: Meiner, 1977). Husserl argues that the dominance of Galilean metaphors has caused a dangerous split between the natural sciences and the humanities, and confusion in the social sciences. An essay stressing some connections between physics and the early history of the social sciences is Louis Dumont, *Homo Aequalis*,

Genese et Epanouissement de l'Ideologie Economique (Paris: Gallimard, 1977). Similar points are made by H. Richards in 'Adam Smith, Milton Friedman y la Etica Cristiana', *Mensaje*, vol. 28 (1979) p. 214.

John Stuart Mill wrote: The Social Science, therefore (which, by a convenient barbarism, has been termed Sociology), is a deductive science; not, indeed, after the model of geometry, but after that of the higher physical sciences.... A science is thus constructed, which has received the name of Political Economy' J. S. Mill, *A System of Logic* (London: Parker, 1846, 2nd edn) vol. II, pp. 567–76). Durkheim's method is somewhat different, but his search for laws expressing relationships among 'forces that determine the individual' shows that *vis* is, for Durkheim too, the governing metaphor. See E. Durkheim, *Les Regles de la Methode Sociologique* (Paris: F. Alcan, 1895), and the preface to *Le Suicide* (Paris: F. Alcan, 1897).

For a parallel discussion of methodological issues in hermeneutic (interpretative) sociology, see Anthony Giddens, *New Rules of Sociological Method* (London: Hutchinson, 1976).

For that part of the history of *vis* which spans the gap between Mill's *Logic* and contemporary statistical methods in psychology and educational research, by way of Galton, the founder of social statistics, see David Hamilton's essay in W. B. Dockrell and David Hamilton (eds), *Rethinking Educational Research* (Toronto: Hodder & Stoughton, 1980).

For a sample of the immense literature seeking to re-establish recognition of the pervasiveness of *kratos* in social research, see Jurgen Habermas, *Erkenntnis und Interesse* (Frankfurt: Suhrkamp, 1977); Orlando Fals Borda, 'El Problema de como Investigar la Realidad para Transformarla', in the Proceedings of the World Congress on Social Science Methods, held at Cartagena, Colombia, in 1977, published as *Critica y Politica en Ciencias Sociales* (Bogota: Editorial Punto de Lanza, 1978); J. W. Freiberg (ed.), *Critical Sociology* (New York: Irvington, 1979).

With respect to the charge that the systems approach dominates by imposing a language, cf. the discussion of 'capital symbolique' in Pierre Bourdieu *Le Sens Pratique* (Paris: Minuit, 1980) pp. 209–31.

For a discussion of dialectics and hermeneutics in contemporary social science, see Gerard Radnitzky, *Contemporary Schools of Metascience* (Göteborg, Sweden: Akademiforlaget, 1968).

17 The Radio Station's Birthday Party

> There are many eyes watching us. They are setting traps for us.
>
> An announcer of The Voice of the Coast whose name had best not be mentioned.

One must live for some considerable time in Osorno to begin to decipher the hermeneutics of conflict. Some people never do. Most people, indeed, in Osorno and elsewhere, go through life without ever learning to distinguish hermeneutics from strawberries. For their benefit, it should be explained at the outset that 'hermeneutics' refers to the interpretation of meanings, while 'strawberries' refers to a small, juicy, red, edible fruit. Hence 'the hermeneutics of conflict' refers to interpreting meanings in a context of conflict.

For example, if a newcomer to Osorno were to take a *colectivo* (a taxi that travels on a fixed route and accepts and discharges passengers as if it were a bus) from the railway station to the upper residential district, driven by a thin taxi driver with indigenous features who has the car radio tuned to The Voice of the Coast, but who, as the *colectivo* approaches the corner beside the Bank of Osorno, where an elegant and portly gentleman is waiting, switches the dial to Radio SAGO (the radio of the Society of Agriculture of Osorno), and stays tuned to Radio SAGO for the duration of the elegant gentleman's ride, switching back to The Voice of the Coast after the gentleman gets out of the car, the newcomer would probably think nothing of it.

On the other hand, anyone who has lived in Osorno long enough to decipher the hermeneutics of conflict knows that even the birthdays of the radio stations are very meaningful events,

214

occasions of complex and subtle political infighting. There are just the two radio stations in Osorno: Radio SAGO, of the *huasos*, the landowners, and The Voice of the Coast, the station of the *campesinos*. They celebrate their respective birthdays a week apart, in the first and second weeks of October, and on the evening of the birthday celebration, each fills the street in front of its studios with crowds of supporters, while local celebrities give speeches and local entertainers entertain from a balcony special-ly constructed for the occasion, a sort of bandstand to which one gains entrance by going up stairs to the second story of the studio, passing from the second story to the balcony above the crowd.

The Voice of the Coast celebrated its birthday on 15 October 1980, a week after a similar event sponsored by Radio SAGO, which had featured rock music, free refreshments, and honking of the horns of the autos of the gilded youth of Osorno.

The birthday celebration of The Voice of the Coast began in the morning with holy mass celebrated at the spacious (and often, as on this occasion, unfilled) cathedral on the town square. Father Winfredo was among those who were absent. The celebrant was the bishop himself, a tall man with a long grey beard reaching nearly to his waist. He wore under the sac-ramental robe, donned for the duration of the mass, his custom-ary attire – an old-fashioned, brown, Franciscan robe and a pair of leather sandals. He is an octogenarian who, in the summer, still drives his late-model Plymouth at great speed along the dusty roads of his diocese. The bishop comes from an aristocratic family. His ancestors held land grants from the king of Spain, but at the moment, his branch of the aristocracy has been pushed aside by the ruling military junta.

The bishop's homily was about names. We are all, he said – assuming, no doubt correctly, that his audience consisted entire-ly of Roman Catholics – named after saints. We should not consider our names as merely labels to distinguish us from each other, but as creating a special relationship with the saint whose name we bear, as a sort of dedication of our lives to the saint and the ideals manifested in the saint's life.

Practitioners of the hermeneutics of conflict will sense that, in the bishop's choice of that particular subject for that particular occasion, there is more than is conveyed by the light waves that fall on the eye or the sound waves that fall on the ear. Although I do not always understand everything, I can provide certain essential background information.

When PPH came to Osorno, it also came to The Voice of the Coast. Although overall headquarters for PPH are at CIDE in Santiago, FREDER, the Osorno charitable foundation headed by Father Winfredo, was the local sponsor of PPH, and also the operator of the radio station, The Voice of the Coast. The PPH style and ideology were resisted by the station manager, who resigned. Father Winfredo chose as his successor Celedino Fierro, a person who, until the time when he became the manager of the radio station, was Jorge Zuleta's administrative assistant at the PPH office. Thus authority to run the radio station was conferred upon a member of the PPH team. The former manager because the Cassandra of the program and of the station, although he was not alone, for many people with influence in the church and the government viewed the spirit of PPH with alarm. The bishop, in whom is vested (as we have not yet had occasion to mention) ultimate legal authority over FREDER and The Voice of the Coast, became the man in the middle, pulled right by the Cassandras and left by the Winfredos.

To return to the homily at the station's birthday mass, the bishop went on to give thanks that a charitable contribution had provided the diocese with a radio station, pointing out that it had been dedicated to Saint Clair, as we are dedicated to the saint whose name we bear, be it Juan, Monica or Pedro. Since the station belongs to Clair, it has a high spiritual calling, independent of the worldly influences which seek to deflect it to the right or to the left of the course charted according to the ideals that inspired its founding.

During the same month, a different point of view had become symbolized in a new 80-metre-high steel transmitting tower. Winfredo and the station staff had sold 'share certificates' to the peasants, at the rate of 25 pesos per centimetre, entitling the bearer to consider himself the 'owner' of a fraction of the tower, in a successful fund-raising campaign that financed the tower's construction, and dramatically strengthened the concept that the station belongs to the peasants.

The next big event of the birthday celebration, after the morning mass, was the reception for local dignitaries in the afternoon, although, as might be expected, The Voice of the

Coast broadcast congratulatory messages to itself all day long. This year, something unexpected happened; the new military governor of Osorno sent congratulations to be read on the air. It had also been noticed that at a patriotic celebration, the new governor had deliberately bypassed the SAGO microphones to answer the questions of a Voice of the Coast reporter. The meaning of the governor's gesture remained unclear.

The reception was at the rambling pink stucco house on Los Carrera Street, and it featured soda pop, table wine, avocado hors d'ouevres and potato chips. For the most part, the radio staff and the PPH staff kept each other company, in the absence of most of the distinguished citizens, who had been invited but who did not come. The new governor saved the reception, not by coming himself, but by sending a police captain as his representative. The captain mingled somewhat uneasily with PPH sector-coordinators, some of whom had been arrested not long ago. I conversed with a pious accountant, who was one of the few solid citizens present; whatever I said, he steered the conversation back to the Osorno Chamber Music Society, of which he was a leading member. Observing the reception was like trying to see a pattern in tea leaves; I tried to discern from the presences and absences, from who was talking to whom and about what, whether Winfredo's support was growing or dwindling, who was on whose side, who was standing firm and who was giving in to pressure – whether or not a crackdown on PPH was in the offing.

I realized that I was in water over my head. My research had got to the point where I saw that the question of how long PPH would be tolerated depended on complex patterns of local politics, complexly intertwined with national and international politics. I could decipher the hermeneutics of conflict up to a point, but I soon lost track of the significance of words and gestures, and lost all ability to discern the motives of the actors.

I turned my thoughts to a smaller issue, that I thought I could cope with – reluctantly, and making a promise to myself not to abandon permanently attempts to understand and deal with politics. Indeed, one might well say that in order to evaluate cultural action programs, the first questions should concern the larger political situation and the program's role in it. Very true. But there are situations where such questions are hard to answer, and where the answers cannot be published. The smaller issue to which I turned, was how best to simplify illuminative evaluation. I remembered the question of a nun in Toronto: 'Our order has a school in Bolivia that requires evaluation. How can we evaluate it simply and cheaply?'

Almost any piece of research is a very rough approximation to some sort of ideal of what research should be. How one approximates, what one considers essential, and what one lets go by the board as desirable but dispensable, depends to a large extent on what ideal one had in the first place, before one started stripping down the principles of methodology because there is no money, and the report was due yesterday. The question then arises: 'what would a stripped down illuminative evaluation of cultural action include?' I decided to propose an answer to this question, and to offer an example. The answer is: (i) some interviews, (ii) some concrete examples, (iii) some triangulation. The example, which Horacio Walker and I later developed, and which is presented below, was to be an evaluation of the radio station – more specifically, of the influence of PPH on the radio station.

THE SHORT EVALUATION: INTERVIEWS

Interviews provide a picture of the situation, in the words of its principal actors. They also clarify what the issues are. Here is one of Horacio's interviews with a Voice of the Coast staff-member.

Ernesto Barra began to work at The Voice of the Coast in May 1968, three months before the station went on the air for the first time. His first work consisted of travelling through the country-side, organizing groups that study by radio school by listening to broadcast lessons. For two years now (up to 1980), he has been the script-writer and master of ceremonies for the program 'FREDER Reports'. He summarizes the history of the radio station as follows.

'I would distinguish three stages in the history of the station. The first, since its creation in 1968 until 1971, was characterized by great vitality and enthusiasm. Perhaps it was because we were starting something new. Also, we were encouraged by the fact that we were providing support for the peasantry, for people overwhelmed by mud and poverty.

'We worked through radio schools at two levels: the community and the family. The programs were mainly the equivalent of formal schooling, covering literacy, Spanish and mathematics, plus other subjects, such as health.'

'The second stage, 1971–3 was, as in the whole country, eminently political. There was much disorientation among the peasantry. At first, we continued the radio schools, while carrying out a cooperative program with the Ministry of Education, which sent teachers and provided materials for the courses. In 1973, we stopped doing formal schooling that covered the subjects I just mentioned. We began to do training courses based on agricultural problems.' [FREDER has provided courses for peasants such as beekeeping, pruning, rabbit-raising, etc.]

'The third stage began in 1973. I would define it as one of great disorientation for the station. We have been changing direction, according to the views of the various managers we have had. We burned our bridges with the country people. The radio station became urban. We had an élitist idea of what radio should be. We were supposed to aim at pure classical music and academic language. To play on the air a dialogue with a peasant was thought to expose the radio to ridicule. I was reprimanded once because on "FREDER Reports", some words were broadcast pronounced with the accent of the peasants. They told me it was impossible for things like that to go out on the air.

'PPH has been a very important means for uniting, for establishing again this bridge with the people that had been burned. Now you can see how the country people drop into the studios to see us when they are in town. [Note: the passerby observes that there is almost always a group of peasants in the doorway of the studios.] You can see the change in the messages we broadcast on our message service, which is a very good indicator for measuring our reception in the countryside. The sector-coordinators of PPH have been crucial for the change at the radio station. They bring us closer to reality with the sensibility of the country-person. Today we have, for example, PPH Radio Theatre. As script-writers, the coordinators have become the best journalists; they are from the country themselves, and know their own *milieu*. The station now has a file of 72 cassettes of *teatros* composed and performed mainly by the sector-coordinators. Since March 1980, i.e. since about half-way through PPH, "FREDER Reports" has been a programme closely linked to the peasantry. The change came about fundamentally because PPH needed a way to send out information about meetings; it was made possible through the link with the country provided by the sector-coordinators. When the change in "FREDER Reports" first happened, there was a tendency to depend too much on PPH. Today, we try to involve other activities in the countryside as well. The majority of letters that come to us are from PPH participants, although in their letters they speak also of other things. The sector-coordinators do the interviews in the country, and I use their tapes to put the program together here in the studio. Sometimes I myself go to the countryside.'

Horacio and I had planned to study attitude change at The Voice of the Coast as a result of its involvement with PPH, by the method of negotiation of accounts. That is to say, we planned to interview separately the principal actors in the drama, and then to work with two or more of them at a time in order to reduce the discrepancies among their several accounts. The method is called 'negotiation' because the process of agreeing on a common version of the story is similar to bargaining. However, as it turned out, the accounts provided by the five people we interviewed separately were not substantially inconsistent with each other, so there were no discrepancies to reduce by negotiation.

THE SHORT EVALUATION: CONCRETE EXAMPLES

Even if their number is small, concrete examples of typical phenomena have high information value. They give meaning to abstract words used in reports based on interviews. They show the process or mechanism by which something works, and are therefore rich in implications concerning what is needed, what went wrong, what can be expected in the future, and how likely it is that results are achieved.

In our short evaluation, the interviews gave us only one main point to illuminate with concrete examples – the way The Voice of the Coast has changed by becoming a channel through which peasants communicate with each other. We selected, as examples, a script from 'FREDER Reports' and a taped PPH Radio Theatre.

Here is the first page of a script selected at random from the archives of the program 'FREDER Reports'.

Program: FREDER Reports
Radio: The Voice of the Coast
Time: 1.00 pm to 1.30 pm
Thursday, 6 November 1980
Script Number: 167/80

Announcer 1: Friends in the country and friends in the city, may you all have a very good afternoon. A great big special hello to everybody who has a birthday today and of course for all those whose Saint's Day it is, and since today all the Leonards are celebrating their Saint's Day, for everyone who bears the name of Leonard, many happy returns of the day.

Engineer: Musical backdrop for 4 seconds.

Announcer 2: We have a message for the coordinators of Los Hualles, that they have a retreat for evaluation on the 7th and 8th at the community building in Los Hualles, to which they are earnestly begged to go, and to be on time; and for the coordinators of Pucoihue: they should wait on the road for the vehicle that will take them to the meeting.

We expect that you who are a participant in the Parents and Children Program will do us the favour of telling the coordinators about this message, given to us by Maria Catriyao, PPH sector-coordinator. We believe that you will keep faith with your coordinator and will all be present, yes all the volunteer base-coordinators will be present the 7th and 8th of November.

Engineer: Cassettes, Theme 4, side A, PPH.

Announcer 1: That was nothing less than our own well-known group 'The Ploughboys', singing one of their own songs about the program they love so much, the Parents and Children Program.

Announcer 2: But, what do you say to reading something from our mailbag? No doubt you are asking: 'Who might be the person writing us a letter?' Well let's stop beating around the bush and get to the point immediately. The author is our good friend Viviana Lemuy. Mrs Lemuy is very active as always, and now let's see in the letter what she tells us.

Announcer 1: Dear 'FREDER Reports': The motive for writing you is to promote something about our Regional Festival of

Country Music, organized by our radio station, The Voice of the Coast. There is something about it very important to make known: the singing there will be in different categories, the songs that will be sung by our country brothers and sisters on the day of the festival, but the crafts fair is also a part of the festival, the crafts that are part of country folklore, part of our know-how, recording with our own hands our culture and our knowledge.

Announcer 2: We want to make a special call to all the participants in the different *centros* of PPH, for them to prepare their exhibits, which they have been working on during the whole year.

Here ends our sample text from 'FREDER Reports'. The following is a sample from PPH Radio Theatre. We set out here the first part of the first page and the last part of the last page of an eight-page script.

The Case of a Person Who Becomes Ill

Music

Narrator: Here we are going to present the case of what happens in a family when they have someone who is sick out in the countryside.

Girl: Ay! Ay! Mummy! I can't stand this headache anymore!

Jacinta: What's the matter my little girl? Ay! Rupertino! The girl is sick. She has a high fever.

Rupertino: And how are we going to carry her at this hour to the hospital? [Here we omit more than 7 pages.]

Music

Narrator: Back at home, she meets her husband and explains to him to the following.

Rupertino: How did it go, dear?

Jacinta: So-so, they got around to seeing us at two in the afternoon, and I had a grumpy doctor, and he gave me four aspirins and told me it was nothing serious, and he told me to keep the girl in bed for a week.

Rupertino: Better I buy the aspirins, and we don't carry the girl to the hospital, it makes her sicker.

Jacinta: Yes, and there they asked me for my social security papers, and they wouldn't stamp my prescription [i.e. stamp it to authorize her to obtain free medicine], they told me I had to pay 160 pesos [$4.00], I told them I didn't have the money.

Rupertino: My God! If we don't get our papers in order, the children are going to die on us.

Jacinta: That's the way it's going to be.

Rupertino: And how are we going to get our papers in order [i.e. catch up on the payments] if there is no work?

Jacinta: I don't know what we are going to do.

Music

Narrator: And so as in this case, as it happened to this family, it happens to many in the country.

THE SHORT EVALUATION: TRIANGULATION

Triangulation provides a check of the veracity of the interview data, and a rough answer to the question 'how much?'. (In the latter connection, it may help to recall that we estimate that 20 to 30 thousand people listen to the station on any given day.)

If our image of the influence of PPH on the radio station is accurate, there should be an observable increase in the amount of horizontal (i.e. peasant to peasant) as opposed to vertical (i.e. dominant culture to peasant) communication. The Bolivian communications specialist Luis Ramiro Beltran defines 'horizontal' communication as follows: 'Horizontal communication is a process of democractic social interaction, based on the exchange of symbols, through which human beings voluntarily share experiences in conditions of freedom and equality of access, dialogue, and participation.' On the basis of Beltran's concept, we defined four levels of horizontality.

Level One: Horizontal – Although perhaps no program is perfectly horizontal, we put three Voice of the Coast programs in this category: the Messages program that reads on the air messages delivered to the station by listeners; PPH Radio Theatre; 'FREDER Reports' in the period subsequent to the changes discussed above.

Level Two: Quasi-horizontal – This category includes only one program, 'Children's World' (described in Chapter 2). Prior to PPH, it featured only city children; now it often includes country children.

Level Three: Occasional Horizontality – These are mainly programs run, and to some extent improvised, by disc jockeys who, since PPH started, have increasingly incorporated into their programs spur of the moment chats with peasants who happen to drop into the studio, or the reading of letters from listeners, sometimes including poems and tapes of singing.

Level Four: Not Horizontal – These are programs that originate in Santiago, or taped special features brought in 'canned' from outside the region, as well as musical programs run by disc jockeys who have not yet caught the spirit of PPH to any considerable degree.

The basic weekday programming schedule of The Voice of the Coast did not change during 1979–80, the period of the PPH program, except for the addition of a daily (sometimes twice daily) PPH Radio Theatre. For this reason, we can produce an estimate of how much time is spent on programs at each of our levels, by analysing the programs broadcast on a single representative day. Below, we show the 1980 weekday Voice of the Coast broadcasting schedule, indicating beside the name of each program its level of horizontality according to the criteria stated above. Where there was a change during the 1979–80 period, we give two numbers, one indicating the prior level of horizontality, the other the post-PPH level.

Voice of the Coast programming, weekday schedule, 1980

Time	Program	Level of horizontality
7 am	Thought for the Day (canned)	4
8.15	Folk Music	4
8.30	Messages	1
9	A Bit of Everything	4 – 3
9.30	Take Care of your Health (canned)	4
10	PPH Radio Theatre	Did not exist – 1
10.30	This Little World Called Home	4 – 3
12.30 pm	Messages	1
12.45	Ninety-on-your-dial News	3
1	FREDER Reports	3 – 1

Time	Program	Level of horizontality
1.30	National and International News	4
2.15	Music for After Lunch	4
2.30	Radio School Course	4
3	Studio 80	4 – 3
3.30	Messages	1
3.35	Studio 80 (continued)	4 – 3
5.30	Children's World	3 – 2
6	Home Again	4 – 3
6.30	Messages	1
7	Ploughing	4
7.30	The Voice of the Communities	4
8	Ninety-on-your-dial News	3
8.15	Looking at Sports	4
8.30	Music and Words	4
9	Messages	1
9.05	The Point of the Plough	4
9.15	The Country People and the Night	4 – 3
10.30	We Keep you Company	4
10.55	God comes to Man (canned)	4
11	Sign Off	

It should be mentioned that Celedino Fierro and others on the staff have a number of interesting intentions they have not yet implemented. They include making the 7.30 pm program 'The Voice of the Communities', a participatory program recorded in the countryside; using local artists preparing for the annual Country Music Festival as the source of folk music for broadcast; and creating a program by and for the indigenous population in the Mapuche language.

The birthday celebration ended in the evening, when thousands of *campesinos* gathered in the street in front of the studios of The Voice of the Coast. They filled the street and overflowed into the surrounding streets. The parade of entertainers featured 'The Ploughboys' and Ponciano Rumian with his 'Young People of the Land'. The parade of speeches by local celebrities featured Uncle José of 'Childrens World', and PPH sector-coordinators. Everybody greeted everybody else with *cariño*. (Father Patricio Cariola of CIDE in Santiago once astutely commented that PPH is based on *cariño* because *cariño* is what the peasants have to give.) The peasants stood there for several hours with no refreshments, duly applauding every performer and every speaker, loyally supporting with the presence of their bodies the institution that supports them. At the end, after the last chord and the last *cariño*, when the crowd dispersed, a peasant-woman, a volunteer base-coordinator from Huampatué said to me: 'Today was a great victory for the *campesinos*. Our crowd was bigger than Radio SAGO's, and better behaved.'

18   Projections

When I left Chile at the end of November 1980, the Reasonable Social Scientist was still there, wandering somewhere in the countryside, doing I know not what. It seemed unlikely to me that she would stay there until Christmas. She would want to be with her relatives in Kirchheim unter Teck for the holidays, and then would return to New York, unless she had been fired from her job because her superiors had ceased to believe her excuses for remaining away from the office.

On a morning in June 1981, it happened, quite by accident, as a result of one of those unusual situations that sometimes occur in life, that I was in New York City. I thought to myself: 'Perhaps I could have lunch with the Reasonable Social Scientist, and talk about evaluation.' As soon as the idea occurred to me, I telephoned her. I was pleasantly surprised to find that she was in, back at her old job as I had supposed she would be. She was eager to talk to me; I sensed that she wanted my advice concerning an important matter. When I invited her to lunch she said: 'Would you like to go for a hamburger or to some place bourgeois?'

Since I believe that intellectuals who intend to serve the people should be willing to share the suffering of the people, I regarded her suggestion as an appeal to my conscience, and there ensued a brief debate between my conscience and my stomach, in which, I am sorry to say, my conscience did not win a clear-cut victory. My stomach let it be known that it would tolerate Horn and Hardart, the automat, and in a moment I heard myself suggesting Horn and Hardart to the RSS. I had to say something to her; I could not just stand there holding the receiver, since, after all, I had called her. The RSS agreed, and my conscience, as consciences often do, allowed itself to be overruled in practice, without conceding the principle.

I was delighted to see her when we met on 38th Street in front of a Horn and Hardart. We selected a table in a back corner. If one wishes to have a conversation at Horn and Hardart, one must choose one's table carefully, and tip the waiter. I decided to have a light lunch of lemon meringue pie and black coffee; as it turned out, I ate only half my piece of pie, since I spent most of my time talking, in response to the Reasonable Social Scientist's urgent questions.

'How did the peasants and the CIDE staff respond to your evaluation?' she asked.

'Actually, it wasn't my evaluation. It was our evaluation since they helped me do it,' I said, deftly avoiding a direct answer to her question. 'We turned the evaluation into a series of conversations. In the end we reached consensus on the conclusions.'

The RSS was not satisfied by my evasion. I could tell she was not satisfied, because she stared gravely at the wall while she stirred her macaroni cheese with a fork. 'The truth is,' she said, 'that you are a hypocrite. Because,' she went on, 'you pretend to facilitate an evaluation which the program participants themselves conduct, while in fact participation is slight, and the research is under the control of an outside evaluator.'

I asked myself: 'What would Jean-Paul Sartre do in a situation like this?' He would, I thought, offer a broad philosophical analysis, from which it would follow, as a conclusion, that his personal conduct had not been entirely despicable.

'One might,' I said, 'divide criteria for the evaluation of evaluations into three categories, as follows. It may be difficult for a study to rank high in all three categories at once.

(i) Democratic control – the extent to which the participants strengthen themselves and their organizations by conducting the research.

(ii) Method – the extent to which the research is done in a way that ascertains important truths about the programme.

(iii) Credibility – the confidence of outsiders (or insiders) who use the report in the preparers of the report.

'However one judges the level of democratic control of the present study, surely most readers will find the level of peasant control higher than average, as studies go. There is, moreover, a connection between democratic control and method. A systems or input–output method does not need peasant participation – it needs only to measure the results. The peasants can learn how to measure results, and achieving a higher level of democratic control would be a good reason for teaching them how. However, it is possible to measure results without them. It would also be possible for a group of peasants to learn output-measuring skills, and then to decline to share their skills – thus becoming intellectually a *comprador* or *kulak* class.

'An illuminative method, on the other hand, requires the understanding of the process through conversations conducted in the participants' terminology. The participant is an expert whose knowledge is indispensable to learning the truth about the process – which is, in turn, indispensable for making projections concerning what, if anything, in the program might be useful elsewhere.

'Consequently, although the present study is not a paradigm of an ideal level of democratic control, the type of method employed requires some democratic control (since the peasant controls his own expertise concerning the process, and is unlikely to cooperate unless his dignity is respected), and lends itself to more. Further, the use of triangulation lends itself to combining democratic control with credibility.'

'Excuse me,' said the RSS. She stood up and walked across the room to a bank of vending machines. She inserted fifty cents in a slot, and received an apple. Then she walked back to our table, sat down, and silently munched the apple.

Her silence appeared to be an unwillingness to commit herself. She did not want to tell me whether or not she had been convinced by what I had said.

'We reached conclusions of considerable importance,' I went on, attempting to convince her of the merit of the study. 'From the point of view of participation, it is significant that the conclusions are not only judgments made by the evaluator. They are the result of a process in which everyone was involved; this increases the likelihood that the conclusions will be successfully implemented, since their implementation will not be viewed as an imposition from outside.'

'What conclusions did you reach?' she asked.

'The first major conclusion,' I said, 'was that PPH failed to plan from the very beginning for the continuity of the organizing effort that it was destined to become. The most embarrassing question to ask about PPH is: "What happens next?"'

'It is hardly surprising,' said the RSS, 'that the staff would concur in the conclusion that the organizing effort should continue indefinitely. After all, everyone would like permanent employment. You would have a more convincing case if the staff-members concurred in a devastating self-criticism and submitted their resignations.

'That is one way to look at the evaluation,' I said. 'A more sympathetic perspective would highlight the superior capacity of the illuminative approach to penetrate and grasp the full significance of the question "What happens next?" The prisoner of the systems problematic will not plumb the depths of the devastation wrought by this question. He will ask whether the objectives were or were not achieved, but he will not illuminate the hermeneutical and dialectical realities. Hermes,' I said eloquently, 'the deity who lent his name to hermeneutics, would show him, if he would look, that the message transmitted by PPH is *confianza*, *union*, *cariño*, while the message transmitted by shutting down the program after two years is: "We were lying all the time we were talking to you about trust, solidarity, and affection. Actually, it was just a job, and when the funds to pay us ran out, we quit." If we focus our vision on who is in conflict with whom, about what, in the countryside of southern Chile, then we shall see an ephemeral organizing effort. The interests of the peasants would have been served better by no help from outside at all than by help that encourages them to take risks and then abandons them.

'The plan that was funded,' I continued, 'was a course on pre-school education in 50 communities for two years. That was long enough to finish all the lessons. Then the course was to end, and a similar course in 50 other localities, also in the Osorno region, was to begin. Perhaps nobody realized at the beginning of 1979 that by the end of 1980, a pre-school education program would have organized 44 communities. Now, with the benefit of hindsight, we can say that with the kind of *capacitacion* that was done, with the kind of people who were needed to be sector-coordinators (i.e. people with organizing experience), with the kind of motivation that was needed and achieved to inspire volunteers to persist in spite of difficulties, and with the kinds of analyses peasants are likely to make of their problems, the result of any program like PPH will be that, at the grassroots level, people will say, as José Felipe Naguil said (Chapter 2): "May this not be the enthusiasm of a day or a couple of months, but let us continue from here on. Let this be the beginning of our organization, the beginning of our union as people and as neighbours, in order to show our children that we are people."

'PPH ought to be a stage in the development of a permanent institution. It was a mistake to set up PPH *centros*. They should have been FREDER centres, because FREDER, in principle, goes on forever, while PPH, in principle, goes on for 24 months. In Osorno and in the countryside, the entire second year of PPH was marked by depression and discouragement, by protests and silent frustration, by makeshift plans to prolong the project – as PPH waited like a prisoner on death row, fearing not only that there was no future, but fearing that because there was no future, nothing done in the present would have any lasting significance.

'A solution to the problem posed by the inherent instability of human commitments is provided by the sacraments of the church, since the sacraments, such as baptism, require eternal commitments. Sister Thelma Arrogabe, the Argentine nun who observed PPH in Osorno for a month (see Chapter 11), drew this conclusion. She proposes to generate in Argentina a version of PPH closely linked to the church, and explicitly devoted to the service of what she calls "the whole person", by which she means the concrete human person conceived and perceived as a being with transcendental needs. Father Gerry, the director of PPH, agrees with Sister Thelma that PPH has not emphasized religion enough. "The poor people are believers," he says. "We have not responded to or taken into account the importance of religion in the culture of the poor."

'Sister Thelma also proposed employing fewer paid coordinators and using more vehicles. She observed that sector-coordinators lose so much time tramping down muddy roads and waiting for *micros* that two could do the work of ten if each sector-coordinator had a jeep. Father Gerry is aware of the facts noticed by Sister Thelma, but he thinks that more benefits are achieved at the same cost by giving more people the experience of being sector-coordinators.'

'Costs?' exclaimed the RSS. 'Benefits? You are talking like a bureaucrat. In fact,' she went on, 'your study would be much improved by cutting the first five or ten chapters. The cost-effectiveness study and the theoretical discussion of cost-effectiveness are unnecessary. Practitioners of *educacion popular* are unanimous in denying that a cost-effectiveness approach is suitable for evaluating their work, and on a theoretical level, Rolland Paulston and others have already drawn attention to a growing trend to move evaluation away from the cost-effectiveness paradigm.'[1]

I reminded her that she herself had called for a cost-effectiveness study. 'You should have disregarded my advice,' she said. 'After all, you invented me in order to have someone to argue with. If you were going to invent me at all, you should have given me better arguments.'

'Actually,' I replied, 'your arguments are rather cogent and quite necessary. There is an important truth in the cost-effectiveness paradigm that needs to be integrated into a more adequate approach rather than discarded. The important truth is that somebody (or some people), somewhere (or at some places), some time (or continuously over various times), must decide to use resources for one activity rather than another. An evaluation which provides no help in projecting the likely benefits of alternative courses of action is incomplete. Running through the usual ways in which attempts are made to quantify and weigh the benefits of alternative programs, with a view to surpassing them in the direction of a more adequate viewpoint, is therefore a useful exercise, not an irrelevant one.

'Moreover, there is a conceptual link between the cost-effectiveness analysis, the attitude study, and cultural action. The points of view of the actors, and the notion of human action as potentially deliberative, need to be introduced precisely to fill in the gaps that the cost-effectiveness approach shows to be important. But the gaps cannot be filled within the limits of the cost-effectiveness approach itself, since the study of attitude change requires the understanding of the process through which it occurs – which is not accessible to the measurement of input and output variables. The discussion of the cost-effectiveness paradigm is needed in order to point out its limits and what is needed to go beyond it.

'Furthermore, the analysis of the process employs a neo-Aristotelian claim about human action – human action is activity guided by language. (One should be ready here to construe the word "language" broadly, to include, for example, the role of dance and body movement noticed by Freire in

Africa.) Consequently, the outcome of the argument that begins
with a discussion of cost-effectiveness is not, as appears to be the
case with some authors, to emphasize that at this point in the
history of project evaluation, many models of evaluation must be
regarded as respectable. The conclusion is not that evaluation
should "let a hundred flowers bloom, a hundred schools of
thought contend". It is that evaluation should employ the
interpretation of symbols that operate in the reality under study
because human action is symbol guided.'

I could tell as I spoke that the Reasonable Social Scientist had
something else on her mind that she was not yet ready to talk
about. She posed her next question mechanically, as if it were a
substitute for the question she really wanted to ask. 'Well, what
happened? Did PPH live on in the old centres in spite of the
expiration of its funding, or did it die?'

'For the most part it died,' I answered, 'but there are some
signs of life *desde la ultratomba* (from beyond the tomb). In San
Juan de la Costa, the sector-coordinator, Ponciano Rumian, and
several base-coordinators, have transformed PPH into the first
step in a revival of Mapuche music and the Mapuche language.
FREDER is reorganizing itself in order to serve as best it can the
new constituency that PPH gave it. Job descriptions have been
shuffled in such a way that two sector-coordinators have been
kept on (contrary to the original plan) with schedules such that
they will be able to visit some of the old centres that, according to
the original conception of the project, ought to cease to exist.
Ponciano Rumian is one sector-coordinator whose employment
is prolonged, ostensibly as "Director of Indigenous Affairs".
Miguel Oyarzun is the other, ostensibly as "chauffeur".

'Meanwhile, PPH is cranking up its machinery to implement
in the same area the second phase of the program authorized by
the proposals approved by the funding agencies: 50 new centres
with 10 new sector-coordinators. The credibility of the program
in the new centres will doubtlessly be affected by the treatment
accorded to the old centres.

'The treatment accorded to the old centres, in turn, will
depend to a large extent on the attitudes of the people who earn
their daily bread in the offices in the rambling old pink stucco
house on Los Carrera Street. FREDER, like any institution large
or small, is a congeries of personalities, each craving respect and
fearing humiliation. After the ending of PPH, it would be easy

for a programmer of rabbit-raising courses, or for a teacher of rug-weaving, to assume the attitude of a sailor at sea after a dangerous storm has passed. PPH was an implicit threat to the regular FREDER beekeeping course, and now that it is over (in certain places), the threat has passed; no longer need the specialist in animal diseases fear that he may be told some day that the peasants like their volunteer base-coordinators better than they like him. PPH is over, the sea is calm, the storm clouds are gone, the threat to the prestige of rabbit-raisers, rug-weavers, beekeepers and animal-curers is a thing of the past.

'A member of the FREDER staff, in charge of a regular part of FREDER's course offerings for *campesinos*, might well say, when a gnarled old man from Pucopio walks in the door and announces that he represents the Board of Directors of PPH-Pucopio, which has decided that Pucopio needs a course on how to get chickens to lay more eggs, that PPH in Pucopio is over, that if a few people continue to hold private meetings then that is not an official concern of FREDER, and, by the way, several peasants have said in confidence that PPH was a pretty useless course of study compared to a good rabbit-raising or quilt-weaving course, which may be why its funding was not renewed, and in any case – although nobody has anything against ex-PPH centres – FREDER cannot play favourites, and Pucopio will have to wait in line for a course the same as any other locality. The gnarled old man may well decide that life has deceived him once again, and that *chicha* is his best friend after all.

'On the other hand, FREDER might make it its policy to consider an organized community a superior recipient for a course – one more likely than the average community to raise the money to buy the materials needed for the course (most FREDER courses require materials, such as yarn to weave, or bees to keep); more likely to follow through after the course by actually raising chickens in better ways; and more likely to generate spin-off benefits in solidarity and further grassroots initiatives. If such is FREDER's policy and the attitude of its personnel, then the people in the new communities where PPH is trying to get started will not perceive abandonment two years down the road as the probable end result of the organizing effort they are being asked to undertake. Word gets around.'

I noticed that an elderly lady at a neighbouring table, who was eating a hot dog and a bowl of beans for lunch, had taken an interest in my discourse. Encouraged by her attention, I quoted Blaise Pascal: 'Exclusion is the source of all error.' Continuing along Pascalian lines, and speaking loudly for the benefit of my new audience, I remarked that a second general conclusion – regarding a problem almost as pervasive as the devastating question 'What happens next?', is that the spirit of PPH makes it difficult for PPH to assimilate specialized knowledge. 'PPH-Osorno is a peasant program,' I went on, 'dedicated to promoting the dignity of the country people, and inevitably tending to exclude whatever is not part of their culture. Its strength is its weakness. The dignity of the people tends to connote the truth of their ideas; the truth of their ideas suggests that they do not need to learn.

'Another important reason for the lack of expert knowledge in PPH is the experience the project has had with schoolteachers. In the early years of PPH, not in Osorno in 1979–80 but in the province of Aconcagua in 1972–5, PPH functioned through the local schoolmaster instead of through volunteer base-coordinators. The teachers, according to the stories told by PPH personnel at CIDE headquarters in Santiago, took a "vertical" attitude toward the peasantry. They thought knowledge came from science above to be delivered to the unwashed below; they, the teachers, being a little lower than the high and a little higher than the low, looked upon themselves as the authorized representatives of occidental civilization in the countryside. Anyone who does not consider the switch from schoolteachers to volunteer base-coordinators the best move PPH ever made, does not possess the spirit.

'The staff has now reached the conclusion that in reacting against the knowledge establishment, they may have inadvertently sometimes reacted against knowledge. Having reached the stage of tears for their sins (a stage regarded by Saint Ignatius as a prerequisite to reform), they are eager to strengthen those parts of the program that require the systematic use of knowledge. Whether it will be possible to find *técnicos* who have also reached the stage of tears for their sins, who are suited by background and temperament to relate "horizontally" to peasants, remains to be seen.

'In any case, we arrived at the following recommendations with great misgivings, because we realized that the problem of putting science at the service of the people, without letting scientific knowledge be a source of power used to dominate the people, has not yet been solved. Nothing would be easier than to destroy PPH's strengths under the guise of correcting its weaknesses.'

1. In any future PPH programs projected by CIDE, members of the group of child-development specialists who made the worksheets (who separated from the staff after intra-staff disagreements) should be brought back in.
2. The material on alcoholism should be circulated for comment (perhaps by mail) among specialists on alcoholism. Similar consultations should be held on other topics.
3. A system should be devised for handling conflicts (see Chapter 16) with the advice of volunteer lawyers.
4. The legal status of the *centros* and of the buildings some *centros* have built should be studied by a lawyer.
5. An effort should be made to recruit a panel of volunteer experts of various kinds who can help answer questions raised by peasants, for example, why their chickens do not lay eggs, why many people have eye diseases (shortsightedness). In principle, PPH should be able to increase the benefits from professional knowledge by communicating it in such a way that the probability that good advice will be followed is high. This is true because PPH has developed a methodology for facilitating peasants learning in their own language in a supportive atmosphere with people they trust, and for complementing and testing knowledge inputs from outside with contributions from the peasants' own experience and common sense.
6. All professional people who work with PPH should learn the methodology through suitable *capacitaciones*.
7. The information content (*contenidos*) of Units 7–12 should be enriched. Units 1–6 should remain practically without *contenidos*.
8. Schoolteachers should be invited (when and if it is possible) to be *capacitados* too.

'The last point is meant to avoid an unfortunate result that has already appeared in some villages. Volunteer base-coordinators acquire rather sophisticated pedagogical skills, while the teacher at the schoolhouse carries on in the old-fashioned way; the parents complain that the children learn more at home than at school, accusing the teacher of incompetence; the teacher retaliates against PPH with whatever weapons he has – the most readily available weapon being the charge that the program is subversive.'

'Do you remember Max?' the Reasonable Social Scientist suddenly asked.

'No,' I replied.

'I mentioned him to you once,' she said. 'He's my boss.'

'Oh yes, of course,' I said. 'He thinks Paulo Freire is a nice man.'

'Something has got to be done about Max,' she said. 'He is launching a ten-year thirty-nation follow-up of the PPH evaluation, to test the following hypotheses.

1. There will be no significant difference in the success of popular education programs in environments where the government is hostile to the program compared to those in environments where the government is friendly to the programme.
2. There will be no significant difference in the success of popular education programs in rural settings, compared to those in urban settings.
3. There will be no significant difference in the success of popular education programs in settings where there is a prior history of popular organization, compared to those in settings where there is no such prior history.
4. There will be no significant difference in the success of popular education programs supported by radio broadcasts, compared to those not supported by radio broadcasts.'

'On the whole,' I said, 'I think more light will be shed on the questions Max is interested in, such as how PPH works without radio or how it would be different in different political circumstances, by the detailed study of particular programs, rather than by the hypothesis-testing that Max proposes.'

'But Max believes he is rational,' the Reasonable Social Scientist said. 'Max believes that the rational approach is not to find out what words mean to peasants, but to define the variables operationally. By "operational definition" he means he will specify the operations to be used to measure the variable. As long as all researchers use the same operations to measure the variable, it is operationally defined. He plans to devote the first year of his ten-year study to the operational definition of "hostile government", "friendly government", "rural setting", "urban setting", "prior history of popular organization", "radio broadcast" and "success of popular education program.'

The elderly lady at a neighbouring table was peering at us intently. She wore granny glasses and a shabby black coat; her grey hair was cut short and tinted slightly blue.

'Max did not read the chapter about Jorge Zuleta,' I said, 'or if he did read it, he did not read it properly, that is he did not read it sympathetically. In understanding a social reality, it is less important that researchers agree among themselves how to measure, than it is to interpret the themes that play an active role in the culture, such as *cariño, unidad, egoísta, sacar conclusiones,* you have to drink to be a man, friendship, *firme,* the radio belongs to the peasants. Operational definitions are invader themes; their sphere of application is outside the language of the people. Operational definitions are not among the meanings that can be causes.'

'In Max's mind,' said the Reasonable Social Scientist, 'questions of cause and effect are embedded in a frame of reference different from yours. He thinks it is the business of science to establish significant relationships among variables. He thinks the reason why a follow-up of the PPH evaluation is needed is that the existing study provided only interesting anecdotal material, without establishing significant relationships among variables.'

'Social science does not need an equation to identify a cause,' I said. Then I reminded the Reasonable Social Scientist of the cause of the sewing of winter coats at Bahia Mansa, which was the ladies of the *centro* deciding to do it, at Ruth Cofré's suggestion. I also said that a cause of the new policy at the radio station was the resignation of the old manager and the hiring of a new manager with a new ideology, although I was sorry I had been unable to trace the hermeneutics of the radio station conflict dialectically, through its connections with the main and subsidiary struggles of the times we live in.

'Max would say,' the Reasonable Social Scientist went on, 'that even if one does not identify the explanation with the impact of a variable on a variable, still, whatever type of explanation one gives, it must be tested. If you hypothesize, for example, that the *conclusiones* of discussion groups are the causes of actions, then the *conclusiones* must at least correctly predict actions. If A (whatever A is) supposedly causes B, and then A happens but B does not, then your claim that A is the cause of B is false.'

'In some sense, Max must be right,' I said. 'There is no point in explaining something that does not exist. However, A may be a mechanism that produces B, which does not produce it in a given case because something else, C or D, interferes. For example, the use of the PPH worksheets produces readiness for first grade, but in a given case, a given child may be socially unready for first grade because his father drinks too much and when drunk beats his children, or intellectually unready because the child has brain damage from undernourishment, or because the child only pretended to do the worksheets, which were really done by the mother. Conversely, a control group child may be readier than a PPH child because the child's parents are literate people who help and encourage the child. In principle, it would be possible to sort out all these possibilities by defining all the relevant variables, measuring them all for suitable numbers of children and studying the measurement data – assuming you have identified all the relevant variables (an assumption that is always false because except in a simple physical system, like a pendulum, one never knows all the relevant variables). But it is more practical and logical to examine the concrete cases of particular children. The reason I say it is more logical, is that when you define a variable, you always place concrete individuals in an abstract category – which means you throw away information. You throw away whatever you know about that individual that does not fit in a pigeonhole provided by the rules of your measuring scheme.'

'Max would say that evaluation has to be quantitative. The information is not useful for decision-making unless you know the dimensions of what you are talking about.'

'Yes,' I said, 'but you do not have to tie your causal analysis to your estimate of the size of the phenomenon. We give rough answers to the question "How much?" in the course of triangulating interpretations of interviews, in the course of listing grassroots initiatives, in the course of ratifying the verbal image in the *centros*, and in the course of measuring the degree of horizontality of the radio station's programming.'

'Max says that is all very interesting, but it is not an evaluation. You began be rejecting the procedure of comparing the results of a program with its stated objectives. Then you rejected the comparison of the benefits of the program with those of alternative programs. In the end, you settle for a description of the program compiled from statements by various informants, and partly confirmed by various checks. But a description is not an evaluation. An evaluation must compare the thing described to some standard.'

'Descriptions are usually evaluations. When a peasant-woman says, for example, "We had a problem finding a place for our *centro* to meet', she does not separate her statement into a descriptive component and an evaluative component.

'The propositions that statements can be classified as descriptive or evaluative, that social science can describe without evaluating, and that evaluation is an activity separate from describing, are doctrines taught by certain philosophers and social scientists. Following the doctrines does not come naturally to ordinary speakers of Spanish or English. Evaluation is normally so embedded in description, that the attempt to purify description by refining out evaluation is arduous work. (Whether it is possible to succeed in describing without evaluating is a question that need not be answered here.)

'Reliance on what may be called "natural" evaluations, that is those embedded in descriptions provided by participants, has certain advantages, as compared to applying a standard (a yardstick, so to speak) to the reality under study. The natural evaluations express the knowledge and opinions of the participants, which would not come to light if evaluation were couched in terms of standards composed by outsiders. (One might, of course, teach the peasants how to compose standards, i.e. to restate their views in terms of (i) description, (ii) standard, and (iii) comparison of (i) with (ii). But this would be more trouble than it would be worth.) Further, many evaluative nuances implicit in natural language descriptions would be lost in a necessarily rather short, necessarily rather crude, list of standards.

'Our study does not, however, rely entirely on evaluations implicit in descriptions. Explicit attention is focused on results usually regarded as benefits, such as children's readiness for school, and on results usually regarded as failures, such as the abandonment of a *centro* due to the peasants' lack of interest.'

'But Max says,' the RSS said, 'that your descriptions are useless for planning. He believes that a planner should project what the costs and benefits will be of some program X at some place Y by consulting research which establishes relationships between independent and dependent variables. That tells you the cost of achieving the objectives. You fund a budget sufficient to achieve the results desired, given the initial state of the system.'

'However,' I said, 'it would seem likely that Z (where Z is, for example, Teofilo Guzman), who has a detailed knowledge of place Y (say north-eastern Panama), where a program X (say *Escuelas para la Producción* – schools with productive farms and shops) is proposed, will be helped to project what in PPH and other programs will be useful for X at Y by reading illuminative studies of PPH and other programs. The wisdom of Z will not be greatly augmented by reading about the impacts of operationally-defined variables on each other.'

'You are fortunate,' said the Reasonable Social Scientist, 'that you do not have to live in the real world. You academic philosophers can speculate about what meaning is, and what a cause is, and whether a meaning can be a cause, but when you live in the real world you have to do what your boss tells you to do. My boss happens to be Max.'

'You could reason with him,' I suggested.

'Impossible,' she said. 'He's got a grant.'

'That is a serious matter,' I said. 'Many otherwise reasonable people cease to be reasonable when they get grants.'

It was time for the Reasonable Social Scientist to return to her office. Since I found myself hungrier than I had been at first, and had my eye on a cheese sandwich that was tempting me through the glass window of a vending machine, I bid *adieu* to the Reasonable Social Scientist, and watched her go out through the revolving door to face the real world.

The elderly lady with the bluish hair took the liberty of approaching me and engaging me in conversation. 'That was fascinating!' she said. 'You always meet such nice people at Horn and Hardart! You are a lawyer, aren't you?' She did not wait for a reply. 'The woman with you was a lawyer too. I could tell by the way you were talking. My son was a lawyer you know.'

I treated her to a cup of tea, and for an hour we discussed her memories. Her son had been killed in a car accident many years ago. She did not say exactly how long ago, but she gave me the impression that when her son was killed, Eisenhower was president. The lady's name was Mrs Higgins.

'You are a fine young man,' said Mrs Higgins. 'Most young people don't have time to pay attention to the elderly these days.'

'*Cariño* is what we have to give each other,' I said, momentarily lapsing by accident into Spanish. She did not seem to mind, or even to notice, that I had spoken to her in a foreign language.

Mrs Higgins said she would invite me to visit her, but she is living on a pension and her apartment is small. However, she has lunch at Horn and Hardart every day, and would be pleased to see me some other day at lunchtime.

Then Mrs Higgins, too, went out of the door.

Everything seemed clear to me in retrospect. The evaluation of a programme, I now saw, consists to a large extent of describing it in an illuminating way, in a way that helps the reader to see it as if he or she were there. The description should first be expressed in the language of the participants themselves. To see how and why cultural change takes place, the viewpoints of the actors who are changing, and an understanding of the conflicts they are involved in, are indispensable. A quantitative estimate of how much change is taking place and checking – triangulating – to improve the accuracy of the picture emerging from the description, are important but secondary.

The participants' viewpoints are needed in any study of attitude change, but when the program to be studied is a cultural action program the need is especially clear. Cultural action requires illuminative evaluation, because it is a form of social change that consists of strengthening the consciousness of human beings, in order to empower them to assert greater control over historical forces. The illuminative evaluation method is appropriate to cultural action because the interview method discerns meanings, and meanings explain how a program works because they are the stuff that cultural action works with, and works on. The resulting description is an interpretation – an attempt by the evaluators to interpret for some audience, events that are significant for the actors. Accounts of benefits achieved, costs and administrative problems, are illuminated by being embedded in such a description of how a program works.

NOTES AND REFERENCES

1. Rolland Paulston, 'Multiple Approaches to the Evaluation of Educational Reform: from Cost-Benefit to Power-Benefit Analysis', paper presented at the seminar on organization of education reform at the local level, held by the International Institute of Educational Planning, Paris (November 27–30, 1979).

Index